Price 35 Cents.

CHARLES DICKENS.

The Story of his Life.

BY THE

AUTHOR OF THE "LIFE OF THACKERAY."

BLEAK HOUSE, AT BROADSTAIRS.

WITH ILLUSTRATIONS AND FACSIMILES.

NEW YORK:
HARPER & BROTHERS, PUBLISHERS,
FRANKLIN SQUARE.
1870.

DICTIONARIES AND WORKS OF REFERENCE,

PUBLISHED BY

HARPER & BROTHERS, New York.

ANDREWS'S LATIN - ENGLISH LEXICON. Founded on the larger German-Latin Lexicon of Dr. WM. FREUND. With Additions and Corrections from the Lexicons of Gesner, Facciolati, Scheller, Georges, &c. Royal 8vo, Sheep extra, $7 50.

ANTHON'S CLASSICAL DICTIONARY. Containing an Account of the principal Proper Names mentioned in Ancient Authors, and intended to elucidate all the important Points connected with the Geography, History, Biography, Mythology, and Fine Arts of the Greeks and Romans, together with an Account of the Coins, Weights, and Measures of the Ancients, with Tabular Values of the same. Royal 8vo, Sheep extra, $6 00.

ANTHON'S SMITH'S CLASSICAL DICTIONARY. A New Classical Dictionary of Greek and Roman Biography, Mythology, and Geography. Partly based upon the Dictionary of Greek and Roman Biography and Mythology. By WM. SMITH, LL.D. Revised, with numerous Corrections and Additions, by CHARLES ANTHON, LL.D. Royal 8vo, Sheep extra, $5 00.

ANTHON'S SMITH'S DICTIONARY OF ANTIQUITIES. A Dictionary of Greek and Roman Antiquities. Edited by WM. SMITH, LL.D., and Illustrated by numerous Engravings on Wood. Third American Edition, carefully revised, and containing also numerous additional Articles relative to the Botany, Mineralogy, and Zoology of the Ancients. By CHARLES ANTHON, LL.D. Royal 8vo, Sheep extra, $6 00.

ANTHON'S LATIN - ENGLISH AND ENGLISH-LATIN DICTIONARY. A Latin-English and English-Latin Dictionary, for the use of Schools. Chiefly from the Lexicons of Freund, Georges, and Kaltschmidt. Small 4to, Sheep, $3 50.

ANTHON'S RIDDLE AND ARNOLD'S ENGLISH-LATIN LEXICON. A Copious and Critical English-Latin Lexicon, founded on the German-Latin Dictionary of Dr. C. E. GEORGES. By Rev. JOSEPH ESMOND RIDDLE, M.A., and Rev. THOMAS KERCHEVER ARNOLD, D.D. First American Edition, carefully revised, and containing a copious Dictionary of Proper Names from the best Sources. By CHARLES ANTHON, LL.D. Royal 8vo, Sheep extra, $5 00.

CRABB'S ENGLISH SYNONYMS. English Synonyms, with copious Illustrations and Explanations, drawn from the best Writers. By GEORGE CRABB, M.A., Author of the "Technological Dictionary" and the "Universal Historical Dictionary." 8vo, Sheep extra, $2 50.

ENGLISHMAN'S GREEK CONCORDANCE. The Englishman's Greek Concordance of the New Testament: being an Attempt at a Verbal Connection between the Greek and the English Texts; including a Concordance to the Proper Names, with Indexes, Greek - English and English - Greek. 8vo, Cloth, $5 00.

FOWLER'S ENGLISH LANGUAGE. The English Language in its Elements and Forms. With a History of its Origin and Development, and a full Grammar. Designed for Use in Colleges and Schools. Revised and Enlarged. By WILLIAM C. FOWLER, LL.D., late Professor in Amherst College. 8vo, Cloth, $2 50.

HAYDN'S DICTIONARY OF DATES. Haydn's Dictionary of Dates, relating to all Ages and Nations. For Universal Reference. Edited by BENJAMIN VINCENT, Assistant Secretary and Keeper of the Library of the Royal Institution of Great Britain; and Revised for the Use of American Readers. 8vo, Cloth, $5 00; Sheep, $6 00.

LIDDELL AND SCOTT'S GREEK - ENGLISH LEXICON. Based on the German Work of FRANCOIS PASSOW. With Corrections and Additions, and the Insertion, in Alphabetical Order, of the Proper Names occurring in the principal Greek Authors, by HENRY DRISLER, LL.D. Royal 8vo, Sheep extra, $7 50.

M'CLINTOCK AND STRONG'S CYCLOPÆDIA of Biblical, Theological, and Ecclesiastical Literature. By Rev. JOHN M'CLINTOCK, D.D., and JAMES STRONG, S.T.D. With Maps and numerous Illustrations. To be completed in about Six Volumes, Royal 8vo, of about One Thousand Pages each. Vols. I., II., and III., comprising the Letters A to G, are now ready. The remaining Volumes are in progress. Price, per Volume, Cloth, $5 00; Sheep, $6 00; Half Morocco, $8 00.

MARCH'S ANGLO-SAXON GRAMMAR. A Comparative Grammar of the Anglo-Saxon Language, in which its Forms are Illustrated by those of the Sanskrit, Greek, Latin, Gothic, Old Saxon, Old Friesic, Old Norse, and Old High-German. By FRANCIS A. MARCH, Professor of the English Language and Comparative Philology in Lafayette College, Author of "Method of Philological Study of the English Language," "A Parser and Analyzer for Beginners," &c. Crown 8vo, Cloth, $2 50.

ROBINSON'S GREEK LEXICON OF THE TESTAMENT. A Greek and English Lexicon of the New Testament. By EDWARD ROBINSON, D.D., LL.D., late Professor of Biblical Literature in the Union Theological Seminary, N. Y. A New Edition, revised, and in great part rewritten. Royal 8vo, Cloth, $6 00.

YONGE'S ENGLISH-GREEK LEXICON. An English-Greek Lexicon. By C. D. YONGE. With many New Articles, an Appendix of Proper Names, and Pillon's Greek Synonyms. To which is prefixed an Essay on the Order of Words in Attic-Greek Prose, by Charles Short, LL.D., Professor of Latin in Columbia College, N. Y. Edited by HENRY DRISLER, LL.D., Professor of Greek in Columbia College, Editor of "Liddell and Scott's Greek-English Lexicon," &c. 8vo, Sheep extra, $7 00.

☞ HARPER & BROTHERS *will send either of the above books by mail, postage prepaid, to any part of the United States, on receipt of the price.*

CHARLES DICKENS as "CAPTAIN BOBADIL."
From the original painting by C. R. Leslie, R.A.

Devonshire Terrace
Second January 1844.

My Dear Sir

That is a very horrible case you tell me of. I would to God I could get at the parental heart of ———, in which event I would so scarify it that he should writhe again. But if I were to put such a father as he into a book, all the fathers going (and especially the bad ones) would hold up their hands and protest against the unnatural caricature. I find that a great many people (particularly those who might have sat for the character) consider even Mr Pecksniff, a grotesque

Fac-simile of

MR. DICKENS'S HANDWRITING.

Part of a Letter to a Friend.

CHARLES DICKENS,

At the age of 29.

From a Drawing by Count D'Orsay, taken on the completion of "The Old Curiosity Shop."

CHARLES DICKENS.

The Story of his Life.

BY THE

AUTHOR OF THE "LIFE OF THACKERAY."

BLEAK HOUSE, AT BROADSTAIRS.

WITH ILLUSTRATIONS AND FACSIMILES.

NEW YORK:
HARPER & BROTHERS, PUBLISHERS,
FRANKLIN SQUARE.
1870.

"OH, potent wizard! painter of great skill!
   Blending with life's realities the hues
   Of a rich fancy: sweetest of all singers!
Charming the public ear, and, at thy will,
   Searching the soul of him thou dost amuse,
   And the warm heart's recess, where mem'ry lingers,
And child-like love, and sympathy, and truth,
   And every blessed feeling which the world
   Had frozen or repressed with its stern apathy
For human suffering! 'Crabbed age and youth,'
   And beauty, smiling tearful, turn to thee,
Whose 'Carol' is an allegory fine,
The burden of whose 'Chimes' is holy and benign!"

                            DOUGLAS JERROLD'S *Magazine.*

PRELIMINARY.

THE following brief Memoir of the late Mr. Charles Dickens may, perhaps, be acceptable as filling an intermediate place between the newspaper or review article and the more elaborate biography which may be expected in due course. The writer had some peculiar means of acquiring information for the purpose of his sketch; and to this he has added such particulars as have been already made public in English and foreign publications and other scattered sources.

The common complaints against memoirs of this necessarily hasty and incomplete character will not be repeated by those who are accustomed to test questions in morals by the principles which underlie them. That there is nothing necessarily indelicate or improper in the desire of the public to obtain some personal knowledge of the great and good who have just passed away, is assumed by every daily, weekly, and quarterly journal, which, on occasions of this kind, furnish their readers with such details as they are able to obtain, and which in no case confine themselves strictly to the public career of the deceased.

Although some facts in the private life of Mr. Dickens will be found to be touched upon in these pages, the writer is not conscious of having written a line which could give pain to others.

In view of a second edition—should one be called for—the writer will be obliged by the receipt of any additional particulars which may assist in completing the outline memoir which now leaves his hand.

He can not, however, conclude without acknowledging the kind assistance he has received in furnishing anecdotes and other particulars from Mr. Arthur Locker, Mr. E. S. Dallas, Mr. Blanchard Jerrold, Mr. James Grant, Dr. Charles Mackay, Mr. Mitchell, of Bond Street (for permission to make reductions of Leslie's beautiful picture, and Count D'Orsay's characteristic portrait), Mr. Edmund Ollier, Mr. E. P. Hingston, Mr. Allen, Mr. J. Colam (Secretary to the Society for the Prevention of Cruelty to Animals), the writers of interesting articles in the "Daily News" and the "Observer," and to Mr. Hablot K. Browne, for his admirable study of the chief characters drawn by him for the late Mr. Dickens's works.

It would have been impossible to have given the data contained in this little book, in the rather short time occupied in its preparation, but for the hearty assistance of Mr. H. T. Taverner, an industrious *littérateur*, who had already gathered some particulars of the great novelist's public career.

LONDON, 29th June, 1870.

A TRIBUTE
TO
CHARLES DICKENS.

BY THE HON. MRS. NORTON.

(*From* ALBERT SCHLOSS'S "*English Bijou Almanac*" *for* 1842.)

"Not merely thine the tribute praise,
 Which greets an author's progress here;
Not merely thine the fabled bays,
 Whose verdure brightens his career;
Thine the pure triumph to have taught
 Thy brother man a gentle part;
In every line a fervent thought,
 Which gushes from thy generous heart:
For thine are words which rouse up all
 The dormant good among us found—
Like drops which from a fountain fall,
 To bless and fertilize the ground!"

CONTENTS.

CHAPTER I.
Early Career........................Page 11

CHAPTER II.
Publication of the "Pickwick Papers".... 17

CHAPTER III.
Popularity of the "Pickwick Papers"..... 22

CHAPTER IV.
Dickens as a Dramatist.—"Oliver Twist".. 25

CHAPTER V.
The Copyright of "Oliver Twist"......... 28

CHAPTER VI.
"Nicholas Nickleby"..................... 30

CHAPTER VII.
Publication of "The Old Curiosity Shop" and "Barnaby Rudge."—Dickens's Ravens.—"Barnaby Rudge" Dramatized.—"The Picnic Papers".................... 32

CHAPTER VIII.
Dickens's Visit to America................ 36

CHAPTER IX.
Further American Experiences............ 40

CHAPTER X.
"Martin Chuzzlewit"..................... 42

CHAPTER XI.
The "Christmas Carol".................. 45

CHAPTER XII.
Visit to Italy.—"The Chimes"............ 48

CHAPTER XIII.
Dickens as an Actor...................... 50

CHAPTER XIV.
Dickens as a Journalist ....Page 52

CHAPTER XV.
Appearance of "Dombey and Son"........ 53

CHAPTER XVI.
Victor Hugo.—"The Haunted Man"...... 55

CHAPTER XVII.
Dickens and Thackeray.—"David Copperfield."—On Capital Punishment.......... 57

CHAPTER XVIII.
"Household Words."—The Guild of Literature................................... 60

CHAPTER XIX.
"Bleak House."—Leigh Hunt............. 64

CHAPTER XX.
American Publishers.—The First Reading.. 66

CHAPTER XXI.
"Hard Times."—"Seven Poor Travellers."—The Dinner to Thackeray.—Johnson's Goddaughter.—"Holly-tree Inn"........ 68

CHAPTER XXII.
"Little Dorrit."—"Travelling Abroad."—Tavistock House Theatricals............. 70

CHAPTER XXIII.
Works translated into French.—Dickens and Thackeray........................... 73

CHAPTER XXIV.
Royal Dramatic College.—Discontinuance of "Household Words."—"All the Year Round"................................. 77

CHAPTER XXV.
"The Uncommercial Traveller"........... 80

CHAPTER XXVI.

Mr. Dickens and the Electors of Finsbury.—"Tom Tiddler's Ground."—"Somebody's Luggage."—"Mrs. Lirriper's Lodgings."—"Pincher".......................Page 81

CHAPTER XXVII.

"Our Mutual Friend." — The Staplehurst Accident.—"Miss Berwick."—"Dr. Marigold's Prescriptions." — Dickens at the Mansion House. — Clarkson Stanfield.— The Printers' Readers................... 84

CHAPTER XXVIII.

Second Visit to America.—Pedestrian Tastes 88

CHAPTER XXIX.

The Farewell Readings.—Failing Health.... 92

CHAPTER XXX.

Interview with the Queen.—Last Illness.—Death.—Burial in Westminster Abbey.—Funeral Sermon.—His last Resting-place. 96

APPENDIX.

ANECDOTES AND REMINISCENCES.

The First Hint of "Pickwick" ....Page 103
Dickens and the "Morning Chronicle".... 103
Portraits of Dickens...................... 104
The Names of Dickens's Characters........ 105
Description of "Boz" in 1844............. 105
Description of Dickens in 1852........... 105
Boz's Table Habits....................... 105
The MS. of "Oliver Twist"............... 106
Dickens's Benevolence.................... 106
Hook and Dickens......................... 106
Methodical Habits and Perseverance....... 106
Manner of Literary Composition........... 106
"The Chief"............................. 107
Blue Ink................................. 107
Dickens in Private Life.................. 107
Sympathy with Working-men 107
A Beggar's Estimate of his Generosity..... 107
Paragraph Disease........................ 107
Dickens and Thackeray.................... 107
Anecdote of Abraham Lincoln............. 108
The Contributors to "Household Words". 108
"The Mystery of Edwin Drood".......... 109
Gad's Hill House......................... 109

CHARLES DICKENS:

THE STORY OF HIS LIFE.

ROCHESTER CASTLE, AS SEEN FROM THE RAILWAY BRIDGE.

CHAPTER I.

EARLY CAREER.

THE "Story of the Life" of England's greatest novelist requires but little introduction. Of his ancestors but few particulars are recorded, and these are entirely without interest as having any connection with the late illustrious bearer of the name.

CHARLES DICKENS* was born at Landport, Portsmouth, on the 7th February, 1812, his father, Mr. John Dickens, being a clerk in the Navy Pay Office at that sea-port. His duties required that he should reside from time to time in different naval stations—now at Plymouth, now at Portsmouth, and then at Sheerness and Chatham. "In the glorious days" of war with France those towns were full of life, bustle, and

* He was christened Charles *John Hougham* Dickens, but the full name (taken partly from the father and partly from his mother's side) was too high-sounding for his simple tastes, and so he never used it, preferring the plainer form. He once remarked that, had he been a fashionable doctor, he might have thought differently about the matter.

character, and the father of the author of "Pickwick" was at times fond of dilating upon the strange scenes he had witnessed. One of the stories described a sitting-room he once enjoyed at Blue Town, Sheerness, abutting on the theatre. Of an evening he used to sit in his room and could hear what was passing on the stage, and join in the chorus of "God save the King" and "Britannia Rules the Waves"—then the favorite song of Englishmen.

On the termination of the war in 1815, a large reduction was made in the number of clerks in this office, and Mr. Dickens receiving his pension, removed to London with his wife and seven children. Possessing considerable abilities, and unwilling to remain idle, he became parliamentary reporter on the "Morning Chronicle."*

Charles remained at home until he was seven years of age, and was then sent to a private school at Chatham, the late Rev. Wm. Giles, F. R. A. S., being his instructor. As an evidence of young Dickens's kindly disposition, it may be mentioned that, some years ago, when such fame as he had acquired would cause most men to have forgotten their former old associations, Dickens joined some other old scholars in the presentation of a service of plate to Mr. Giles, accompanied by a most gratifying testimonial of regard, to which he attached his well-known bold autograph. A fellow-scholar, who was at school at the same time with Dickens (there being only two years difference in their ages), used often to speak of the marked geniality of Dickens's character as a boy, and of his proficiency in all boyish sports, such as cricket, etc. Ultimately he completed his education at a good school in or near London.

At an early age he commenced to read the

* The old gentleman died in Keppel Street, Russell Square, on 31st March, 1851, aged 65.

standard works of the best authors. In the preface to "Nicholas Nickleby," speaking of how he first heard of the cruelties of the Yorkshire schools, he describes himself as being "a not very robust child, sitting in by-places, near Rochester Castle, with a head full of Partridge, Strap, Tom Pipes, and Sancho Panza." In "David Copperfield" (a book one can hardly help fancying is in some respects autobiographical), he says (omitting a few words): "From that blessed little room Roderick Random, Peregrine Pickle, Humphry Clinker, Tom Jones, the Vicar of Wakefield, Don Quixote, Gil Blas, and Robinson Crusoe, came out, a glorious host, to keep me company. They kept alive my fancy—they, and the 'Arabian Nights,' and the 'Tales of the Genii,'—and did me no harm; for whatever harm there was in some of them, was not there for me; *I* knew nothing of it. * * * I have seen Tom Jones (a child's Tom Jones, a harmless creature) for a week together. I have sustained my own idea of Roderick Random for a month at a stretch, I verily believe. I had a greedy relish for a few volumes of voyages and travels, and for days and days I can remember to have gone about my region of our house armed with a centre-piece out of an old set of boot-trees—the perfect realization of Captain Somebody, of the Royal British Navy, in danger of being beset by savages, and resolved to sell his life at a great price. The Captain never lost dignity from having his ears boxed with the Latin Grammar. I did; but the Captain was a captain and a hero, in despite of all the grammars of all the languages in the world, dead or alive."

His career at school having concluded, his father was desirous that he should be articled to the law, and he entered a solicitor's office for that purpose. Dunning (afterwards Lord Ashburton) once said: "The study of the law is generally ridiculed as dry and uninteresting; but a mind anxious for the discovery of truth and information will be amply gratified for the toil of investigating the origin and progress of jurisprudence which has the good of the people for its basis, and the accumulated wisdom of ages for its improvement." But to young Dickens it was ill calculated to accord with the literary tastes he had formed, and thus imbued with the kindred feelings of some of his distinguished contemporaries—Disraeli, Layard, Harrison Ainsworth, and Westland Marston, all of whom passed a portion of their early days at an attorney's desk—he became disgusted with the tedious routine of the profession, and, resigning all ideas of propitiating Thetis (the goddess of lawyers), determined to become a reporter, like his father, who, finding how strong his son's ideas were on the subject, wisely placed no obstacle in his path, but removed him from his uncongenial employment, and placed him with the Messrs. Gurney, the parliamentary short-hand writers of Abingdon Street, Westminster. It is said that during his probation, and while practising short-hand writing, Dickens passed the leisure hours of some two years in the Library of the British Museum.

The manner in which the difficulties of stenography were overcome had best be told in his own words: "I did not allow my resolution with respect to the parliamentary debates to cool. It was one of the irons I began to heat immediately, and one of the irons I kept hot and hammered at with a perseverance I may honestly admire. I bought an approved scheme of the noble art and mystery of stenography (which cost me ten-and-sixpence),* and plunged into a sea of perplexity, that brought me in a few weeks to the confines of distraction. The changes that were rung upon dots, which in one position meant such a thing, and in another position something else entirely different; the wonderful vagaries that were played by circles; the unaccountable consequences that resulted from marks like fly's legs; the tremendous effects from a curve in the wrong place; not only troubled my waking hours, but reappeared before me in my sleep. When I had groped my way blindly through these difficulties, and had mastered the alphabet, which was an Egyptian temple in itself, there then appeared a procession of new horrors, called arbitrary characters—the most despotic characters I had ever known; who insisted, for instance, that the thing like the beginning of a cobweb meant expectation, that a pen-and-ink sky-rocket stood for disadvantageous. When I had fixed these wretches in my mind, I found that they had driven every thing else out of it; then, beginning again, I forgot them; while I was picking them up, I dropped the other fragments of the system; in short, it was almost heart-breaking."

Occupying the Chair at the second Anniversary of the Newspaper Press Fund, on 20th May, 1865, and referring to his early reporting days, he said:

"I went into the gallery of the House of Commons as a parliamentary reporter when I was a boy not eighteen, and I left it—I can hardly believe the inexorable truth—nigh thirty years ago; and I have pursued the calling of a

---

* This was "Gurney's System of Short-hand," the 16th edition of which is now selling at the old price, 10s. 6d.

reporter under circumstances of which many of my brethren at home in England here—many of my brethren's successors—can form no adequate conception. I have often transcribed for the printer from my short-hand notes important public speeches in which the strictest accuracy was required, and a mistake in which would have been to a young man severely compromising, writing on the palm of my hand by the light of a dark lantern in a post-chaise and four, galloping through a wild country, through the dead of the night, at the then surprising rate of fifteen miles an hour. The very last time I was at Exeter I strolled into the castle-yard there to identify, for the amusement of a friend, the spot on which I once 'took,' as we used to call it, an election speech of my noble friend Lord Russell, in the midst of a lively fight maintained by all the vagabonds in that division of the county, and under such pelting rain, that I remember two good-natured colleagues, who chanced to be at leisure, held a pocket-handkerchief over my note-book after the manner of a state canopy in an ecclesiastical procession. I have worn my knees by writing on them on the old back row of the old gallery of the old House of Commons; and I have worn my feet by standing to write in a preposterous pen in the old House of Lords, where we used to be huddled like so many sheep kept in waiting till the wool-sack might want restuffing. Returning home from excited political meetings in the country to the waiting press in London, I do verily believe I have been upset in almost every description of vehicle known in this country. I have been in my time belated on miry by-roads towards the small hours, forty or fifty miles from London, in a rickety carriage, with exhausted horses and drunken post-boys, and have got back in time before publication, to be received with never-forgotten compliments by Mr. Black, in the broadest of Scotch, coming from the broadest of hearts I ever knew. I mention these trivial things as an assurance to you that I never have forgotten the fascination of that old pursuit. The pleasure that I used to feel in the rapidity and dexterity of its exercise has never faded out of my breast. Whatever little cunning of hand or head I took to it or acquired in it, I have so retained as that I fully believe I could resume it to-morrow. To this present year of my life, when I sit in this hall, or where not, hearing a dull speech—the phenomenon does occur—I sometimes beguile the tedium of the moment by mentally following the speaker in the old, old way; and sometimes, if you can believe me, I even find my hand going on the table-cloth. Accept these little truths as a confirmation of what I know, as a confirmation of my interest in this old calling. I verily believe, I am sure, that if I had never quitted my old calling, I should have been foremost and zealous in the interest of this institution, believing it to be a sound, a wholesome, and a good one."

"That there was no exaggeration in this statement," writes a personal friend,* "he proved, in the course of that very year, by giving a series of lessons in short-hand to a young man, a connection of his, when his fluency and perspicuity were found to be as great as ever." To the same writer he once told a curious anecdote of his reporting days: "The late Earl of Derby, then Lord Stanley, had on some important occasion made a grand speech in the House of Commons. This speech, of immense length, it was found necessary to compress, but so admirably had its pith and marrow been given in the 'Morning Chronicle,' that Lord Stanley sent to the office, requesting that the gentleman who had reported it would wait upon him at his residence in Carlton House Terrace, that he might then and there take down the speech in its entirety from his lordship's lips, Lord Stanley being desirous of having a perfect transcript of it. The reporter was Charles Dickens. He attended, took down the speech, and received Lord Stanley's compliments on his work. Many years after, Mr. Dickens, dining for the first time with a friend in Carlton House Terrace, found the aspect of the dining-room strangely familiar to him, and, on making inquiries, discovered that the house had previously belonged to Lord Derby, and that that was the very room in which he had taken down Lord Stanley's speech." It is understood that our author practised reporting in the law Courts before going to the Houses of Parliament.

The first paper he obtained an engagement on was "The True Sun," with the managers of which he soon became noted for the succinctness of his reports, and the judicious, though somewhat ruthless, style with which he cut down unnecessary verbiage, displaying the substance to the best advantage, and exemplifying the well-known maxim of Perry, the famous chief of the "Morning Chronicle," that "Speeches can not be made long enough for the speakers, *nor short enough for the readers*."

Remaining for a brief period on the staff of "The True Sun," he seceded to the "Mirror of Parliament," which had started with the express object of reporting the debates *verbatim*. Mr. Barrow, Dickens's uncle, was the conductor; its downfall, however, was rapid, as it only existed two sessions.

---

* In the "Observer," 12th June, 1870.

Through his father's influence he was next secured an appointment on the "Morning Chronicle," a newspaper originally established on Whig principles, by Woodfall, in 1769. By a remarkable coincidence, three of its chief parliamentary reporters afterwards attained to eminent positions. The late Lord Chancellor Campbell commenced his career on its staff; on his resignation William Hazlitt (the celebrated essayist) supplied his place, who was in turn succeeded by Mr. Charles Dickens.

While Dickens was reporting for the "Morning Chronicle," it fell in the way of his duty to go down into Devonshire, where Lord John Russell—who had accepted the post of Secretary of State in the new Melbourne cabinet—was seeking re-election (May, 1835) from his old constituency. As his lordship had been instrumental in getting Peel and the tories out of office, his constituents resented the act by returning another member in his place. It is to this noisy election that Dickens alludes in the extract from his speech on "reporting" given above. In those days of coaching and slow letter-post, Dickens had to keep his editor fully informed of the best and quickest transit for his "reports;" and, by the kindness of the then sub-editor, who received Dickens's letters, and, believing in the man as heartily as the great John Black did, has carefully preserved them to the present time, I am enabled to give an extract from the identical letter received from him when on this journey. He writes from the Bush Inn at Bristol, a famous hostelry for commercial travellers, and a noted "coaching" house for persons bound to the West of England. The letter was dated Tuesday morning:

"The conclusion of Russell's dinner will be forwarded by Cooper's company's coach, which leaves here at half past six to-morrow morning. The report of the Bath dinner shall be forwarded by the first Bath coach on Thursday morning —what time it starts we have no means of ascertaining till we reach Bath; but you will receive it as early as possible, as we will indorse the parcel 'Pay the porter 2s. 6d. extra for immediate delivery.' Beard will go over to Bath from here to-morrow morning, and I shall come back by the mail from Marlborough. I need not say that it will be sharp work, and will require two of us; for we shall both be up the whole of the previous night, and shall have to sit up all night again to get it off in time.

"As soon as we have had a little sleep, we shall return to town as quickly as we can, for we have (if the express succeeds) to stop at two or three places along the road, to pay money and express satisfaction. You may imagine that we are extremely anxious to know the result of the arrangement. Pray direct to one of us at the 'White Hart,' Bath, and inform us in a parcel *sent by the* FIRST COACH *after you receive this*, exactly at *what hour* it arrived. Do not fail on any account.

"We joined with the 'Herald' (I say this in reference to the first part of your letter) precisely on the principle you at first laid down—economy; not pushed so far, however, as to interfere with the efficiency of the express. As the conclusion of the dinner was to be done, we all thought the best plan we could pursue would be to leave two men behind, and trust Russell to the others. I have no doubt, if he makes a speech of any ordinary dimensions, it can be done by the time we reach Marlborough; and taking into consideration the immense importance of having the addition of saddle-horses from thence, it is beyond all doubt worth an effort. Believe me (for self and Beard),

"Very sincerely yours,
"CHARLES DICKENS.

"*⁎* I thought of putting the accompanying letter to my brother in the post. Will you have the kindness to send a boy with it?"

This is, in all likelihood, the only letter of Dickens's reporting days now in existence. As a record of his industry and business foresight it is most interesting, and the glimpses that it gives of the wild life led by a reporter in those days, show us the source of that wonderful knowledge of those old coaching days and that old tavern life that have passed out of actual existence, to live forever in Dickens's pages. We may just say that it is Mr. Thomas Beard, one of the first reporters in England, and Dickens's dear friend, who is alluded to in the letter; the Mr. Frank Beard, who attended the great novelist in his last moments, is, we believe, a brother of this gentleman.

Concerning Dickens's earliest printed writings, Mr. James Grant, the well-known journalist and author, has supplied us with an account which differs much from what has been elsewhere said upon this part of our author's career. "It is everywhere stated," says Mr. Grant, "that the earliest productions from his pen made their appearance in the columns of the 'Morning Chronicle,' and that Mr. John Black, then editor of that journal, was the first to discover and duly to appreciate the genius of Mr. Dickens. The fact was not so. It is true that he wrote 'Sketches' afterwards in the 'Morning Chronicle,' but he did not begin them in that journal. Mr. Dickens first became connected with the 'Morning Chronicle' as a reporter in the gallery of the House of Commons. This was in 1835-'36; but Mr. Dickens had been previously engaged, while in his nineteenth year, as a reporter for a publication entitled the 'Mirror of Parliament,' in which capacity he occupied the very highest rank among the eighty or ninety reporters for the press then in Parliament. While in the gallery of the House of Commons, he was exceedingly reserved in his manners. Though interchanging the usual courtesies of life with all with whom he came into contact in the discharge of his professional duties, the only gentleman at that time in the gallery of the House of Commons with whom he formed a close personal intimacy was Mr. Thomas Beard, then a reporter for the 'Morning Herald,' and now connected with the newspaper press generally, as furnishing the court intelligence in the morning journals. The friendship thus formed between Mr. Dickens and Mr. Beard so far back as the year 1832 was, I believe, continued till the death of Mr. Dickens.

"It was about the year 1833-'34, before Mr. Dickens's connection with the 'Morning Chronicle,' and before Mr. Black, then editor of that journal, had ever met with him, that he commenced his literary career as an amateur writer. He made his *début* in the latter end of 1834 or beginning of 1835, in the 'Old Monthly Magazine,' then conducted by Captain Holland, an intimate friend of mine. The 'Old Monthly Magazine' had been started more than a quarter of a century before by Sir Richard Philips, and was for many years a periodical of large circulation and high literary reputation—a fact which might be inferred from another fact, namely, that the 'New Monthly Magazine,' started by Mr. Colburn, under the editorial auspices of Mr. Thomas Campbell, author of 'The Pleasures of Hope,' appropriated the larger portion of its title. The 'Old Monthly Magazine' was published at half a crown, being the same price as 'Blackwood,' 'Fraser,' and 'Bentley's' magazines are at the present day.

"It was, as I have said, in this monthly periodical—not in the columns of the 'Morning Chronicle'—that Mr. Dickens first appeared in the realms of literature. He sent, in the first instance, his contributions to that periodical anonymously. These consisted of sketches, chiefly of a humorous character, and were simply signed 'Boz.' For a long time they did not attract any special attention, but were generally spoken of in newspaper notices of the magazine as 'clever,' 'graphic,' and so forth.

"Early in 1836 the editorship of the 'Monthly Magazine'—the adjective 'Old' having been by this time dropped—came into my hands; and in making the necessary arrangements for its transfer from Captain Holland—then, I should have mentioned, proprietor as well as editor—I expressed my great admiration of the series of 'Sketches by Boz,' which had appeared in the 'Monthly,' and said I should like to make an arrangement with the writer for a continuance of them under my editorship. With that view I asked him the name of the author. It will sound strange in most ears when I state, that a name which has for so many years filled the whole civilized world with its fame was not remembered by Captain Holland. But he added, after expressing his regret that he could not at the moment recollect the real name of 'Boz,' that he had received a letter from him a few days previously, and that if I would meet him at the same time and place next day, he would bring me that letter, because it related to the 'Sketches' of the writer in the 'Monthly Magazine.' As Captain Holland knew I was at the time a parliamentary reporter on the 'Morning Chronicle,' then a journal of high literary reputation, and of great political influence, he supplemented his remark by saying that 'Boz' was a parliamentary reporter; on which I observed that I must, in that case, know him, at least by sight, as I was acquainted, in that respect, more or less, with all the reporters in the gallery of the House of Commons.

"Captain Holland and I met, according to appointment, on the following day, when he brought me the letter to which he had referred. I then found that the name of the author of 'Sketches by Boz' was Charles Dickens. The letter was written in the most moderate terms. It was simply to the effect that as he (Mr. Dickens) had hitherto given all his contributions—those signed 'Boz'—gratuitously, he would be glad if Captain Holland thought his 'Sketches' to be worthy of any small remuneration, as otherwise he would be obliged to discontinue them, because he was going very soon to get married, and therefore would be subjected to more expenses than he was while living alone, which he was during the time, in Furnival's Inn.

"It was not quite clear from Mr. Dickens's letter to Captain Holland, whether he meant he would be glad to receive any small consideration for the series of 'Sketches,' about a dozen in number, which he had furnished to the 'Monthly Magazine' without making any charge, or whether he only expected to be paid for those he might afterwards send. Neither do I know whether Captain Holland furnished him with any pecuniary expression of his admiration of

THE HOUSE IN FURNIVAL'S INN (1833-'36).

[Our Author's earliest London home, after leaving his father's house. Here he had chambers when a reporter, and some time before he received any appointment as a writer for the press. Here the "Sketches by Boz" were written, and the largest portion of his best-known work, the inimitable "Pickwick Papers."]

the 'Sketches by Boz' which had appeared in the 'Monthly.' But immediately on receiving Mr. Dickens's letter, I wrote to him, saying that the editorship of the 'Monthly Magazine' had come into my hands, and that, greatly admiring his 'Sketches' under the signature of 'Boz,' I should be glad if we could come to any arrangement for a continuance of them. I concluded my note by expressing a hope that he would, at his earliest convenience, let me know on what terms per sheet he would be willing to furnish me with similar sketches every month for an indefinite period.

"By return of post I received a letter from Mr. Dickens, to the effect that he had just entered into an arrangement with Messrs. Chapman & Hall to write a monthly serial. He did not name the work, but I found in a few weeks it was none other than the 'Pickwick Papers.' He added, that as this serial would occupy much of his spare time from his duties as a reporter, he could not undertake to furnish me with the proposed sketches for less than eight guineas per sheet, which was at the rate of half a guinea per page.

"I wrote to him in reply, that the price was not too much, but that I could not get the proprietor to give the amount, because when the 'Monthly Magazine' came into his hands it was not in the same flourishing state as it once had been. I was myself, at this time, getting ten guineas a sheet from Captain Marryat for writing for his 'Metropolitan Magazine,' which was started by Thomas Campbell and Tom Moore, in opposition to the 'New Monthly Magazine,' and at the rate of twenty guineas per sheet for my contributions to the 'Penny Cyclopædia.'

"Only imagine," concludes Mr. Grant, with pardonable fervor, "Mr. Dickens offering to furnish me with a continuation, for any length of time which I might have named, of his 'Sketches by Boz' for eight guineas a sheet, whereas in little more than six months from that date he could—so great in the interval had his popularity become—have got 100 guineas per sheet of sixteen pages from any of the leading periodicals of the day!"*

Dr. Charles Mackay writes to us: "John Black, of the 'Morning Chronicle,' was always keen to discover young genius, and to help it onward in the struggle of life. He very early discovered the talents of Dickens—not only as a reporter, but as a writer." Dr. Mackay was sub-editor of the 'Morning Chronicle' when Dickens was a reporter. He continues: "I have often heard Black speak of him, and predict his future fame. When Dickens had become famous, Black exerted all his influence with Sir John Easthope, principal proprietor of the 'Chronicle,' to have Dickens engaged as a writer of leading articles. He (Black) had his wish, and Dickens wrote several articles; but he did not seem to take kindly to such work, and did not long continue at it."

And Mr. Gruneisen writes: "I believe I must add my name to the remaining list of editorial workers who became acquainted with Charles Dickens when he was in the Gallery. I hope my memory is not deceiving me when I claim for Vincent Dowling, once a reporter, and for years the respected editor of 'Bell's Life in London,' the credit of having been the first to discover the genius for sketching charac-

---

* "Morning Advertiser," 13th June, 1870.

ters of Dickens. 'J. G.' may remember that the proprietary of the 'Morning Chronicle,' the 'Observer,' and 'Bell's Life' was in the hands, if I remember rightly, exclusively of Mr. Perry, and the publication of the several papers was at the Strand office. I have a distinct recollection that Dr. Black's notice of Dickens was based on writings which had been in print prior to his joining the reporting staff of the 'Morning Chronicle.' Dr. Black was always very emphatic in his prognostications of the brilliant future of Charles Dickens. In 1835 the famed novelist was spoken of among his colleagues as a man of mark. The 'Boz' sketches, if not the rage of the general public, had attracted the attention of the literary circles of the day.

"Respecting the marvellous facility of Dickens as a reporter, many versions of his notetaking of a speech of the late Lord Derby (when Lord Stanley) have been current, and I had a correspondence with Dickens on the subject only some months since, he promising to give me the accurate record of his stenographic feat when he met me. This promise he fulfilled the last time, alas! I ever saw him alive, at the anniversary dinner of the News-venders' Benevolent Institution, when he took the Chair in Free-masons' Hall—the last banquet at which he presided. It was in consequence of a reporter having broken down for the 'Mirror of Parliament' that the late Lord Derby, after complimenting Dickens for his report in the 'Chronicle,' dictated to him his speech—the 'Mirror,' as you are aware, giving in those days *verbatim* reports."

When Charles Dickens first became acquainted with Mr. Vincent Dowling, editor of "Bell's Life"—or "Sleepless Life," as he facetiously termed it, from its Latin heading, "*Nunquam Dormio*" ("wide awake")—he would generally stop at old Tom Goodwin's oyster and refreshment rooms, opposite the office, in the Strand. On one occasion, Mr. Dowling, not knowing who had called, desired that the gentleman would leave his name, to be sent over to the office, whereupon young Dickens wrote:

"CHARLES DICKENS,
"*Resurrectionist*,
"*In search of a Subject.*"

Some recent cases of body-snatching had then made the matter a general topic for public discussion, and Goodwin pasted up the strange address-card for the amusement of the medical students who patronized his oysters. It was still upon his wall when "Pickwick" had made Dickens famous, and the old man was never tired of pointing it out to those whom he was pleased to call his "bivalve demolishers!"

We may just mention that it was Dowling who rushed down from the reporters' gallery and seized Bellingham, after his assassination of Spencer Perceval.

The late Mr. Jerdan used to describe how he caught the Prime Minister in his arms.

CHAPTER II.

PUBLICATION OF THE "PICKWICK PAPERS."

WE have thought it right to give Mr. Grant's personal account of Dickens's early career *entire*, but it is only fair to other friends of the deceased novelist, who have favored us with particulars, that their recollections should find a place in these pages. From them we learn that in the year 1835 our author made his *début* as a writer, "with the exception of certain tragedies achieved at the mature age of eight or ten, and represented with great applause to overflowing nurseries." His first sketch, entitled "Mrs. Joseph Porter," was inserted in the "Old Monthly Magazine." In the preface to the "Pickwick Papers," mention is made of the effect its publication had on him:

"— My first effusion—dropped stealthily one evening at twilight, with fear and trembling, into a dark letter-box, in a dark office, up a dark court in Fleet Street—appeared in all the glory of print; on which occasion, by-the-by —how well I recollect it!—I walked down to Westminster Hall, and turned into it for half an hour, because my eyes were so dimmed with joy and pride that they could not bear the street, and were not fit to be seen there." A number of other papers were sent to the same magazine, and subsequently he contributed a similar series to the evening edition of the "Morning Chronicle."

The pseudonym adopted was "Boz," which quaint signature subsequently gave rise to the epigram:

"Who the dickens 'Boz!' could be
Puzzled many a curious elf;
Till time unveil'd the mystery,
And 'Boz' appear'd as Dickens' self."

And Tom Hood, in the character of an "uneducated poet," says:

"Arn't that 'ere 'Boz' a tip-top feller!
Lots writes well, but he writes Weller!"

The reason for such a singular *nom-de-plume* is thus told by the author himself: "*Boz* was the nickname of a pet child, a younger brother, whom I had dubbed Moses, in honor of 'The Vicar of Wakefield;' which being facetiously pronounced through the nose, became Boses, and being shortened became Boz. *Boz* was a very familiar household word to me long before I was an author, and so I came to adopt it."

The reception the "Sketches" met with was, we are assured, immense; and it has been truly said: "They were the first of their class. Dickens was the first to unite the delicately-playful thread of Charles Lamb's street musings —half experiences, half bookish phantasies— with the vigorous wit, and humor, and observation of Goldsmith's 'Citizen of the World,' his 'Indigent Philosopher,' and 'Man in Black,' and twine them together in that golden cord of Essay, which combines literature with philosophy, humor with morality, amusement with instruction." The wonderful fund of humor and picturesque word-painting contained in them surprises, even in these days, most persons who read them for the first time. They are, as Pope wrote:

"From grave to gay, from lively to severe."

The most thrilling and impressive are, undoubtedly, "A Visit to Newgate" and "The Drunkard's Death," while perhaps the best comic ones are the celebrated "Election for Beadle," "Greenwich Fair," and "Miss Evans at the Eagle."

In February, 1836, the first series, in two volumes, illustrated by George Cruikshank, was published in a collected form by Macrone, of St. James's Square, and in the December following the second series was issued. Macrone, shortly afterwards, being in distressed circumstances, sold the copyright to Messrs. Chapman and Hall for £1100. At the present day their popularity still remains unabated, and it is seldom, at a Penny Reading or entertainment by an Elocution Class, that one or more of them is not selected as a staple attraction in the programme.

To show how persons at times may take a mistaken and bigoted view of things in general, and how apt they are to look with jaundiced eyes on humorous writing, we may be pardoned for mentioning that, at one of the Penny Readings at Stowmarket, Suffolk, some nine years since, on the announcement of a Mr. Gudgeon's intention to read "The Bloomsbury Christening," he received this epistle from the horrified rector:

"Stowmarket Vicarage, Feb. 25, 1861.

"Sir,—My attention has been directed to a piece called 'The Bloomsbury Christening,' which you propose to read this evening. Without presuming to claim any interference in the arrangement of the Readings, I would suggest to you whether you have, on this occasion, sufficiently considered the character of the composition you have selected. I quite appreciate the laudable motive of the promoters of the Readings to raise the moral tone and direct this taste in a familiar and pleasant manner. 'The Bloomsbury Christening' can not possibly do this. It trifles with a sacred ordinance, and the language and style, instead of improving the taste, has a direct tendency to lower it.

"I appeal to your right feeling whether it be desirable to give publicity to that which must shock several of your audience, and create a smile among others, to be indulged in only by violating the conscientious scruples of their neighbors.

"The ordinance which is here exposed to ridicule is one which is much misunderstood and neglected among many families belonging to the Church of England, and the mode in which it is treated in this chapter can not fail to appear as giving a sanction to, or at least excusing, such neglect.

"Although you are pledged to the public to give this subject, yet I can not but believe that they would fully justify your substitution of it by another, did they know the circumstances. An abridgment would only lessen the evil, as it is not only the style of the writing, but the subject itself, which is objectionable.

"Excuse me for troubling you, but I felt that, in common with yourself, I have a grave responsibility in the matter, and I am,

"Most truly yours, T. S. Coles.

"To Mr. J. Gudgeon."

It is not generally known that some time before "Pickwick" had been thought of by either publisher or author, Dickens was engaged upon a novel, the fate of which we may now never know. The success of the "Sketches" was such—a *second* edition being called for immediately after they were issued—that Macrone entered into an arrangement with "Boz" to publish this work in the regular three-volume form. The title was to be "Gabriel Vardon"—and a new novel by the author of "Sketches by Boz" was at once advertised by the publisher, and continued to be so announced until the commencement of 1837, when Macrone failed in business, and the advertisement was withdrawn. Could the novel have been laid aside to appear, four years later, in the altered form of "Barnaby Rudge," in which—as the reader may remember—"Gabriel Varden" (not *Vardon*), the father of Dolly, is one of the principal characters?

It has been recently stated, in more than one journal, that "The Sketches by Boz" were not republished in a collective form until *after* the success of "Pickwick." This is a mistake. It was in the month following the publication of the "Sketches"—in March, 1836—that the first number of the "Pickwick Papers" was issued, and in the following year the work was published in a complete form, and dedicated to Mr. Serjeant Talfourd, an old and attached friend, and one of the first to recognize Dickens's extraordinary genius. He it was that presided at the monthly dinner, at the conclusion of which the proof of the forthcoming number of "Pickwick" was read by him (Talfourd). The guests—some half a dozen literary and personal friends—expressed their opinions, suggested changes, etc., which the author took kindly, and often availed himself of.

His friend, the late Mr. Maclise, often told how that he, John Forster, and Charles Dickens used to meet at "Jack Straw's Castle," Hampstead Heath, and there Dickens would read to them that which he had written during the week; and this done, the rest of the time would be passed in a pleasant commingling of good cheer and genial criticism. "But this," the great artist would add, "was in the good old days gone by, when we were all young, and had the world before us."

Subsequently, in sending a complete copy of the work to his friend Talfourd, he took occasion to speak of his learned friend's exertions to secure to authors an extended term of copyright in their works:

"If I had not enjoyed the happiness of your private friendship, I should still have dedicated this work to you, as a slight and most inadequate acknowledgment of the inestimable services you are rendering to the literature of your country. * * * Many a fevered head and palsied hand will gather new vigor in the hour of sickness and distress from your excellent exertions; many a widowed mother and orphan child, who would otherwise reap nothing from the fame of departed genius but its too frequent legacy of poverty and suffering, will bear, in their altered condition, higher testimony to the value of your labors than the most lavish encomium from lip or pen could ever afford.

"Besides such tributes, any avowal of feeling from me on the question to which you have devoted the combined advantages of your eloquence, character, and genius, would be powerless indeed. Nevertheless, in thus publicly expressing my deep and grateful sense of your efforts in behalf of English literature, and of those who devote themselves to the most precarious of all pursuits, I do but imperfect justice to my own strong feelings on the subject, if I do no service to you."

The entire letter was printed as an introduction to the old, original, and large-size edition of "Pickwick," but it has been omitted in the "Charles Dickens Edition" recently issued.

An amusing anecdote is remembered of our author and the learned Serjeant. At a public dinner, some years afterwards, Mr. Talfourd, regretting the absence of his friend Dickens, paid an appropriate and well-merited compliment to the breadth of surface over which the life, character, and general knowledge contained in his works extended. The reporter, not rightly hearing this, or not attending to it, but probably saying to himself, "Oh, it's about Dickens —one can't go wrong," gave a version of the learned Serjeant's speech in the next morning's paper, to the effect that Mr. Dickens's genius comprised that of all the greatest minds of the time put together, and that *his* works represented all *their* works. The high ideal and imaginative—the improvements in the steam-engine and machinery—all the new discoveries in anatomy, geology, and electricity, with the prize cartoons, and history and philosophy thrown into the bargain—one had only to search from the "Sketches by Boz" down to "Martin Chuzzlewit" to find, in some shape or other— "properly understood"—all these, and much more; in fact, every thing valuable which the world of letters elsewhere contains! We need hardly say that no reader of this astounding report was more amused than was Mr. Dickens himself, when he glanced over his newspaper on the following morning.

A great deal has been said of the origin of Pickwick and his Club, but notwithstanding the accounts given by both author and artist are perplexingly circumstantial, the reader will have but little difficulty in coming to a conclusion upon the matter.

The artist's account, given in the introduction to the last edition of "Seymour's Sketches," is this: "Seymour was very fond of horticultural pursuits, and took great pains in cultivating a very nice garden which was attached to his house. Being rather disappointed with the effect of his gardening operations, it was suggested to him that the misfortunes of an amateur gardener might be made the subject of some humorous drawings. After revolving the idea in his mind for a short time, he resolved upon converting it into something of a sporting character, and said it should be 'Pickwick and his Club.' His first notion was to bring it out on a similar plan to that of the 'Heiress,' which appeared in 1830, and he proposed the subject to Mr. M'Lean. This was in the autumn of 1835, during which Mr. Spooner frequently called at Seymour's house to ascertain the progress of the plates for the 'Book of Christmas,' and on one of these occasions Seymour brought forward the project of 'Pickwick,' which Spooner highly approved; and, in talking the matter over between them, it was decided that it would be an improvement to add letter-press. The undertaking was so far put in motion that Seymour etched four plates from the drawings which he had made, and Mr. Spooner suggested that Theodore Hook should, if possible, be engaged for the letter-press. In consequence of Spooner being very much occupied in the production of the 'Book of Christmas,' which, through the author's (T. K. Hervey's) dilatoriness, came out a month later than it should have done, 'Pickwick' lay in abeyance, and the four plates that were etched remained in the artist's drawer for about three months, so that Seymour began to think that if he did not soon hear from Spooner he would bring out the work on his own account, and get H. Mayhew or Moncrieff to write for it. In February, 1836, Mr. Chapman, the publisher, called on Seymour and asked him to make a drawing for a wood-cut, which Seymour undertook on the express condition that it should be engraved by a certain engraver whom he named. At this interview he mentioned the 'Pickwick' design to Mr. Chapman, and showed him the plates. Chapman very soon closed with his offer, proposing at first that it should be brought out in half-guinea volumes; but Seymour, who desired the widest circulation, insisted on his original plan, for it was his own idea that it should be in shilling monthly numbers. The publisher then asked Seymour if he had engaged an author to do the writing, and upon receiving an answer in the negative, mentioned Mr. Clarke, the author of 'Three Courses and a Dessert.' This writer, however, the artist objected to, for a private reason. Chapman then spoke of 'Boz' (Mr. Dickens's pseudonym), and having in his hand one of the 'Pickwick' drawings, which was a representation of a poor author's troubles (afterwards converted into the 'Stroller's Tale'), he ended the matter by some pleasantry about the proverbial poverty of literary men, and expressed a hope that he would see Mr. Dickens, and lay his views of the matter before him. Soon after an interview took place between the parties, and the sum of £15 per month was agreed on as Dickens's recompense. The artist, however, soon found, like Winkle on the tall horse, that it was a difficult thing to direct the motions of an author who had his own views to consult. Seymour's scheme was certainly a form of narrative in which the principal incidents should be of a sporting character, something, as Mr. Dickens describes it, 'a Nimrod Club, the members of which were to go out shooting, fishing, and so forth.' Whether this design involves such a pastoral simplicity, and restricts the range of description so much as Mr. Dickens seems to imply, is perhaps capable of being disproved. Certain it is that sketches to illustrate the 'Pickwick Papers' were designed a considerable time before the letter-press was arranged for; and the well-known portrait of the founder of the club existed on paper at least five years prior to Mr. Chapman's visit to Seymour, when the artist unfolded his views. In the second plate of the 'Heiress' series, published March 1st, 1830, Mr. Pickwick introduces the modest girl, just arrived from the country, to Lady Dashfort, who exclaims, 'And blushing too—how very amusing!' The figure of Pickwick was a favorite character, a sort of stock-piece with Seymour—just as Mr. Briggs and Paterfamilias were favorites of John Leech, or as that stout elderly gentleman, with well-brushed whiskers, and invariably attired in a buttoned-up frock-coat, is of Mr. Charles Keene. In Sketch 114 of 'Seymour's Sketches,' a figure very closely resembling the well-known form of Pickwick may be seen. It should here be stated that the original designs were in some degree modified, as it is certain, from an entry in the artist's books, that 'the first four plates were re-etched. By whatever combination of counsels it happened, the first number of 'Pickwick' came out April 1st, and was very successful. Mr. Dickens wrote to Seymour the following letter:

"'MY DEAR SIR,—I had intended to write you to say how much gratified I feel by the pains you have bestowed on our mutual friend Mr. Pickwick, and how much the result of your labors has surpassed my expectations. I am happy to be able to congratulate you, the publishers, and myself on the success of the undertaking, which appears to have been most complete.

"'I have now another reason for troubling you. It is this: I am extremely anxious about the "Stroller's Tale," the more especially as many literary friends, on whose judgment I place great reliance, think it will create considerable sensation. I have seen your design for an etching to accompany it. I think it extremely good, but still it is not quite my idea; and as I feel so very solicitous to have it as complete as possible, I shall feel personally obliged if you will make another drawing. It will give me great pleasure to see you, as well as the drawing, when it is completed. With this view I have asked Chapman and Hall to take a glass of grog with me on Sunday evening (the only night I am disengaged), when I hope you will be able to look in.

"'The alteration I want I will endeavor to explain. I think the woman should be younger—the dismal man decidedly should, and he should be less miserable in appearance. To communicate an interest to the plate, his whole appearance should express more sympathy and solicitude; and while I represented the sick man as emaciated and dying, I would not make him too repulsive. The furniture of the room you have depicted *admirably*. I have ventured to make these suggestions, feeling assured that you will consider them in the spirit in which I submit them to your judgment. I shall be happy to hear from you that I may expect to see you on Sunday evening. Dear sir, very truly yours, CHARLES DICKENS.'

"In compliance with this wish, Seymour made a new drawing for the 'Stroller's Tale,' which he etched on steel, and gave it into the hands of Mr. Dickens on the Sunday evening appointed. This was the last illustration the artist did for 'Pickwick.' His sad death, which took place April 20th, 1836, is perhaps known to the reader.

"The second number of the 'Pickwick Papers' contained the following just eulogium: 'Some time must elapse before the void the deceased gentleman has left in his profession can be filled up. The blank his death has occasioned in the society which his amiable nature won and his talents adorned we hardly hope to see supplied. We do not allude to this distressing event in the vain hope of adding, by any eulogium of ours, to the respect in which the late Mr. Seymour's memory is held by all who ever knew him.'

"Mr. Dickens adds: 'Some apology is due to our readers with only three plates. When we say they comprise Mr. Seymour's last efforts, and that upon one of them, in particular (the embellishments of the "Stroller's Tale"), he was engaged to a late hour of the night preceding his death, we feel confident the excuse will be deemed a sufficient one.' This, however, is incorrect. We have already said that this plate, which was certainly the last Seymour did for 'Pickwick,' was given to Mr. Dickens on the Sunday evening on which Seymour met him at Furnival's Inn, about a fortnight before."

Such is the artist's account.

As recently as March, 1866, a letter concerning this subject appeared in the "Athenæum," signed "R. Seymour." This was from the son of the artist who drew those inimitable caricatures of George IV. and his Ministry, and who, as we have seen, was associated with Dickens in the production of Pickwick.

The following was Mr. Dickens's reply, sent to the editor of the "Athenæum:"

"Gad's Hill Place, March 28, 1866.

"As the author of the 'Pickwick Papers' (and of one or two other books), I send you a few facts, and no comments, having reference to a letter signed 'R. Seymour,' which in your editorial discretion you published last week.

"Mr. Seymour, the artist, never originated, suggested, or in any way had to do with, save as illustrator of what I devised, an incident, a character (except the sporting tastes of Mr. Winkle), a name, a phrase, or a word, to be found in the 'Pickwick Papers.'

"I never saw Mr. Seymour's handwriting, I believe, in my life.

"I never even saw Mr. Seymour but once in my life, and that was within eight-and-forty hours of his untimely death. Two persons, both still living, were present on that short occasion.

"Mr. Seymour died when only the first twenty-four printed pages of the 'Pickwick Papers' were published; I think before the next three or four pages were completely written; I am sure before one subsequent line of the book was invented.

"In the Preface to the cheap edition of the 'Pickwick Papers,' published in October, 1847, I thus described the origin of that work: 'I was a young man of three-and-twenty when the present publishers, attracted by some pieces I was at that time writing in the "Morning Chronicle" newspaper (of which one series had lately been collected and published in two volumes, illustrated by my esteemed friend Mr. George Cruikshank), waited upon me to propose a something that should be published in shilling numbers—then only known to me, or, I believe, to any body else, by a dim recollection of certain interminable novels in that form, which used, some five-and-twenty years ago, to be carried about the country by peddlers, and over some of which I remember to have shed innumerable tears before I served my apprenticeship to Life. * * * The idea propounded to me was that the monthly something should be a vehicle for certain plates, to be executed by Mr. Seymour; and there was a notion, either on the part of that admirable humorous artist, or of my visitor (I forgot which), that a "Nimrod Club," the members of which were to go out shooting, fishing, and so forth, and getting themselves into difficulties through their want of dexterity, would be the best means of introducing these. I objected, on consideration that, although born and partly bred in the country, I was no great sportsman, except in regard of all kinds of locomotion; that the idea was not novel, and had been already much used; that it would be infinitely better for the plates to arise naturally out of the text; and that I should like to take my own way, with a freer range of English scenes and people, and was afraid I should ultimately do so in any case, whatever course I might prescribe to myself at starting. My views being deferred to, I thought of Mr. Pickwick, and wrote the first number; from the proof-sheets of which Mr. Seymour made his drawing of the Club, and that happy portrait of its founder, by which he is always recognized, and which may be said to have made him a reality. I connected Mr. Pickwick with a club because of the original suggestion, and I put in Mr. Winkle expressly for the use of Mr. Seymour. We started with a number of twenty-four pages instead of thirty-two, and four illustrations in lieu of a couple. Mr. Seymour's sudden and lamented death before the second number was published brought about a quick decision upon a point already in agitation; the number became one of thirty-two pages with two illustrations, and remained so to the end.'

"In July, 1849, some incoherent assertions made by the widow of Mr. Seymour, in the course of certain endeavors of hers to raise money, induced me to address a letter to Mr. Edward Chapman, then the only surviving business partner in the original firm of Chapman & Hall, who first published the 'Pickwick Papers,' requesting him to inform me in writing whether the foregoing statement was correct.

"In Mr. Chapman's confirmatory answer, immediately written, he reminded me that I had given Mr. Seymour more credit than was his due. 'As this letter is to be historical,' he wrote, 'I may as well claim what little belongs to me in the matter, and that is, the figure of Pickwick. Seymour's first sketch' (made from the proof of my first chapter) 'was for a long thin man. The present immortal one he made from my description of a friend of mine at Richmond.'"

CHAPTER III.

POPULARITY OF THE "PICKWICK PAPERS."

Mr. James Grant's account of Dickens's earliest writings we have already given. The same gentleman has favored us with some personal recollections of the fortune which attended the first publication of "Pickwick:"

"In connection with the rapidity of Mr. Dickens's rise, and the heights to which he soared in the regions of literature, I may mention a few facts which have not before found their way into print. The terms on which he concluded an arrangement with Messrs. Chapman & Hall for the publication of the 'Pickwick Papers' were fifteen guineas for each number, the number consisting of two sheets, or thirty-two pages. That was a rather smaller sum than that at which he offered, just at the same time, to contribute to the 'Monthly Magazine,' then under my editorship.

"For the first five months of its existence Mr. Dickens's first serial, the 'Pickwick Papers,' was a signal failure, and notwithstanding the fact that Mr. Charles Tilt, at that time a publisher of considerable eminence, made extraordinary exertions, out of friendship for Messrs. Chapman & Hall, to insure its success. He sent out, on what is called sale or return, to all parts of the provinces, no fewer than fifteen hundred copies of each of the first five numbers. This gave the 'Pickwick Papers' a very extensive publicity, yet Mr. Tilt's only result was an average sale of about fifty copies of each of the five parts. A certain number of copies sold, of course, through other channels, but commercially the publication was a decided failure. Two months before this Mr. Seymour, the artist, died suddenly, but left sketches for two parts more, and the question was then debated by the publishers whether they ought not to discontinue the publication of the serial. But just while the matter was under their consideration, Sam Weller, who had been introduced in the previous number, began to attract great attention, and to call forth much admiration. The press was all but unanimous in praising 'Samivel' as an entirely original character, whom none but a great genius could have created; and all of a sudden, in consequence of 'Samivel's' popularity, the 'Pickwick Papers' rose to an unheard-of popularity. The back numbers of the work were ordered to a large extent, and of course all idea of discontinuing it was abandoned.

"No one can read these interesting incidents without being struck with the fact that the future literary career of Mr. Dickens should have been for a brief season placed in circumstances of so much risk of proving a failure; for there can be no doubt that, had the publication of his serial been discontinued at this particular period, there was little or no probability that other publishers would have undertaken the risk of any other literary venture of his. And he might consequently have lived and died, great as his gifts and genius were, without being known in the world of literature. How true it is that there is a tide in the affairs of men!

"By the time the 'Pickwick Papers' had reached their twelfth number, that being half of the numbers of which it was originally intended the work should consist, Messrs. Chapman & Hall were so gratified with the signal success to which it had now attained, that they sent Mr. Dickens a check for £500, as a practical expression of their satisfaction with the sale. The work continued steadily to increase in circulation until its completion, when the sale had all but reached 40,000 copies. In the interval between the twelfth and concluding number, Messrs. Chapman & Hall sent Mr. Dickens several checks, amounting in all to £3000, in addition to the fifteen guineas per number which they had engaged at the beginning to give him. It was understood at the time that Messrs. Chapman & Hall made a clear profit of nearly £20,000 by the sale of the 'Pickwick Papers,' after paying Mr. Dickens in round numbers £3500.

"Probably," concludes Mr. Grant, "there are few instances on record in the annals of literature in which an author rose so rapidly to popularity and attained so great a height in it as Mr. Dickens. His popularity was all the more remarkable because it was reached while yet a mere youth. He was incomparably the most popular author of his day before he had attained his twenty-sixth year; and what is even more extraordinary still, he retained the distinction of being the most brilliant author of the age until the very hour of his death—a period of no less than thirty-five years."

Since the illustrious author's decease even the book-binders who have had the charge of "Pickwick" have been claiming the honor of stitching the sheets together, and giving their recollections to the newspapers. It having been stated in the "Daily Telegraph" newspaper that "it was a question between Messrs. Chapman and Hall and their binder, Mr. Bone," "whether a greater or less number than seven hundred copies should be stitched in wrappers; instead of hundreds, it soon became necessary to provide for the sale of thousands; and the green covers of 'Pickwick' were seen all over the country," a Mr. Joseph Aked, of Green Street, Leicester Square, on the following day sent this correction to the same journal:

"SIR,—In your sketch of the Life and Death of Mr. Charles Dickens, in yesterday's 'Telegraph,' you state that the first order given to the binder for Part I. of the 'Pickwick' was seven hundred copies, and it was a question between Messrs. Chapman & Hall, and Mr. Bone, the binder, whether a greater or less number than seven hundred should be stitched in wrapper.

"The first order for Part I. of the 'Pickwick' was for four hundred copies only, and the order was given to myself to execute (not to Mr. Bone) by Messrs. Chapman & Hall, the publishers, who in those days did not consult the binder about the number of copies they would require. Also the first number, stitched and put in the green cover, was done by myself, my work-people having left off work for the day.

"Before the completion of the work the sale amounted to nearly 40,000, the orders being given to myself and to Mr. Bone."

Readers of "Pickwick" found the style so fresh and novel, so totally unlike the forced fun and unreal laughter of the other light reading of their time, that the smallest scrap from any portion of the work was deemed worthy of frequent quotation—a gem in itself. We have seen a little book—now very rare, and not to be found in the British Museum—of which thousands and thousands of copies must have been sold by Mr. Park, of Long Lane, and Mr. Catnach, of Seven Dials, bearing the title of "Beauties of Pickwick."

The famed Pickwick cigar—the "Penny Pickwick" of our childhood—is too well known to need any comment. It was a "brand" originally made by a manufacturer in Leman Street, Minories, and sold in boxes and papers decorated with Mr. Pickwick, hat off, bowing to you in the politest manner, and offering for your notice a long scroll, setting forth the excellence of the cigar—a small cheroot, and containing about one-half of the tobacco used in a cigar of this kind sold at 2d. At the present day "Pickwicks" are patronized almost entirely by cab-drivers.

Then there were "Pickwick" hats, with narrow brims curved up at the sides, as in the figure of the immortal possessor of that name; "Pickwick" canes, with tassels; and "Pickwick" coats, with brass and horn buttons, and the cloth invariably dark green or dark plum. The name "Pickwick" is said to have been taken from the hamlet or cluster of houses which formed the last resting-stage for coaches going to Bath,* which town, it will be remembered, was the scene of Sam Weller's chaffing of "Blazes," the red-breeched footman.

But to return to the work as a literary composition. "The Pickwick Papers" stand alone from all Dickens's works. Like "Robinson Crusoe," "Tom Jones," "Gulliver," "Rabelais," "Tristram Shandy," "The Vicar of Wakefield," and half a score more, it will never die out or be forgotten. It is crammed with rollicking fun and drollery. You may read it fifty times and never tire of it. Open it at whatever page you will, the charm is such that one can not put it down without feeling thoroughly amused and delighted. We may remark that the well-known song, "The Ivy Green," which William Henry Russell used to sing with such *éclat* five-and-twenty years since, first appeared in "Pickwick." It is the only poetry contained in any of Dickens's novels. Judging from its merits, the author would doubtlessly have taken a very fair stand as a poet. In "Shy Neighborhoods" ("Uncommercial Traveller"), speaking of walking one night half-asleep, dozing heavily, and slumbering continually, he observes, "I made immense quantities of verses on that pedestrian occasion (of course I never make any when I am in my right senses)."

Concerning the inimitable "Pickwick," "Blackwood," many years since, in an article entitled "A Remonstrance with Dickens," thus bears testimony: "As to what the best bits are, only he who brings a virgin palate is, perhaps, qualified to discriminate, of so rich materials is the whole compounded; and to this day we are lost in admiration of the wealth of humor which could go on, page after page, chapter after chapter, month after month, to the close of a long work, pouring forth, from a source seemingly inexhaustible, fun, and incident, and description, and character, ever fresh, vivid, and new, which, if distributed with a thrifty hand, would have served to relieve and enliven, perhaps immortalize, twenty sober romances. The very plan of the work (if plan it can be called where plan seems none) evinces the writer's extraordinary confidence in his resources, where a knot of individuals, connected with the loosest tie, and interesting only from their unconscious drollery, are cast loose upon the world to wander through scenes of every-day life, in which, though constantly getting more absurd and weak, they yet gain a firm hold on the reader's affection; so that at length we take leave of Mr. Pickwick, in his rural retirement at Dulwich, with a lingering fondness, such as we have never felt for any of those young and handsome miracles of sense and spirit upon whose heroic career the vicissitudes of three thrilling volumes are suspended. * * * But so much geniality of all kinds is displayed in the book, that probably no appreciative reader ever rose from its perusal without a strong feeling of personal regard for the author—an element generally omitted in the estimate of a writer's genius, to which we always attach great importance."

A writer, whose name we have forgotten, remarked that "Pickwick" was made up of "two pounds of Smollett, three ounces of Sterne, a handful of Hook, a dash of the grammatical Pierce Egan—incidents at pleasure, served with an *original sauce piquante*." And Lady Chatterton, in one of her works, remarked: "Mr. Davy, who accompanied Colonel Chesney up the Euphrates, has recently been in the service of Mohammed Ali Pacha. 'Pickwick' happening to reach Davy while he was at Damascus, he read a part of it to the Pacha, who was so delighted with it, that Davy was on one occasion summoned to him in the middle of the night, to finish the reading of some part in which they had been interrupted. Mr. Davy read in Egypt, upon another occasion, some passages from these unrivalled papers to a blind Englishman, who was in such ecstasy with what he had heard, that he exclaimed he was almost thankful he could not see he was in a foreign country, for that, while he listened, he felt completely as though he were again in England."

"Pickwick" was attacked in the "Quarterly Review," which declared that "indications are not wanting that the peculiar vein of humor which has hitherto yielded such attractive metal is worn out;" but the rancorous article did not change public opinion, and the work continued just as popular as ever.

James Smith (one of the authors of "The Rejected Addresses"), according to the "Law Magazine," one day made the bold assertion that *he* clearly preceded Mr. Dickens in the line which first acquired "The Pickwick Papers" their popularity.

Sydney Smith had two tests for the goodness of a novel: "Does it make you deaf to the dinner-bell?

"While reading it, do you forget to answer, even if a bishop should speak to you?"

---

* "PICKWICK (97 m.).—A degree of importance is attached to this small place, from its contiguity to Corsham House (1 m.), the celebrated seat of Paul Cobb Methuen, Esq., whose superb collection of paintings are the theme and admiration of every visitor. On the right of Pickwick stands Hartham Park, the seat of —— Jay, Esq., and Pickwick Lodge, belonging to Caleb Dickenson, Esq."—"Walks through Bath." By PIERCE EGAN, 1819.

Moncrieff, the famous author of "Tom and Jerry," and a hundred farces and light comedies, dramatized "Pickwick" long before it was finished, for the Strand Theatre, where it was performed under the title of "Sam Weller; or, The Pickwickians;" Mr. W. J. Hammond sustaining the character of Sam Weller. The termination of the drama was very different to that given in the book itself, as will be readily seen. The adapter caused Mrs. Bardell to be tried and found guilty of attempted bigamy, her husband being Alfred Jingle. Messrs. Dodson & Fogg, the Freeman Court sharks, were sent to Newgate for conspiracy, and only released upon payment of the sum of £300 or thereabouts, which Mr. Pickwick, on receiving, very generously handed to Jingle to start afresh in the world—the curtain falling with a herald entering and announcing the accession of Queen Victoria, which occurred about this time!

Another version was acted, with indifferent success, at the Adelphi, Yates representing Mr. Pickwick, and John Reeve Sam Weller. In February, 1838, Mr. G. W. M. Reynolds started a monthly "Pickwick Abroad; or, A Tour in France," illustrated by Alfred Crowquill. As a curiosity, it deserves to be read, if only to see the immense difference existing between the two books.

CHAPTER IV.

DICKENS AS A DRAMATIST.—"OLIVER TWIST."

It was in the year 1836 that Mr. Thackeray, according to an anecdote related by himself, offered Mr. Dickens to undertake the task of illustrating one of his works. The story was told by the former at an anniversary dinner of the Royal Academy a few years since, Mr. Dickens being present on the occasion. "I can remember (said Mr. Thackeray) when Mr. Dickens was a very young man, and had commenced delighting the world with some charming humorous works in covers which were colored light green, and came out once a month, that this young man wanted an artist to illustrate his writings; and I recollect walking up to his chambers in Furnival's Inn, with two or three drawings in my hand, which, strange to say, he did not find suitable. But for the unfortunate blight which came over my artistical existence, it would have been my pride and my pleasure to have endeavored one day to find a place on these walls for one of my performances." The work referred to was the "Pickwick Papers." Seymour, the illustrator, having destroyed himself in a fit of derangement, a new artist was wanted, and the result was the singular interview between the two men whose names, though representing schools of fiction so widely different, were destined to become constantly associated in the public mind.

A leading article in a morning newspaper on the occasion of Mr. Thackeray's death, in telling the anecdote of his attempt to illustrate "Pickwick," adds that, disappointed at the rejection of his offer, he exclaimed, "Well, if you will not let me draw, I will write;" and from that hour determined to compete with his illustrious brother novelist for public favor. Nothing could be more opposed to the facts than this colored version of the anecdote. It was not for a year or two after the event referred to that he began seriously to devote himself to literary labor; and his articles, published anonymously, and only now for the first time brought into notice, because recognized from their *noms-de-plume* to have been written by him, contain the best evidences that he felt no shadow of ill-will for a rejection which he always good-humoredly alluded to as "Mr. Pickwick's lucky escape!"*

The artists eventually engaged to take Seymour's place were, first Mr. Buss, and then Mr. Hablot Knight Browne, who had, in wood-cut, illustrated a small pamphlet by Mr. Charles Dickens, now out of print and extremely scarce, on the subject of the Sabbath in London, and bearing the title of "Sunday under three Heads." As is well known, the same artist, under the quaint signature of "Phiz," apparently intended to match the author's own *nom-de-plume*, "Boz," continued to etch the plates for Mr. Dickens's monthly numbers for many years afterwards. Poor Tom Hood used to stumble at the name: "Fizz, Whizz, or something of that sort," he would say.

During the publication of "The Pickwick Papers" St. James's Theatre was opened, September 29th, 1836, with a burletta entitled "The Strange Gentleman," written by "Boz;" Pritt Harley acted the *Strange Gentleman;* and "Boz," himself, on one occasion took a part. The piece ran until December, when it was withdrawn for an operatic burletta, "The Village Coquettes," by the same author, the music by John Hullah. The parts were sustained by Messrs. Harley (as Martin Stokes), Braham (as Squire Norton), Bennett (as George Edmunds), and John Parry; Mesdames Smith, Rainsforth (as Lucy Benson), and others. It met with a marked reception; and Braham, for a long time after, at different concerts, sang "The Child and the Old Man sat alone," invariably getting

---

* Theodore Taylor's "Life of Thackeray," p. 63.

encored most enthusiastically. Three other songs in the burletta were great favorites, viz., "Love is not a Feeling to pass away," "Autumn Leaves," and "There's a Charm in Spring." The book of the words was published by Mr. Bentley, and dedicated to J. Pritt Harley in the following terms:

"My dramatic bantlings are no sooner born than you father them. You have made my Strange Gentleman exclusively your own; you have adopted Martin Stokes with equal readiness."

The author, "Boz," excuses himself for appearing before the public as the composer of an operatic burletta in the following words:

"'Either the Honorable Gentleman is in the right, or he is not,' is a phrase in very common use within the walls of Parliament. This drama may have a plot, or it may not; and the songs may be poetry, or they may not; and the whole affair, from beginning to end, may be great nonsense, or it may not; just as the honorable gentleman or lady who reads it may happen to think. So, retaining his own private and particular opinion upon the subject (an opinion which he formed upwards of a year ago, when he wrote the piece), the author leaves every gentleman or lady to form his or hers, as he or she may think proper, without saying one word to influence or conciliate them.

"All he wishes to say is this—that he hopes Mr. Braham, and all the performers who assisted in the representation of this Opera, will accept his warmest thanks for the interest they evinced in it from its very first rehearsal, and for their zealous efforts in his behalf—efforts which have crowned it with a degree of success far exceeding his most sanguine anticipations, and of which no form of words could speak his acknowledgment.

"It is needless to add, that the *libretto* of an Opera must be, to a certain extent, a mere vehicle for the music; and that it is scarcely fair or reasonable to judge it by those strict rules of criticism which would be justly applicable to a five-act tragedy or a finished comedy."

About this time (in 1837, we believe) Mr. Dickens married Miss Catherine Hogarth, a daughter of Mr. George Hogarth, musical and dramatic critic of the "Morning Chronicle," author of "Memoirs of the Musical Drama," and formerly a writer to the "Signet" in Scotland. Dickens now left his old chambers in Furnival's Inn, and took the house, No. 48 Doughty Street, Mecklenburg Square. Soon after he was installed editor of "Bentley's Miscellany," and he began therein "Oliver Twist," subsequently published in a complete form by

NO. 48 DOUGHTY ST., MECKLENBURG SQUARE (1837-'40).

[When Mr. Dickens got married, he removed from Furnival's Inn to this house. Here were written the concluding numbers of "Pickwick," "Oliver Twist," and "Nicholas Nickleby."]

Mr. Bentley in November, 1838, illustrated by some of the finest etchings that ever sprang from the magic needle of George Cruikshank. Any criticism upon the work at this time is at least needless, if not impertinent; but we may be forgiven in saying that the work abounds in touches of surpassing pathos, picturesque description, and dramatic effect, while the sombre parts are relieved by a rich vein of irresistible humor. The death of Bill Sykes, after the barbarous murder of poor Nancy, is one of the most thrilling and effective chapters in the book. Bumble the Beadle has attained a world-wide reputation. The scene of his courtship with Mrs. Corney—first prudently ascertaining the value of the spoons, etc.—is perhaps the best "bit" of all.

In proof of Dickens's accuracy in all matters of detail, an eminent medical authority assures us that his description of hectic, given in "Oliver Twist," has found its way into more than one standard English work,[*] in both medicine

---

[*] Miller's "Principles of Surgery," second edition, p. 46; also Dr. Aitkin's "Practice of Medicine," third edition, vol. i. p. 111.

and surgery, also into several American and French books of medicine.

The preface to "The Charles Dickens Edition" (1867) speaks of Alderman Laurie having called in question the existence of such a place as Jacob's Island, and declares that even then, in 1867, it may be seen in almost the same squalid and filthy state as it was when first described. "Oliver Twist" was directed with great effect against the Poor-law and work-house system. It will be remembered by many that a great outcry was raised at the time of its original publication, and statements respecting its "gross untruth" and "distorted facts" were freely made. Can any one, reading the shocking and disgraceful disclosures made during the last three or four years, still maintain that erroneous opinion?

A meeting was held at Willis's Rooms, on 3d March, 1866, to promote the establishment of an Association for the Improvement of the Infirmaries of the London Work-houses. Mr. Ernest Hart, the Secretary, had invited Dickens to attend the meeting and take part in the proceedings. In his reply, the author of "Oliver Twist" said:

"An annual engagement which I can not possibly forego will prevent my attending next Saturday's meeting, and (consequently) my seconding the resolution proposed to be intrusted to me for that purpose. My knowledge of the general condition of sick poor in work-houses is not of yesterday, nor are my efforts in my vocation to call merciful attention to it. Few anomalies in England are so horrible to me as the unchecked existence of many shameful sick-wards for paupers side by side with the constantly increasing expansion of conventional wonder that the poor should creep into corners and die rather than fester and rot in those infamous places.

"You know what they are, and have manfully told what they are, to the awakening at last, it would seem, of rather more than the seven distinguished sleepers. If any subscriptions should be opened to advance the objects of our association, do me the kindness to set me down for £20."

Mr. Sheldon M'Kenzie, in the American "Round Table," relates this anecdote of "Oliver Twist:"

"In London I was intimate with the brothers Cruikshank, Robert and George, but more particularly with the latter. Having called upon him one day at his house (it then was in Mydleton Terrace, Pentonville), I had to wait while he was finishing an etching, for which a printer's boy was waiting. To while away the time, I gladly complied with his suggestion that I should look over a port-folio crowded with etchings, proofs, and drawings, which lay upon the sofa. Among these, carelessly tied together in a wrap of brown paper, was a series of some twenty-five or thirty drawings, very carefully finished, through most of which were carried the well-known portraits of Fagin, Bill Sykes and his dog, Nancy, the Artful Dodger, and Master Charles Bates—all well known to the readers of 'Oliver Twist.' There was no mistake about it; and when Cruikshank turned round, his work finished, I said as much. He told me that it had long been in his mind to show the life of a London thief by a series of drawings engraved by himself, in which, without a single line of letter-press, the story would be strikingly and clearly told. 'Dickens,' he continued, 'dropped in here one day, just as you have done, and, while waiting until I could speak with him, took up that identical port-folio, and ferreted out that bundle of drawings. When he came to that one which represents Fagin in the condemned cell, he studied it for half an hour, and told me that he was tempted to change the whole plot of his story; not to carry Oliver Twist through adventures in the country, but to take him up into the thieves' den in London, show what their life was, and bring Oliver through it without sin or shame. I consented to let him write up to as many of the designs as he thought would suit his purpose; and that was the way in which Fagin, Sykes, and Nancy were created. My drawings suggested them, rather than individuality suggesting my drawings.'"

How the remarkable figure of Fagin was first conceived Mr. Hodder tells us. The reader will remember the picture of the Jew malefactor in the condemned cell, biting his nails in the torture of remorse. Cruikshank had been laboring at the subject for several days, and thought the task hopeless, when, sitting up in his bed one morning, with his hand on his chin and his fingers in his mouth, the whole attitude expressive of despair, he saw his face in the cheval glass.

"That's it!" he exclaimed, "that's the expression I want!" and he soon finished the picture.

Thackeray, in "The Newcomes," remarked that "a profane work, called 'Oliver Twist,' having appeared, which George read out to his family with admirable emphasis, it is a fact that Lady Walham became so interested in the parish-boy's progress, that she took his history into her bedroom (where it was discovered, under Blatherwick's 'Voice from Mesopotamia,' by her ladyship's maid); and that Kew laughed so immensely at Mr. Bumble, the Beadle, as to endanger the reopening of his wound."

And again, in "Fraser's Magazine" for February, 1840, at the end of a clever satire upon the Newgate Calendar school of romance, purporting to be written by Ikey Solomons, Jun., Thackeray thus remarks upon "Oliver Twist:" "No man has read that remarkable tale without being interested in poor Nancy and her murderer, and especially amused and tickled by the gambols of the skillful Dodger and his companions. The power of the writer is so amazing, that the reader at once becomes his captive, and must follow him whithersoever he leads: and to what are we led? Breathless to watch all the crimes of Fagin, tenderly to deplore the errors of Nancy, to have for Bill Sykes a kind of pity and admiration, and an absolute love for the society of the Dodger. All these heroes stepped from the novel on to the stage; and the whole London public, from peers to chimney-sweeps, were interested about a set of ruffians whose occupations are thievery, murder, and prostitution. A most agreeable set of rascals, indeed, who have their virtues, too, but not good company for any man. We had better pass them by in decent silence; for, as no writer can or dare tell the *whole* truth concerning them, and faithfully explain their vices, there is no need to give *ex parte* statements of their virtues. * * * The pathos of the workhouse scenes in 'Oliver Twist,' of the Fleet Prison descriptions in 'Pickwick,' is genuine and pure—as much of this as you please; as tender a hand to the poor, as kindly a word to the unhappy as you will, but in the name of common sense let us not expend our sympathies on cut-throats and other such prodigies of evil!"

Albert Smith, in his "Adventures of Mr. Ledbury," observed that, "in the year 1840, he found an Italian translator of the book had placarded the name of the poor parish orphan of England against the walls of the Ducal Palace of Venice!"

In May, 1838, an adaptation of the story was produced at the Pavilion Theatre, and at the Surrey on November 19th following, and met with great success. The representations of "Oliver Twist" and "Jack Sheppard," being considered as entailing great mischief, were accordingly prohibited; but Mr. John Oxenford's version (specially licensed), in three acts, was produced at the New Queen's Theatre, in April, 1868, and attracted large audiences, Mr. J. L. Toole playing the Artful Dodger, and Miss Nelly Moore, Nancy. It was this version that became the subject of a Parliamentary discussion:

Dr. Brady asked the Secretary of State whether the Lord Chamberlain had refused to license a play dramatized by Mr. Oxenford from Mr. Dickens's celebrated work of "Oliver Twist;" and whether all plays from the same work were interdicted in London as being offensive to parish beadles; and whether he approved of the Lord Chamberlain's consideration for the feelings of the parish authorities.

Mr. Hardy: The parish beadles have not the influence with the Lord Chamberlain which the hon. member supposes. Formerly, "Oliver Twist" and "Jack Sheppard" were prohibited, but Mr. Oxenford's play has been licensed by the Lord Chamberlain.

Representations also took place at the Surrey, Victoria, Pavilion, and other theatres.

CHAPTER V.

THE COPYRIGHT OF "OLIVER TWIST."

HERE we come to a matter connected with the transfer of the copyright of "Oliver Twist" back into Mr. Dickens's own possession, which, many years later, occasioned a controversy in the public papers. Mr. Jerdan, the once famous editor of the "Literary Gazette," in his rambling autobiography, published in 1853, mentions (vol. iv.) that—"Bulwer, I believe, paid Mr. Bentley £750 to recover a small portion of copyright which he wished, in order to possess an entire property in his work; and, nearly at the same time, Mr. Dickens took a like step to repurchase a share of the copyright of 'Oliver Twist,' after it had launched "Bentley's Miscellany" prosperously on the popular tide, and gone through two or three profitable editions. The compensation was referred to Mr. John Forster and myself, and upon my table the sum of £2250 was handed over to Mr. Bentley, and both parties perfectly satisfied. But was not 'the trade' fortunate in so easily adding to handsome preceding emoluments, the total of no less than £3000?"

Mr. Bentley, in a letter to "The Critic" (now defunct, which had reviewed the book, and quoted the above paragraph), replied:

"MR. JERDAN'S AUTOBIOGRAPHY.

"SIR,—In your last number, while reviewing the concluding volume of Mr. Jerdan's Autobiography, you quote a statement made by him relative to two transactions—one with Sir Edward Bulwer Lytton, and the other with Mr. Charles Dickens and myself—which, if left uncontradicted, is calculated to be injurious to me. This statement, I distinctly assert, is *grossly incorrect;* and I have thought it necessary to call upon Mr. Jerdan to cancel it altogether.

"I greatly regret, for Mr. Jerdan's sake, as well as the parties referred to, that he should have ventured to commit such an indiscretion.

"Yours faithfully, RICHARD BENTLEY.
"New Burlington Street, Jan. 12, 1854."

To which Jerdan, in turn, wrote:

"MR. BENTLEY AND MR. JERDAN.
"*To the Editor of* 'The Critic' *London Literary Journal.*

"SIR,—Having admitted a letter from Mr. Bentley to your columns, impugning a statement you did me the honor to quote in your notice of the fourth volume of my Autobiography, I beg your permission to insert the following observations on the complaint:

"If I could have supposed, for an instant, that the facts related were calculated to do Mr. Bentley the slightest injury, I never would have published them; but, on the most earnest consideration of the matter, I must say that such an idea is perfectly incomprehensible.

"In the one instance, I mention a report that Sir Edward Lytton Bulwer had paid a certain sum to Mr. Bentley for the restoration of a particular copyright; and, in the other, I state from my own knowledge the circumstance of Mr. Dickens having paid a larger sum for a similar reassignment.

"Now, I would ask, to what does this amount? It may go to prove the truism that publishers are more likely than authors to keep their coaches; but all the rest simply amounts to the commonest commercial arrangement, viz., that Sir Edward Bulwer Lytton and Mr. Dickens paid Mr. Bentley a fair price for what they desired to purchase, and which he had no higher or more profitable object in wishing to retain. In the more important case I was his own arbiter, and surely I would not accuse myself of having been a party to a transaction injurious to my principal or to Mr. Dickens, by sanctioning a disreputable arbitration, of which I may add, that it had the rare good fortune, at the time, to be perfectly satisfactory to all concerned.

"As for any breach of confidence, you, sir, are far too conversant with the literary world to suppose that these matters were not the common talk of every circle in London, and that the attempt to represent them as secrets is very preposterous.

"I am indeed sorry that Mr. Bentley's feelings or *amour propre* have been disturbed; but I am sure that few persons, except himself, will think that I have cast a blot on his publishing scutcheon. I am, sir, yours obediently,
"W. JERDAN.
"January 25th."

Another letter from Mr. Bentley closed the controversy:

"*To the Editor of* 'The Critic.'

"New Burlington Street, February 13, 1854.

"SIR,—You will oblige me by giving insertion in your journal to the accompanying letter from Mr. Forster, which has been handsomely sent to me without any solicitation on my part.

"Yours faithfully, RICHARD BENTLEY."

[*Copy inclosed.*]

"58 Lincoln's Inn Fields, January 31, 1854.

"DEAR SIR,—I perceive that the 'Morning Herald' which I have just received, comes from you, and I can not doubt that it is sent to me because it contains a correspondence between yourself and Mr. Jerdan, in reference to a statement on the part of the latter, in which my name is introduced.

"I feel it right, in confirmation of your opinion, expressed in that correspondence, to state to you my own opinion, that the negotiation was undoubtedly of a private nature, and one with which the public have no concern.

"Further, there were matters in dispute between yourself and Mr. Dickens, the fair adjustment of which was taken into account when the the sum of £2250 was fixed upon as the price at which he should purchase back from you the copyright of 'Oliver Twist.'

"This matter having been brought before the public without any fault of yours, it is just towards you that I should write these few words; and I do so with the knowledge and consent of Mr. Dickens himself. Yours very truly,
"JOHN FORSTER.
"R. BENTLEY, Esq."

"Oliver Twist" completed, Dickens resigned the editorship to Mr. W. Harrison Ainsworth, who, we believe, still occupies that position. Just before the last installment was published, there appeared in "Bentley's Miscellany" this:

"POETICAL EPISTLE FROM FATHER PROUT TO BOZ.

I.

"A RHYME! a rhyme! from a distant clime—from the
    gulf of the Genoese:
O'er the rugged scalps of the Julian Alps, dear Boz!
    I send you these,

To light the *Wick* your candlestick holds up, or, should you list,
To usher in the yarn you spin concerning Oliver Twist.

II.

"Immense applause you've gained, O Boz! through Continental Europe;
You'll make Pickwick œcumenick;* of fame you have a sure hope;
For here your books are found, gadzooks! in greater *luxe* than any
That have issued yet, hotpress'd or wet, from the types of GALIGNANI.

III.

"But neither, when you sport your pen, O potent mirth-compeller!
Winning our hearts 'in monthly parts,' can Pickwick or Sam Weller
Cause us to weep with pathos deep, or shake with laugh spasmodical,
As when you drain your copious vein for Bentley's periodical.

IV.

"Folks all enjoy your Parish Boy—so truly you depict him:
But I, alack! while thus you track your stinted Poor-law's victim,
Must think of some poor nearer home—poor who, unheeded, perish,
By squires despoiled, by 'patriots' gulled—I mean the starving Irish.

V.

"Yet there's no dearth of Irish mirth, which, to a mind of feeling,
Seemeth to be the Helot's glee before the Spartan reeling:
Such gloomy thought o'ercometh not the glow of England's humor,
Thrice happy isle! long may the smile of genuine joy illume her!

VI.

"Write on, young sage! still o'er the page pour forth the flood of fancy;
Wax still more droll, wave o'er the soul Wit's wand of necromancy.
Behold! e'en now around your brow th' immortal laurel thickens;
Yea, SWIFT or STERNE might gladly learn a thing or two from DICKENS.

VII.

"A rhyme! a rhyme! from a distant clime—a song from the sunny South!
A goodly theme, so Boz but deem the measure not uncouth.
Would, for thy sake, that 'PROUT' could make his bow in fashion finer,
'*Partant*' (from thee) 'pour la Syrie,' for Greece and Asia Minor.
"*Genoa*, 14*th December*, 1837."

CHAPTER VI.

"NICHOLAS NICKLEBY."

IN January, 1838, "The Memoirs of Joseph Grimaldi, the Clown," edited by Dickens, illustrated by Cruikshank, was published by Mr. Bentley, in two volumes. It is amusingly written, full of merriment and quaint anecdotes of the great pantomimist, and has gone through several editions. It was not, however, the composition of Mr. Dickens, being only "edited" by him, as the title-page declares.

The next work—and the second in the "green-leaf" series—was "Nicholas Nickleby," the first number of which appeared 31st March, 1838. It extended to twenty numbers, and was published in a complete form, in the following year, by Messrs. Chapman & Hall, dedicated to Mr. Macready. This novel showed that Dickens was still working for the emancipation of boyhood. In the preface, after mentioning how he first came to hear of the gross mismanagement carried on in the Yorkshire schools, he resolved to go and see what they were like.

"With that intent I went down into Yorkshire before I began this book, in very severe winter-time, which is pretty faithfully described herein. As I wanted to see a schoolmaster or two, and was forewarned that those gentlemen might, in their modesty, be shy of receiving a visit from the author of the 'Pickwick Papers,' I consulted with a professional friend here, who had a Yorkshire connection, and with whom I concerted a pious fraud. He gave me some letters of introduction, in the name, I think, of my travelling companion; they bore reference to a supposititious little boy who had been left with a widowed mother who didn't know what to do with him; the poor lady had thought, as a means of thawing the tardy compassion of her relations in his behalf, of sending him to a Yorkshire school; I was the poor lady's friend, travelling that way; and if the recipient of the letter could inform me of a school in his neighborhood, the writer would be very much obliged.

"I went to several places in that part of the country where I understood these schools to be most plentifully sprinkled, and had no occasion to deliver a letter until I came to a certain town which shall be nameless. The person to whom it was addressed was not at home; but he came down at night, through the snow, to the inn where I was staying. It was after dinner; and he needed little persuasion to sit down by the fire in a warm corner, and take his share of the wine that was on the table.

"I am afraid he is dead now. I recollect he was a jovial, ruddy, broad-faced man; that we got acquainted directly; and that we talked on all kinds of subjects, except the school, which he showed a great anxiety to avoid. Was there any large school near? I asked him, in reference to the letter. 'Oh yes,' he said; 'there was a pratty big 'un.' 'Was it a good

* ειδωλον της γης οικουμενης.

one?' I asked. 'Ey!' he said, 'it was as good as anoother; that was a' a matther of opinion;' and fell to looking at the fire, staring round the room, and whistling a little. On my reverting to some other topic that we had been discussing, he recovered immediately; but, though I tried him again and again, I never approached the question of the school, even if he were in the middle of a laugh, without observing that his countenance fell, and that he became uncomfortable. At last, when we had passed a couple of hours or so very agreeably, he suddenly took up his hat, and, leaning over the table and looking me full in the face, said, in a low voice, 'Weel, Misther, we've been vary pleasant toogather, and ar'll spak' my moind tiv'ee. Dinnot let the weedur send her lattle boy to yan o' our schoolmeasthers, while there's a harse to hoold in a' Lunnun, or a gootther to lie asleep in. Ar wouldn't mak' ill words amang my neeburs, and ar speak tiv'ee quiet loike. But I'm dom'd if ar can gang to bed and not tellee, for weedur's sak', to keep the lattle boy from a' sike scoondrels while there's a harse to hoold in a' Lunnun, or a gootther to lie asleep in!' Repeating these words with great heartiness, and 'with a solemnity on his jolly face that made it look twice as large as before, he shook hands and went away. I never saw him afterwards, but I sometimes imagine that I descry a faint reflection of him in John Browdie."

In reference to these gentry, we may here quote a few words from the original preface to this book:

"It has afforded the author great amusement and satisfaction, during the progress of this work, to learn, from country friends and from a variety of ludicrous statements concerning himself in provincial newspapers, that more than one Yorkshire schoolmaster lays claim to being the original of Mr. Squeers. One worthy, he has reason to believe, has actually consulted authorities learned in the law, as to his having good grounds on which to rest an action for libel; another has meditated a journey to London, for the express purpose of committing an assault and battery on his traducer; a third perfectly remembers being waited on, last January twelve month, by two gentlemen, one of whom held him in conversation while the other took his likeness; and although Mr. Squeers has but one eye, and he has two, and the published sketch does not resemble him (whoever he may be) in any other respect, still he and all his friends and neighbors know at once for whom it is meant, because—the character is *so* like him."

"Nicholas Nickleby" is not quite so popular as some of Dickens's other fictions, although it is certainly not inferior to any of the other works of this illustrious author. The passages describing the deaths of Ralph Nickleby and Gride the Miser are dramatic in the highest degree, and inimitable as pieces of powerful writing. John Browdie, with his hearty laugh and thoroughly English heart, will ever be an immense favorite. Dotheboys Hall and its tenants is a very sad history, and well might Dickens use his utmost endeavors to crush such an infamous hot-bed of misery and torment. Who has not roared at the eccentricities of Mrs. Nickleby, especially in that memorable interview with the gentleman in the small clothes?

It is said that the Brothers Grant, the wealthy cotton-mill owners of Manchester, were the prototypes of the Brothers Cheeryble; both are now dead, the elder one dying in March, 1855. In the original preface, Dickens having stated that they were portraits from life, and were still living, in the preface to a later edition he said: "If I were to attempt to sum up the hundreds of letters from all sorts of people, in all sorts of latitudes and climates, to which this unlucky paragraph has since given rise, I should get into an arithmetical difficulty from which I could not easily extricate myself. Suffice it to say, that I believe the applications for loans, gifts, and offices of profit, that I have been requested to forward to the originals of the Brothers Cheeryble (with whom I never interchanged any communication in my life), would have exhausted the combined patronage of all the lord chancellors since the accession of the House of Brunswick, and would have broken the rest of the Bank of England."

In Mr. Samuel Smiles's admirable "Self Help" (the later editions) is recorded a very touching instance of the kindness and generosity of these gentlemen. However, it is too long to transfer to these pages.

Long before the completion of "Nicholas Nickleby," Mr. Edward Stirling produced a dramatic version of it, and received, in consequence, a sharp reproof in the ensuing number. It was performed at the Adelphi, on November 19th, 1838, as a farce, in two acts, Mr. O. Smith representing *Newman Noggs;* Mr. Yates, *Mantalini;* and Mrs. Keeley, *Smike.* Another adaptation was brought out at the Strand Theatre, under the title of "The Fortunes of Smike." As recently as the end of 1866, Mr. J. L. Toole made a great hit by doubling the parts of Squeers and Newman Noggs, when playing in the provinces with Mrs. Billington, who made a capital Mrs. Squeers, the termagant partner of the school-master.

Sydney Smith, in a letter to Sir George Phillips, about September, 1838, wrote: " 'Nickleby' is very good. I stood out against Mr. Dickens as long as I could, but he has conquered me."

And Thomas Moore, in his Diary, under date April 5, 1835, mentions dining at Messrs. Longmans, in Paternoster Row, the company consisting of Sydney Smith, Canon Tate, Merivale, Dionysius the Tyrant, M'Culloch, and Hayward (the translator of " Faust "). " Conversation turned on Boz, the new comic writer. Was sorry to hear Sydney cry him down, and evidently without having given him a fair trial. Whereas, to me it appears one of the few proofs of good taste that the 'masses,' as they are called, have yet given, there being some as nice humor and fun in the 'Pickwick Papers' as in any work I have seen in our day. Hayward, the only one of the party that stood by me in this opinion, engaged me for a dinner (at his chambers) on Thursday next."

In the following year Sydney Smith had formed an acquaintance with Dickens, and we find him writing to the author of " Nicholas Nickleby :"

"Nobody more—and more justly—talked of than yourself. The Miss Berrys, now at Richmond, live only to become acquainted with you, and have commissioned me to request you to dine with them Friday, the 29th, or Monday, July 1st, to meet a Canon of St. Paul's, the Rector of Combe Florey, and the Vicar of Halberton, all equally well known to you; to say nothing of other and better people. The Miss Berrys and Lady Charlotte Lindsay have not the smallest objection to be put into a number, but, on the contrary, would be proud of the distinction; and Lady Charlotte, in particular, you may marry to Newman Noggs. Pray come; it is as much as my place is worth to send a refusal."

We have already given evidence of Thackeray's hearty appreciation of the author who has chronicled for us the adventures of " Oliver Twist." Later on, in " Fraser's Magazine," when commenting on the Royal Academy Exhibition, we find another interesting reference by Thackeray to Mr. Dickens, with a prophecy of his future greatness: "Look (he says, in the assumed character of Michael Angelo Titmarsh) at the portrait of Mr. Dickens—well arranged as a picture, good in color and light and shadow, and as a likeness perfectly amazing; a looking-glass could not render a better fac-simile. Here we have the real identical man Dickens: the artist must have understood the inward 'Boz' as well as the outward before he made this admirable representation of him. What cheerful intellectuality is about the man's eyes, and a large forehead ! The mouth is too large and full, too eager and active, perhaps; the smile is very sweet and generous. If Monsieur De Balzac, that voluminous physiognomist, could examine this head, he would no doubt interpret every line and wrinkle in it—the nose firm and well placed, the nostrils wide and full, as are the nostrils of all men of genius (this is Monsieur Balzac's maxim). The past and the future, says Jean Paul, are written in every countenance. I think we may promise ourselves a brilliant future from this one. There seems no flagging as yet in it, no sense of fatigue, or consciousness of decaying power. Long mayest thou, O Boz! reign over thy comic kingdom; long may we pay tribute—whether of threepence weekly, or of a shilling monthly, it matters not. Mighty prince ! at thy imperial feet, Titmarsh, humblest of thy servants, offers his vows of loyalty and his humble tribute of praise."

And lecturing on " Week-day Preachers," at St. Martin's Hall,[*] in aid of the Jerrold Fund, Thackeray spoke of the delight which children derived from reading the works of Mr. Dickens, and mentioned that one of his own children said to him that she wished he "would write stories like those which Mr. Dickens wrote. The same young lady," he continued, " when she was ten years old, read 'Nicholas Nickleby' morning, noon, and night, beginning it again as soon as she had finished it, and never wearying of its fun."

Concerning the financial success of " Nicholas Nickleby," it may be mentioned that the late Mr. Tegg, the publisher, writing to the " Times," in February, 1840, on copyrights, declared that the work produced the author £3000.

At the Royal Academy Exhibition of 1840, a fine portrait of Dickens, painted by his friend Daniel Maclise, was exhibited. This is the portrait to which Thackeray alludes above. An engraving from it appeared in subsequent editions of " Nicholas Nickleby."

CHAPTER VII.

PUBLICATION OF "THE OLD CURIOSITY SHOP" AND "BARNABY RUDGE."

THE first number of " Master Humphrey's Clock " appeared on the 4th of April, 1840. Not content with the unexampled success which had attended the issue of "Nicholas Nickleby"

---

[*] July, 1857.

in shilling numbers, the publisher conceived the mistaken idea of altering the form of Mr. Dickens's new work. It was not to be in what is technically known as "demy octavo," at one shilling, but in ungainly "imperial octavo," and in weekly numbers, at three-pence each. Messrs. Cattermole and "Phiz" (Hablot K. Browne) had undertaken the illustrations, and the work proceeded, but it soon became a matter of policy, or rather of necessity, to revive the public interest; and this was done by the resuscitation of Mr. Pickwick and of the two Wellers — father and son. Thus helped forward, the new work began to make its way steadily; and the two principal tales, "The Old Curiosity Shop" and "Barnaby Rudge," are among the best and most popular of Mr. Dickens's stories. The work was published in a complete form, in the following year, by Messrs. Chapman & Hall. Eventually the author thought fit to separate the stories, "and 'Master Humphrey's Clock,' as originally constructed," he mentions, "became one of the lost books of the earth—which, we all know, are far more precious than any that can be read for love or money."

The "Old Curiosity Shop" is a splendid and touching story. Little Nelly is a beautiful and delicate creation; so likewise is the poor schoolmaster, and his favorite scholar, who wrote so good a hand with such a very little one. We may here mention a curious fact, to which Mr. R. H. Horne, in his "New Spirit of the Age," first directed attention. He says that the description of Nelly's death, if divided into lines, will form that species of gracefully irregular blank verse which Shelley and Southey often used. Here is a specimen:

"When Death strikes down the innocent and young,
For every fragile form, from which he lets
  The panting spirit free,
  A hundred virtues rise,
In shape of mercy, charity, and love,
  To walk the world and bless it.
  Of every tear
That sorrowing nature sheds on such green graves,
Some good is born, some gentler nature comes."

Of that exquisitely beautiful creation, "Little Nell," Mr. Dickens has himself remarked: "I have a mournful pride in one recollection associated with 'Little Nell.' While she was yet upon her wanderings, not then concluded, there appeared in a literary journal an essay, of which she was the principal theme, so earnestly, so eloquently, and tenderly appreciative of her, and of all her shadowy kith and kin, that it would have been insensibility in me if I could have read it without an unusual glow of pleasure and encouragement. Long afterwards, and when I had come to know him well, and see him, stout of heart, going slowly down into his grave, I knew the writer of that essay to be THOMAS HOOD."

In the course of this review, Hood took occasion to say of the author: "The poor are his especial clients. He delights to show worth in low places—living up a court, for example, with Kit and the industrious washerwoman his mother. To exhibit Honesty holding a gentleman's horse, or Poverty bestowing alms."

Fraser, in 1850, said: "We have been told that when the 'Old Curiosity Shop' was drawing to a close, he received heaps of anonymous letters in female hands, imploring him 'not to kill Little Nell.' The wretch ungallantly persisted in his murderous design; and those gentle readers only wept, and forgave him."

Dick Swiveller is a type and representative of a numerous class of young men not absolutely vicious, but too lazy to work, and who lounge away their lives resorting to all manner of shifts and contrivances to exist, yet, great at the clubs and meetings as he was, as

"Perpetual Grand of the Glorious Apollos."

Quilp is, perhaps, the most carefully-elaborated and highly-finished character of all—a Caliban and wretch, never more delighted than when inflicting pain on his meek wife, Mrs. Jiniwin, his mother-in-law, or that fawning, white-livered hound, Sampson Brass, the attorney of Bevis Marks. To comment further would be to pass a glowing eulogium on every other character in the book. It was dedicated to his friend Samuel Rogers, the Banker Poet.

"Barnaby Rudge" is a history of the notorious "No Popery" riots of 1780, which had hitherto not formed the subject of, or been introduced into, any work of fiction. The tale abounds in vigorous descriptions of the chief misguided actor, Lord George Gordon, and the dreadful scenes that ensued. The sketches of Old Willet, at the Maypole, at Chigwell, and the courtship of Joe Willett and Dolly Varden, are unsurpassed; Sir Edward Chester evidently being intended for the celebrated Lord Chesterfield, the decorously polite but heartless author of a worthless book entitled "Lord Chesterfield's Letters to his Son."

"Will" (writes a friend of the late novelist) "a great living painter of English manners, Mr. W. P. Frith, forgive an allusion to the early days when the success of his admirable picture of 'Dolly Varden' led Charles Dickens to call on him, and, after expressing the warmest thanks for the feeling and appreciation which the artist's handiwork displayed, to give him a commission for other subjects, to be selected from the works of 'Boz?' Dickens," continues the writer, "wanted on canvas, and in hues which should live, the young artist's conception of the imaginary people with whose characteristics England was ringing. His hearty approval of the pictures, when painted, his personal introduction of himself to thank the artist, and his check, with the well-known signature, the 'C' rather like a 'G,' and the elaborate flourish beneath it, exactly as it is given outside the last edition of his works, are, we venture to say, like things of yesterday to Mr. Frith."

It is doubtful if the illustrious author of "Barnaby Rudge" ever knew that the genial Tom Hood—for whom Dickens always had the greatest admiration, we may almost say affection—once wrote an exquisitely beautiful account of that work, as well as of "The Old Curiosity Shop." We know it as a fact, and the reader can judge for himself whether Hood was not the man, above all others, to appreciate Dickens. The reviewer says: "The first chapter pleasantly plants us, not in Cato Street, but on the borders of Epping Forest, at an ancient ruddy Elizabethan inn, with a May-pole for its sign, an antique porch, quaint chimneys, and 'more gable-ends than a crazy man would care to count on a sunny day.' The ornamented eaves are haunted by twittering swallows, and the distorted roof is mobbed by clusters of cooing pigeons. Then for its landlord: there is old John Willett, as square and as slow as a tortoise; and for its parlor customers, Long Parks, Tom Cobb, both taciturn and profound smokers; and Solomon Daisy, that parochial Argus, studded all down his rusty black coat, and his long flapped waistcoat, with little queer buttons, like nothing except his eyes, but so like them, that as they twinkled and glistened in the light of the fire, which shone too in his bright shoe-buckles, he seemed all eyes from head to foot."

. As illustrative of Mr. Dickens's love of animals—of ravens in particular—we may here be permitted to give his own remarks in a preface to the cheap edition of this work: "As it is Mr. Waterton's opinion that ravens are gradually becoming extinct in England, I offer a few words here about mine.

"The raven in this story is a compound of two great originals, of whom I have been, at different times, the proud possessor. The first was in the bloom of his youth, when he was discovered in a modest retirement, in London, by a friend of mine, and given to me. He had from the first, as Sir Hugh Evans says of Anne Page, 'good gifts,' which he improved, by study and attention, in a most exemplary manner. He slept in a stable—generally on horseback—and so terrified a Newfoundland dog by his preternatural sagacity, that he has been known, by the mere superiority of his genius, to walk off unmolested with the dog's dinner from before his face. He was rapidly rising in acquirements and virtues, when, in an evil hour, his stable was newly painted. He observed the workmen closely, saw that they were careful of the paint, and immediately burned to possess it. On their going to dinner, he ate up all they had left behind, consisting of a pound or two of white lead; and this youthful indiscretion terminated in death.

"While I was yet inconsolable for his loss, another friend of mine in Yorkshire discovered an older and more gifted raven at a village public-house, which he prevailed upon the landlord to part with for a consideration, and sent up to me. The first act of this sage was to administer to the effects of his predecessor, by disinterring all the cheese and half-pence he had buried in the garden—a work of immense labor and research, to which he devoted all the energies of his mind. When he had achieved this task, he applied himself to the acquisition of stable language, in which he soon became such an adept, that he would perch outside my window and drive imaginary horses with great skill all day. Perhaps even I never saw him at his best, for his former master sent his duty with him, 'and if I wished the bird to come out very strong, would I be so good as to show him a drunken man'—which I never did, having (fortunately) none but sober people at hand. But I could hardly have respected him more, whatever the stimulating influences of this sight might have been. He had not the slightest respect, I am sorry to say, for me in return, or for any body but the cook; to whom he was attached—but only, I fear, as a policeman might have been. Once I met him unexpectedly, about half a mile off, walking down the middle of the public street, attended by a pretty large crowd, and spontaneously exhibiting the whole of his accomplishments. His gravity under those trying circumstances I never can forget, nor the extraordinary gallantry with which, refusing to be brought home, he defended himself behind a pump, until overpowered by numbers. It may have been that he was too bright a genius to live long, or it may have been that he took some pernicious substance into his bill, and thence into his maw—which is not improbable, seeing that he new-pointed the greater part of the garden wall by digging out the mortar, broke countless squares of glass by scraping away the putty all round the frames, and tore up and swallowed, in splinters, the greater part of a wooden staircase of six steps and a landing— but after some three years he too was taken ill, and died before the kitchen fire. He kept his eye to the last upon the meat as it roasted, and suddenly turned over on his back with a sepulchral cry of 'Cuckoo.' Since then I have been ravenless."

It is just worth while to remark, in connection with this fondness for ravens, that a personal friend, a bad punster, being at a party, and remarking on the mania Dickens seemed to have for these birds, said, "Dickens is *raven mad*." This, being repeated, gave rise to a report, which was industriously spread by his detractors, that "Dickens was raving mad," and "was confined in a madhouse," and other silly rumors.

"Barnaby Rudge" expressed the author's abhorrence to capital punishment, on the principle enunciated by Pistol, in Shakspeare's "King Henry V.:"

"Let gallows gape for dog, let man go free,
And let not hemp his wind-pipe suffocate."

The pathetic scene of the gray-headed old father following the dead body of his only son, merely to touch the lifeless hand of the boy so unjustly hung, also reminds one of Shakspeare's lines:

"If I put out thy light, thou flaming minister,
I can restore it, should I repent me;
But once put out *thy* light, thou cunning'st pattern of excelling nature,
I know not that Promethean heat that can thy light relume."

Some London publisher, about this time, having issued imitations or piracies of some of Dickens's former works and titles, Thomas Hood, writing to the "Athenæum" (June, 1842) on "Copyright and Copywrong," speaks of a conversation he had had with a bookseller on a spurious "Master Humphrey's Clock."

"Sir," said the bookseller, "if you had observed the name, it was *Bos*, not *Boz*—s, sir, not z; and, besides, it would have been no piracy, sir, even with the z, because 'Master Humphrey's Clock,' you see, sir, was not published as by Boz, but by Charles Dickens!"

In the summer of 1841, a dramatized version of the story, by Charles Selby, was produced at the Lyceum, and other versions appeared about the same time at various theatres. More recently, on November 13th, 1866, it was put on the stage at the Princess's, by Messrs. Vining and Watts Phillips, as a four-act drama, Miss Rodgers playing *Barnaby Rudge*, Mrs. John Wood *Miss Miggs*, Mr. Shore *Sir John Chester*. A newspaper critic, speaking of Mrs. Wood's performance, observed: "If any one expected the subdued cough, the small groan, the sigh, the sniff, the spasmodic start, and the constant rubbing and tweaking of the nose to which Miss Miggs had recourse in the frequent moments of her vexation, would have been reproduced by Mrs. John Wood in illustration of the novelist's description, they must have overlooked the peculiarities of that liberty-loving country from which the *débutante* has just come, after a sojourn of some twelve years. It is quite apparent that Mrs. John Wood has been in the habit of representing Miss Miggs repeatedly on the other side the Atlantic, in a version which has been doubtless made by some patriotic American, who believed that the Declaration of Independence secured the right of departing as far as possible from the intentions of the British author. The Miss Miggs who appeared last evening on the stage of the Princess's is a 'Yankee gal' of the familiar Down-East pattern, who sings one of the high-toned ditties characteristic of her class, mixes up grotesque pantomime extravagances with nasal inflections and angular attitudes, and thinks nothing of sprawling on tables and tumbling into tubs. Nor, in personal appearance, will the good-looking, though coarse-mannered, companion of Mrs. Varden at all correspond to the portraiture which was also so long identified with one of the principal figures in 'Master Humphrey's Clock.' The double disappointment thus experienced found audible expression in the course of the performance, and drew the customary expostulation of a first night from Mr. Vining, who took the opportunity of a call at the end of the third act to address the audience. 'On the present occasion,' observed Mr. Vining, 'I do not appear before you as an actor; but from a private box I have seen that a determination to hiss this piece from its commencement has been apparent on the part of a few persons among the audience. I have watched for an expression of public opinion. If you have seen any thing which deserved hissing, hiss away— (cheers)—but some, to the degradation of their manhood, have hissed a lady who was a stranger in the land.'" Mr. George Honey was afterwards substituted to play the part, and the piece ran until January following.

That our author, about this time, was busy in "society" as well as in literature, we have good evidence from the examples of his correspondence which exist in contemporary biography. With the Countess of Blessington he had been acquainted for some time. On one occasion

Dickens fell in with a remarkable clairvoyant—a "magnetic boy," as he is styled, and our author thus writes to the Countess: "Have you seen Townsend's magnetic boy? You heard of him, no doubt, from Count d'Orsay. If you get him to Gore House, don't, I entreat you, have more than eight people—four is a better number—to see him. He fails in a crowd, and is *marvellous* before a few. I am told, that down in Devonshire there are young ladies innumerable who read crabbed manuscripts with the palms of their hands, and who, so to speak, are literary all over. I begin to understand what a blue-stocking means; and have not the slightest doubt that Lady ———, for instance, could write quite as entertaining a book with the sole of her foot as ever she did with her head. I am a believer in earnest, and am sure you would be if you saw this boy, under moderately favorable circumstances, as I hope you will before he leaves England."*

It was about this time that "The Picnic Papers," "by various hands," and edited by Dickens, was issued by Mr. Henry Colburn, in three volumes, with illustrations by George Cruikshank. The work was the result of a series of literary contributions in aid of the family of Mr. Macrone, who had just died. He was described in the preface as "A publisher who died prematurely young, and in the prime and vigor of his years, before he had time or opportunity to make any provision for his wife and infant children, and at the moment when his prospects were the brightest, and the difficulties of his enterprise were nearly overcome." The editor led off with "The Lamplighter's Story." The contributors comprised Messrs. Talfourd, Thomas Moore, W. H. Maxwell, Leitch Ritchie, Michael Honan, John Forster, Allan Cunningham, and W. Harrison Ainsworth. The book served the purpose it was intended for, and realized a large sum. It is now seldom read, and then more for the editor's tale than for any thing else contained in it.

• In the July of this year (1841) a public dinner in honor of Dickens took place at Edinburgh, and went off with great *éclat*, Professor Wilson (the celebrated "Christopher North") presiding.†

---

* Madden's "Life of Lady Blessington," June, 1841.
† Mr. Dickens's speech upon this occasion is given in the great novelist's collected "Speeches," recently published.

CHAPTER VIII.

DICKENS'S VISIT TO AMERICA.

LONG before he fixed any date for his departure, Dickens had promised Washington Irving, and many other correspondents in America, that he would come and see them. The progress of "Oliver Twist," "Nicholas Nickleby," and other works, however, delayed the event, and many of his English admirers did all that lay in their power to keep him at home. "Worked hard," says poor Haydon, the painter, in his Diary, under date of December 10th; "Talfourd said he introduced Dickens to Lady Holland. She hated the Americans, and did not want Dickens to go.

"She said: 'Why can not you go down to Bristol, and see some of the third or fourth-class people, and they'll do just as well?'"

And the genial Thomas Hood, in his article on "Barnaby Rudge," after lamenting the temporary loss of Dickens, thus excuses his absence: "Availing himself of the pause for a little well-earned rest and recreation, the author, it appears, has sailed on a long-projected trip to America; or, according to Mr. Weller, senior, has 'made away with hisself to another, though not a better, world,' though it's called a new one. In fact he is, we hope, paddling prosperously across the Atlantic, while we are sitting down to criticise the characters he has left behind him in his 'Barnaby Rudge.'"

To another journal Hood sent these lines:

TO C. DICKENS, ESQ.,

ON HIS DEPARTURE FOR AMERICA.

"Pshaw! away with leaf and berry,
  And the sober-sided cup!
Bring a goblet, and bright sherry,
  And a bumper fill me up!
Though a pledge I had to shiver,
  And the longest ever was,
Ere his vessel leaves our river,
  I would drink a health to Boz!
Here's success to all his antics,
  Since it pleases him to roam,
And to paddle o'er Atlantics,
  After such a *sale* at home!
May he shun all rocks whatever,
  And each shallow sand that lurks,
And his passage be as clever
  As the best among his works!"

It was on the 3d of January, 1842, that our author and his wife left England for the United States. They went to Liverpool, and crossed the Atlantic in the "Britannia" steam-packet, Captain Hewett. The result of this trip was the publication, by Messrs. Chapman & Hall, in October of the same year, of "American Notes for General Circulation," in two volumes, with a frontispiece by Clarkson Stanfield, R.A.

The dedication was as follows:

"I DEDICATE THIS BOOK
TO THOSE FRIENDS OF MINE IN AMERICA
WHO,
GIVING ME A WELCOME I MUST EVER GRATEFULLY
AND PROUDLY REMEMBER,
LEFT MY JUDGMENT
FREE;
AND WHO, LOVING THEIR COUNTRY,
CAN BEAR THE TRUTH, WHEN IT IS TOLD GOOD-HUMOREDLY, AND IN A KIND SPIRIT."

The publication, however, gave great offense to our author's American readers, and, as he might have foreseen, he got abused and vilified most unmercifully. Judge Haliburton ("Sam Slick"), in one of his works, alluding to the fêtes and receptions given to Dickens, said that, on his homeward passage, he had suffered severely from sea-sickness, and all the kindness he had experienced had been cast overboard.

Whether Dickens had in his mind's eye the advice tendered by old Weller to Sam, when he proposed having a "pianner" to carry Mr. Pickwick from the Fleet Prison, is uncertain:

"There ain't no vurks in it," whispered his father. "It 'ull hold him easy, with his hat and shoes on, and breathe through the legs, vich is holler. Have a passage ready taken for 'Merriker. The 'Merrikin Gov'ment vill never give him up, ven they finds as he's got money to spend, Sammy. Let the gov'ner stop there till Mrs. Bardell's dead, or Mr. Dodson and Fogg's hung, which last ewent I think is the most likely to happen first, Sammy; and then let him come back and write a book about the 'Merrikins as'll pay all his expenses and more, if he blows 'em up enough."

Emerson, in "The Conduct of Life" (in the Essay on "Behavior"), writes:

"Charles Dickens self-sacrificingly undertook the reformation of our American manners in unspeakable particulars. I think the lesson was not quite lost; that it held bad manners up, so that the churls could see the deformity. Unhappily, the book has its own deformities. It ought not to need to print in a reading-room a caution to strangers not to speak loud; nor to persons who look over fine engravings, that they should be handled like cobwebs and butterflies' wings; nor to persons who look at marble statues, that they shall not smite them with their canes."

In publishing a new edition of "American Notes," in 1850, Dickens, in the preface, urged that "prejudiced I have never been, otherwise than in favor of the United States. * * * To represent me as viewing it with ill-nature, animosity, or partisanship, is merely to do a very foolish thing, which is always a very easy one, and which I have disregarded for eight years, and could disregard for eighty more."

Whatever transatlantic critics may have thought of the work, Lord Jeffrey, on the appearance of the first edition, wrote the author a letter, in which he says: "A thousand thanks for your charming book, and for all the pleasure, profit, and *relief* it has afforded me. You have been very tender to our sensitive friends beyond the sea, and really said nothing which will give any serious offense to any moderately rational patriot among them. The *slavers*, of course, will give you no quarter, and of course you did not expect they would. * * * Your account of the silent or solitary imprisonment system is as pathetic and as powerful a piece of writing as I have ever seen, and your sweet airy little snatch of the little woman taking her new babe home to her young husband,* and your manly and feeling appeal in behalf of the poor Irish, or rather the affectionate poor of all races and tongues, who are patient and tender to their children, under circumstances which would make half the exemplary parents among the rich monsters of selfishness and discontent, remind us that we have still among us the creator of Nelly and Smike, and the schoolmaster and his dying pupil, and must continue to win for you still more of that homage of the heart, that love and esteem of the just and the good, which, though it should never be disjoined from them, *should*, I think you must already feel, be better than fortune or fame."

Very recently it has been made known that poor Tom Hood, almost immediately upon its appearance, reviewed the work, under the title of "Boz in America." In his happiest vein of drollery, he conjectures that it would be impossible for Mr. Boz to go to "the States" without losing all his English characteristics, and returning to his friends a regular Down-East Yankee: "So strong, indeed, was this impression, that certain blue-stockinged prophetesses even predicted a new Avatar of the celebrated Mr. Pickwick, in slippers and loose trowsers, a nankeen jacket, and a straw hat as large as an umbrella. Sam Weller was to reappear as his 'help,' instead of a footman, still full of droll sayings, but in a slang more akin to his namesake, the Clock-maker: while Weller, senior, was to revive on the box of a Boston long stage—only calling himself Jonathan, instead of Tony, and spelling it with a G. A Virginian Widow Bardell was as a matter of

---

* See Chapter XII., "American Notes." A very finished and beautiful little incident, related in that natural and truthful manner in which Dickens excels all other writers.

course; and some visionaries even foresaw a slave-owning Mr. Snodgrass, a coon-hunting Mr. Winkle, a wide-awake Joe, and a forest-clearing Bob Sawyer.* But, upon the appearance of the book itself," continues Hood, "the romanticists were in despair, and reluctantly abandoned all hopes of a Pennsylvanian Nicholas Nickleby, affectionately darning his mother—a New Yorkshire Mr. Squeers, flogging creation—a black Smike—a brown Kate—and a Bostonian Newman Noggs, alternately swallowing a *cocktail* and a *cobbler*."

Professor Felton, alluding to the death of Washington Irving, in a speech, in the latter part of the year 1859, gave this interesting reminiscence of the friendship existing between Dickens and Irving:

"The time when I saw the most of Mr. Irving was in the winter of 1842, during the visit of Mr. Charles Dickens in New York. I had known this already distinguished writer in Boston and Cambridge, and, while passing some weeks with my dear and lamented friend, Albert Sumner, I renewed my acquaintance with Mr. Dickens, often meeting him in the brilliant literary society which then made New York a most agreeable resort. Halleck, Bryant, Washington Irving, Davis, and others scarce less attractive by their genius, wit, and social graces, constituted a circle not to be surpassed anywhere in the world. I passed much of the time with Mr. Irving and Mr. Dickens, and it was delightful to witness the cordial intercourse of the young man, in the flush and glory of his youthful genius, and his elder compeer, then in the assured possession of immortal renown. Dickens said, in his frank, hearty manner, that from his childhood he had known the works of Irving; and that, before he thought of coming to this country, he had received a letter from him, expressing the delight he felt in reading the story of 'Little Nell;' and from that day they had shaken hands *autographically* across the Atlantic."

After Professor Felton's reminiscences, it may not be uninteresting to quote the following extract from a letter written by Washington Irving to his niece (Mrs. Storrow), under date May 25, 1841, in which he mentions a letter he had just received from Dickens, in reply to one from himself:

"And now comes the third letter from that glorious fellow, Dickens (Boz), in reply to the one I wrote, expressing my heartfelt delight with his writings, and my yearnings towards himself. See how completely we sympathize in feeling:

"'There is no man in the world,' replies Dickens, 'who could have given me the heartfelt pleasure you have by your kind note of the 13th of last month. There is no living writer, and there are very few among the dead, whose approbation I should feel so proud to earn; and, with every thing you have written upon my shelves, and in my thoughts, and in my heart of hearts, I may honestly and truly say so. If you could know how earnestly I write this, you would be glad to read it—as I hope you will be, faintly guessing at the warmth of the hand I autographically hold out to you over the broad Atlantic.

"'I wish I could find in your welcome letter some hint of an intention to visit England. I can't. I have held it at arm's length, and taken a bird's-eye view of it, after reading it a great many times; but there is no greater encouragement in it, this way, than on a microscopic inspection. I should love to go with you—as I have gone, God knows how often—into Little Britain, and Eastcheap, and Green Arbor Court, and Westminster Abbey. I should like to travel with you, outside the last of the coaches, down to Bracebridge Hall. It would make my heart glad to compare notes with you about that shabby gentleman in the oil-cloth hat and red nose, who sat in the nine-cornered back parlor of the Mason's Arms; and about Robert Preston, and the tallow-chandler's widow, whose sitting-room is second nature to me; and about all those delightful places and people that I used to talk about and dream of in the day-time, when a very small and not-over-particularly-taken-care-of boy. I have a good deal to say, too, about that dashing Alonzo de Ojeda, that you can't help being fonder of than you ought to be; and much to hear concerning Moorish legend, and poor unhappy Boabdil. Diedrich Knickerbocker I have worn to death in my pocket, and yet I should show you his mutilated carcass with a joy past all expression.

"'I have been so accustomed to associate you with my pleasantest and happiest thoughts, and with my leisure hours, that I rush at once into full confidence with you, and fall, as it were naturally, and by the very laws of gravity, into your open arms. Questions come thronging to my pen as to the lips of people who meet after long hoping to do so. I don't know what to say first, or what to leave unsaid, and am constantly disposed to break off and tell you again how glad I am this moment has arrived.

---

* "With the wishes of these admirers of Boz we can in some degree sympathize; for what could be a greater treat, in the reading way, than the perplexities of a *squatting* Mr. Pickwick or a *settling* Mrs. Nickleby?"

"'My dear Washington Irving, I can not thank you enough for your cordial and generous praise, or tell you what deep and lasting gratification it has given me. I hope to have many letters from you, and to exchange a frequent correspondence. I send this to say so. After the first two or three, I shall settle down into a connected style, and become gradually rational.

"'You know what the feeling is, after having written a letter, sealed it, and sent it off. I shall picture you reading this, and answering it, before it has lain one night in the post-office. Ten to one that before the fastest packet could reach New York I shall be writing again.

"'Do you suppose the post-office clerks care to receive letters? I have my doubts. They get into a dreadful habit of indifference. A postman, I imagine, is quite callous. Conceive his delivering one to himself, without being startled by a preliminary double knock!'"

Irving, writing again to Mrs. Storrow, 29th of October following, says:

"What do you think? Dickens is actually *coming to America*. He has engaged passage for himself and his wife in the steam-packet for Boston, for the 4th of January next. He says: 'I look forward to shaking hands with you, with an interest I can not (and I would not if I could) describe. You *can* imagine, I dare say, something of the feelings with which I look forward to being in America. I can hardly believe I am coming.'"

But to return to Professor Felton and his recollections of Irving and Dickens. He continues:

"Great and varied as was the genius of Mr. Irving, there was one thing he shrank with a comical terror from attempting, and that was a *dinner speech*. A great dinner, however, was to be given to Mr. Dickens in New York, as one had already been given in Boston, and it was evident to all that no man like Washington Irving could be thought of to preside. With all his dread of making a speech, he was obliged to obey the universal call, and to accept the painful pre-eminence. I saw him daily during the interval of preparation, either at the lodgings of Dickens, or at dinner, or at evening parties. I hope I showed no want of sympathy with his forebodings, but I could not help being amused with his tragi-comical distress which the thought of that approaching dinner had caused him. His pleasant humor mingled with the real dread, and played with the whimsical horrors of his own position with an irresistible drollery. Whenever it was alluded to, his invariable answer was, 'I shall certainly break down!'—uttered in a half-melancholy tone, the ludicrous effect of which it is impossible to describe. He was haunted, as if by a nightmare; and I could only compare his dismay to that of Mr. Pickwick, who was so alarmed at the prospect of leading about that 'dreadful horse' all day. At length the long-expected evening arrived. A company of the most eminent persons, from all the professions and every walk of life, were assembled, and Mr. Irving took the chair. I had gladly accepted an invitation, making it, however, a condition that I should not be called upon to speak—a thing I then dreaded quite as much as Mr. Irving himself. The direful compulsions of life have since helped me to overcome, in some measure, the post-prandial fright. Under the circumstances—an invited guest, with no impending speech—I sat calmly and watched with interest the imposing scene. I had the honor to be placed next but one to Mr. Irving, and the great pleasure of sharing in his conversation. He had brought the manuscript of his speech, and laid it under his plate. 'I shall certainly break down,' he repeated over and over again. At last the moment arrived. Mr. Irving rose, and was received with deafening and long-continued applause, which by no means lessened his apprehension. He began in his pleasant voice; got through two or three sentences pretty easily, but in the next hesitated; and, after one or two attempts to go on, gave it up, with a graceful allusion to the tournament, and the troop of knights all armed and eager for the fray; and ended with the toast, 'Charles Dickens, the guest of the nation.' 'There!' said he, as he resumed his seat under a repetition of the applause which had saluted his rising—'there! I told you I should break down, and I've done it.'

"There certainly never was a shorter after-dinner speech; and I doubt if there ever was a more successful one. The manuscript seemed to be a dozen or twenty pages long, but the printed speech was not as many lines.

"Mr. Irving often spoke with a good-humored envy of the felicity with which Dickens always acquitted himself on such occasions."*

---

* This speech is given in "The Speeches of Charles Dickens," recently published. Thomas Moore, in his Diary, speaking of running up to London to act as steward of the Literary Fund Dinner at the Freemasons' Tavern, H.R.H. the Prince Consort acting as Chairman, says: "*May* 11*th*, 1842.—By-the-by, Irving had yesterday come to Murray's with the determination, as I found, not to go to the dinner, and all begged of me to use my influence with him to change this resolution. But he told me his mind was made up on the point, that the drinking his health, and the speech he would have to make in return, were more than he durst encounter; that he had broken down at the Dickens Dinner (of which he was Chairman) in America, and obliged to stop short in the middle of his oration, which made him resolve not to encounter another such accident. In vain did I rep-

Immediately after dinner, Irving and Dickens started off together to Washington, to spend a few days, and there took leave of one another. Irving at this time having just received his appointment as Minister to Spain, Dickens wrote to him: "We passed through—literally passed through—this place again to-day. I did not come to see you, for I really had not the heart to say good-bye again, and I felt more than I can tell you when we shook hands last Wednesday. You will not be at Baltimore, I fear? I thought at the time, that you only said you might be there, to make our parting the gayer.

"Wherever you go, God bless you! What pleasure I have had in seeing and talking with you, I will not attempt to say. I shall never forget it as long as I live. What would I give if we could have a quiet walk together! Spain is a lazy place, and its climate an indolent one. But if you have ever leisure under its sunny skies to think of a man who loves you, and holds communion with your spirit oftener, perhaps, than any other person alive—leisure from listlessness, I mean—and will write to me in London, you will give me an inexpressible amount of pleasure."

Dickens took the opportunity, in a number of "All the Year Round," March, 1862 (when the song "A Young Man from the Country" was very popular, and which suggested the article), to remark that what he had originally written about the United States had been fully borne out in the recent events in that great republic.

CHAPTER IX.

FURTHER AMERICAN EXPERIENCES.

IN 1848 there appeared a new edition of an extensive and important work on "Prison Discipline." The author was the Rev. John Field, chaplain of the county jail at Reading, in Berkshire, and well known in literary circles as the author of a "Life of John Howard, the Philanthropist," and editor of the "Howard Correspondence." This work on prison discipline had attracted considerable attention; and as the author, in advocating the advantages of the separate system of imprisonment, took occasion to mention Mr. Dickens's remarks in his "American Notes" upon the Solitary Prison at Philadelphia, the latter felt it his duty to reply:

"As Mr. Field condescends to quote some vaporings about the account given by Mr. Charles Dickens in his 'American Notes' of the Solitary Prison at Philadelphia, he may perhaps really wish for some few words of information on the subject. For this purpose Mr. Charles Dickens has referred to the entry in his Diary, made at the close of that day.

"He left his hotel for the prison at twelve o'clock, being waited on, by appointment, by the gentleman who showed it to him, and he returned between seven and eight at night; dining in the prison in the course of that time, which, according to his calculation, in despite of the Philadelphia newspaper, rather exceeded two hours. He found the prison admirably conducted, extremely clean, and the system administered in a most intelligent, kind, orderly, tender, and careful manner. He did not consider (nor should he, if he were to visit Pentonville to-morrow) that the book in which visitors were expected to record their observations of the place was intended for the insertion of criticisms on the system, but for honest testimony to the manner of its administration, and to that he bore, as an impartial visitor, the highest testimony in his power. In returning thanks for his health being drunk, at the dinner within its walls, he said that what he had seen that day was running in his mind; that he could not help reflecting on it; and that it was an awful punishment. If the American officer who rode with him afterwards should ever see these words, he will perhaps recall his conversation with Mr. Dickens on the road, as to Mr. Dickens having said so very plainly and very strongly. In reference to the ridiculous assertion that Mr. Dickens in his book termed a woman 'quite beautiful' who was a negress, he positively believes that he was shown no negress in the prison, but one who was nursing a woman much diseased, and to whom no reference is made in his published account. In describing three young women, 'all convicted at the same time of a conspiracy,' he may, *possibly*, among many cases, have substituted in his memory, for one of them whom he did not see, some other prisoner, confined for some other crime, whom he did see; but he has not the least doubt of having been guilty of the (American) enormity of detecting beauty in the passive quadroon or mulatto girl, or of having seen exactly what he describes; and he remembers the girl more particularly described in this connection perfectly. Can Mr. Field really suppose Mr. Dickens had any interest or purpose in misrepresenting the system, or that, if he could be

---

resent to him that a few words would be quite sufficient in returning thanks. 'That *Dickens* Dinner,' which he always pronounced with strong emphasis, hammering away all the time with his right arm, *more suo*, 'that *Dickens* Dinner' still haunted his imagination, and I almost gave up all hope of persuading him." The arguments proved irresistible, and Irving went to it.

guilty of such unworthy conduct, or desire to do it any thing but justice, he could have volunteered the narrative of a man's having, of his own choice, undergone it for two years?

"We will not notice the objection of Mr. Field (who strengthens the truth of Mr. Burns to nature, by the testimony of Mr. Pitt!) to the discussion of such a topic as the present in a work of 'mere amusement;' though we had thought we remembered in that book a word or two about slavery, which, although a very amusing, can scarcely be considered an unmitigatedly comic theme. We are quite content to believe, without seeking to make a convert of the Rev. Mr. Field, that no work need be one of 'mere amusement,' and that some works to which he would apply that designation have done a little good in advancing principles to which, we hope and will believe, for the credit of his Christian office, he is not indifferent."

However, all these disputes and "angry recollections" of the America of 1842, were finally disposed of by Mr. Dickens on his arrival home after a second visit to that great country. At the end of this little Memoir we give the great novelist's public testimony of the change in his experiences of America, with the "Postscript" which he then declared should forever after continue to form a part of any new edition of "American Notes."

One of the prime objects in Mr. Dickens's visit to our transatlantic cousins was the endeavor to place the vexed question of International Copyright on a sound and proper footing, and whenever an available occasion presented itself he strenuously urged his ideas and views. Returning to England, he forwarded to the "Athenæum" this letter, for which he had desired the widest publicity, in the hope that it might assist in bringing about the much-desired International Convention. It was inserted with the following editorial note:

"On the subject of literary piracy we have received the following letter from Mr. Charles Dickens. We do not see very clearly the good that would result even from a general adoption of the proposed measures; but the straightforward and hearty way in which the writer has, under the most discouraging circumstances, set himself in opposition to the disgraceful practice, entitles all his suggestions to respectful attention:

"1 Devonshire Terrace, York Gate, Regent's Park, July 7, 1842.

"You may perhaps be aware that, during my stay in America, I lost no opportunity of endeavoring to awaken the public mind to a sense of the unjust and iniquitous state of the law of that country in reference to the wholesale piracy of British works. Having been successful in making the subject one of general discussion in the United States, I carried to Washington, for presentation to Congress by Mr. Clay, a petition from the whole body of American authors, earnestly praying for the enactment of an International Copyright Law. It was signed by Mr. Washington Irving, Mr. Prescott, Mr. Cooper, and every man who had distinguished himself in the literature of America, and has since been referred to a Select Committee of the House of Representatives. To counteract any effect which might be produced by that petition, a meeting was held at Boston—which you will remember is the seat and stronghold of learning and letters in the United States—at which a memorial against any change in the existing state of things in this respect was agreed to, with but one dissentient voice. This document, which, incredible as it may appear to you, was actually forwarded to Congress and received, deliberately stated that, if English authors were invested with any control over the republication of their own books, it would be no longer possible for American editors to alter and adapt them (as they do now) to the American taste. This memorial was without loss of time replied to by Mr. Prescott, who commented, with the natural indignation of a gentleman and a man of letters, upon its extraordinary dishonesty. I am satisfied that this brief mention of its tone and spirit is sufficient to impress you with the conviction that it becomes all those who are in any way connected with the literature of England to take that high stand to which the nature of their pursuits, and the extent of their sphere of usefulness, justly entitle them, to discourage the upholders of such doctrines by every means in their power, and to hold themselves aloof from the remotest participation in a system from which the moral sense and honorable feeling of all just men must instinctively recoil. For myself, I have resolved that I will never from this time enter into any negotiation with any person for the transmission across the Atlantic of early proofs of any thing I may write, and that I will forego all profit derivable from such a source. I do not venture to urge this line of proceeding upon you, but I would beg to suggest, and to lay great stress upon the necessity of observing, one other course of action, to which I can not too emphatically call your attention. The persons who exert themselves to mislead the American public on this question, to put down its discussion, and to suppress and distort the truth in reference to it in every possible way (as you may easily suppose) are those who have a strong interest in the existing system of piracy and plunder; inasmuch as, so long as it continues, they can gain a very comfortable living out of the brains of other men, while they would find it very difficult to find bread by the exercise of their own. These are the editors and proprietors of newspapers almost exclusively devoted to the republication of popular English works. They are, for the most part, men of very low attainments, and of more than indifferent reputation, and I have frequently seen them, in the same sheet in which they boast of the rapid sale of many thousand copies of an English reprint, coarsely and insolently attacking the author of that very book, and heaping scurrility and slander upon his head. I would therefore entreat you, in the name of the honorable pursuit with which you are so intimately connected, never to hold correspondence with any of these men, and never to negotiate with them for the sale of early proofs, over which you have control, but to treat on all occasions with some respectable American publishing house, and with such an establishment only. Our common interest in this subject, and my advocacy of it, single-handed, on every occasion that has presented itself during my absence from Europe, forms my excuse for addressing you.

"I am, etc.,   CHARLES DICKENS."

To revert to the American visit, we may state that for the "Dickens Ball," at New York, on February 14th, 1842, a committee of the citizens recommended, among many other suggestions of a similar character, the following:

ORDER OF DANCES AND TABLEAUX VIVANTS.
1. Grand March.
2. Tableau Vivant..............."A Sketch, by Boz."
3. Amilie Quadrille.
4. Tableau Vivant....."The Seasons," a poem, with music.
5. Quadrille Waltz, selections.
6. Tableau Vivant......The book of "Oliver Twist."
7. Quadrille March..........................Norma.
8. Tableau Vivant..............."The Ivy Green."
9. Victoria Waltz.
10. Tableau Vivant....................."Little Nell."
11. Basket Quadrille.
12. Tableau Vivant...........The book of "Nicholas Nickleby."
13. March.
14. Tableau Vivant..............."A Sketch, by Boz."
15. Spanish Dance.
16. Tableau Vivant.........."The Pickwick Papers."

It is, perhaps, well to remark that "Mrs. Leo Hunter's dinner party" was presented among the *tableaux*, as finally amended. The following report of an actual incident at the ball reads like an extract from the account of the manner in which Martin Chuzzlewit "received" the American Sovereigns at the "National Hotel:"

"As Boz approached, Mr. Philip Hone seized his hand, and said, 'My dear sir, here is a handful of our people—right glad—bright eyes—rejoice—heartfelt welcome—can't express—overpowered—feelings—' to all which Boz most graciously bowed, and placed his hand upon his heart; and then Mr. Hone said "Nine cheers," and, evidently to the astonishment of the hero of the extraordinary scene, the surrounding crowd gave utterance to nine enthusiastic cheers."

"Punch" jokingly said: "We learnt, while having our hair cut at Truefitt's the other day (March, 1842), that that illustrious dealer in fictitious hair had received an immense order from Boz, originating in his desire to gratify the seventeen thousand American young ladies who had honored him with applications for locks from his caput. Two ships have been chartered to convey the sentimental cargo, and will start from the London docks on the 1st day of April."

Soon after his return from America we find Sydney Smith again in active correspondence with our author. Dickens had asked him to dinner, and Sydney Smith replied :*

"I accept your obliging invitation conditionally. If I am invited by any man of greater genius than yourself, or by one in whose works I have been more completely interested, I will repudiate you, and dine with the more splendid phenomenon of the two."

At the end of the year, on the 10th December, "The Patrician's Daughter," by Dr. Westland Marston, was represented at Drury Lane, the beautiful prologue by Dickens being admirably delivered by Mr. Macready.

CHAPTER X.

"MARTIN CHUZZLEWIT."

UNDETERRED by the disapprobation showered down upon him by the Americans, on 1st January, 1843, Dickens issued the first number of "Martin Chuzzlewit."

If there had been any previous doubt as to the general feeling throughout the States, there was none now. No sooner had the new book reached America than the storm burst forth with great violence, and all classes were so touched with Dickens's satire and the fun he had made of them, that a writer some time since said that, when present at the Boston Theatre—the burlesque of "Macbeth" being performed—all sorts

---

* 14th May, 1842.

of worthless articles (Mexican rifles, Pensylvanian bonds, etc.) were pitched into the caldron, in the incantation scene, but nothing provoked louder cheers than when the last work by Dickens was thrown in! The American journals, both literary and political, all united against the common foe, much in the same way as they had united twelve years before against Mrs. Trollope and her "Domestic Manners of the Americans."

In the preface to the cheap edition appearing in 1849, he remarked that the American portions of the book, he had been given to understand from authorities, were considered violent exaggerations, and that the Water-toast Association and eloquence, for example, were beyond all bounds of belief. Nothing, however, but a liberal paraphrase of some reports of public proceedings in the United States (especially of the Brandywine Association), printed in the "Times," in June and July, 1843, had been employed in writing Martin Chuzzlewit, and these formed the material complained of. We may remark that the same "Postscript" as in that of "American Notes" is affixed to the "Charles Dickens Edition" of "Martin Chuzzlewit."

Blackwood affirmed that "Pecksniff owed much of his celebrity, we believe, to his remarkable likeness to the late Sir Robert Peel." "The American Publishers' Circular," in the summer of 1857, stating that Mr. Samuel Carter Hall was about to visit the United States, to deliver a series of lectures, impudently alluded to Mr. Hall as being "the original of Dickens's character," and suggested that if he (Mr. Hall) wished to draw well, he should advertise himself as "the original Pecksniff."

Lord Lytton, in the preface to "Night and Morning," says: "In this work I have sought to lift the mask from the timid selfishness which too often bears with us the name of *Respectability*. Purposely avoiding all attraction that may savor of extravagance, patiently subduing every tone and every hue to the aspect of those whom we meet daily in our thoroughfares, I have shown in Robert Beaufort the man of decorous phrase and bloodless action—the systematic self-server—in whom the world forgives the lack of all that is generous, warm, and noble, in order to respect the passive acquiescence in methodical conventions and hollow forms. And how common such men are with us in this century, and how inviting and how necessary their delineation, may be seen in this—that the popular and pre-eminent Observer of the age in which we live has since placed their prototype in vigorous colors upon imperishable canvas. Need I say that I allude to the 'Pecksniff' of Mr. Dickens?"

The main object of "Martin Chuzzlewit" was to call attention to the system of ship-hospitals, and to work-house nurses; and, as types of the latter, Sarah Gamp, with the no less immortal, though invisible, Mrs. Harris and Betsey Prig, are inimitable. Speaking of the former, a writer said:

"She is, with a vengeance,
'The grave, conceited nurse, of office proud!'

"coarse, greedy, inhuman, jovial — prowling about young wives with a leer, and old men with a look that would fain 'lay them out.' Ready at every festivity 'to put the bottle to her lips,' and at every calamity to squat down and find in it her own account of pickled salmon and cucumber—and crutched up in a sort of sham sympathy and zeal, by the perpetual praises administered to herself by that *Eidolon*, Mrs. Harris—there are not many things of their kind so living in fiction as this nightmare. The touch of exaggeration in her dialect is so skillfully distributed everywhere, that we lose the sense of it as we read."

Sydney Smith, delighted at the manner in which the Americans were pasquinaded, sent him these familiar notes on the merits of the book:

"You have been so used to such impertinences that I believe you will excuse me for saying how very much pleased I am with the first number of your new work. Pecksniff and his daughters, and Pinch, are admirable—quite first-rate painting, such as no one but yourself can execute.

"I did not like your genealogy of the Chuzzlewits, and I must wait a little to see how Martin turns out. I am impatient for the next number.

"Pray come and see me next summer; and believe me ever yours, SYDNEY SMITH.

"P.S.—Chuffey is admirable. I have never read a finer piece of writing; it is deeply pathetic and affecting. Your last number is excellent. Don't give yourself the trouble to answer my impertinent eulogies, only excuse them."

Then, again, under date July 12th, 1843, in acknowledgment of a call from Dickens, and after the receipt of a new number of "Martin Chuzzlewit," he writes:

"Excellent! nothing can be better! You must settle it with the Americans as you can, but I have nothing to do with that. I have only to certify that the number is full of wit, humor, and power of description.

"I am slowly recovering from an attack of the gout in the knee, and am sorry to have missed you."

"Martin Chuzzlewit" was published in a complete form by Messrs. Chapman & Hall, and dedicated to Miss Burdett Coutts. Poor Tom Pinch claims our best sympathy; the boy Bailey, Pecksniff and his chaste daughters, Montague Tigg, Mark Tapley, and Mrs. Lupin, and the Chuzzlewits, old and young, are all admirably sketched. The American characters, Jefferson Brick (war correspondent), Scadder, Colonel Diver, and Hannibal Chollop, are fine food for mirth.

The most melodramatic portion is the murder of Tigg by Jonas Chuzzlewit. The disguise and preparation—the history of the individual mind of the murderer—the steps by which he descends—and the minute particulars which the over-wrought brain of Jonas catches up to use for his horrible purpose (witness the conversation with the doctor), are splendid examples of observation and intuition, as true as nature itself; and the defeat and final extirpation of selfishness in the heart of the hero, Martin, point a most valuable moral. The heroine is, however, weak, and sinks into insignificance by the side of charming little Ruth Pinch.

Remaining true to the resolve contained in his letter to the "Athenæum," the numbers were simultaneously published here in America —Messrs. Harper Brothers, by arrangement, being furnished with a duplicate copy of each number, thereby enabling them to forestall the other American publishers.

A good melodramatic version was produced at the Lyceum, Mr. Robert Keeley enacting *Sairey Gamp;* Mr. Emery, *Jonas;* Frank Matthews, *Pecksniff;* Miss Woolgar and Mrs. Keeley, *Mercy* and *Bailey.*

Very recently, in March, 1868, Mr. Horace Wigan's adaptation at the Olympic met with considerable success, Mr. J. Clarke sustaining the part of *Mrs. Gamp.*

Douglas Jerrold this summer (1843), occupying a cottage near Herne Bay, wrote to Dickens, inviting him to come and see him. The following is an extract from his rejoinder:

"Herne Bay. Hum! I suppose it is no worse than any other place in this weather; but *it* is watery, rather, isn't it? In my mind's eye, I have the sea in a perpetual state of smallpox, and the chalk running down-hill like town milk. But I know the comfort of getting to work in a fresh place, and proposing pious projects to one's self, and having the more substantial advantage of going to bed early, and getting up ditto, and walking about alone. If there were a fine day, I should like to deprive you of the last-named happiness, and take a good long stroll."

During the year, at the inauguration of the Manchester Athenæum, he made an admirable speech—his longest effort up to this time—on the importance and usefulness of Mechanics' Institutes.*

After the publication of "Oliver Twist" and "Martin Chuzzlewit," Dickens's friends were continually reporting to him cases of cruelty and hardship, and begging his attention thereto. In answer to one of these philanthropic appeals, Dickens wrote—he was at that time living in Devonshire terrace:

"That is a very horrible case you tell me of. I would to God I could get at the parental heart of —— ——, in which event I would so scarify it that he should writhe again. But if I were to put such a father as he into a book, all the fathers going (and especially the bad ones) would hold up their hands and protest against the unnatural caricature. I find that a great many people (particularly those who might have sat for the character) consider even Mr. Pecksniff a grotesque impossibility; and Mrs. Nickleby herself, sitting bodily before me in a solid chair, once asked me whether I really believed there was such a woman.

"So ——, reviewing his own case, would not believe in Jonas Chuzzlewit. 'I like "Oliver Twist,"' says ——, 'for I am fond of children. But the book is unnatural; for who would think of being cruel to poor little Oliver Twist?'

"Nevertheless I will bear the dog in my mind. And if I can hit him between the eyes, so that he shall stagger more than you or I have done this Christmas under the combined effects of punch and turkey, I will.

"Thank you cordially for your note. Excuse this scrap of paper. I thought it was a whole sheet, until I turned over."†

The reader will remember Maclise's beautiful portrait of Dickens, familiar to us all as the engraved frontispiece to the large edition of "Nicholas Nickleby." It is the portrait of a literary exquisite thirty years ago; and it is hard to believe that those large effeminate eyes sparkling from beneath flowing locks, that ample black satin scarf, with a diamond union-pin, and that wide velvet collar, can have any thing to do with the hearty, keen-eyed, sailor-like man whose last photographs now look at us from every shop-window! But it is so! they are the portraits of the same great man. Time

---

* Given in Charles Dickens's Speeches, recently published.

† The letter was dated "2d January, 1844." It was published in the "Autographic Mirror" for February, 1864.

alone has worked the change. Of his elegant appearance, when young, Mr. Arthur Locker gives us a reminiscence: "The first time," he says, "I saw the idolized Boz in the flesh was at a Fancy Fair in the Painted Hall of Greenwich Hospital, held, I think, for the benefit of the Shipwrecked Mariners' Society. He was then a handsome young man, with piercing bright eyes and carefully arranged hair—much, in fact, as he is represented in Maclise's picture."

Towards the close of this year another characteristic portrait of our author was taken by Miss M. Gillies; and a fine engraving of it, by Armytage, appeared as a frontispiece to Horne's "New Spirit of the Age," issued early in the new year. It is different to the Maclise picture; the hair is longer and more careless, the face is more thoughtful, the mouth firmer—in fact, there is less of the exquisite and more of the man about it than in the Maclise portrait taken four years before.

CHAPTER XI.

THE "CHRISTMAS CAROL."

His next work was that delightful little book —a better-hearted one never issued from the press—"A Christmas Carol, in prose; being a Ghost Story of Christmas." It appeared in December, 1843, with some admirable illustrations by John Leech. Since the publication of the "Pickwick Papers," no work of Dickens's caused half the sensation this touching and beautiful little story did—it is written with such a hearty appreciation of Christmas, and all the attendant festivities indulged in at that joyous period. The description of Scrooge is wonderfully drawn; his excitement in waking up after his interviews with the spirits, and finding it all a dream—his getting up and nearly cutting his nose off in shaving—buying the big turkey, and sending it off to Bob Cratchit, with a series of chuckles, and giving so handsome a donation to the collector—and, finally, going to the party at Fred's, where that fine fellow Topper and the plump sister played up such grand tricks, and then behaving so unexpectedly to poor Bob the next day—follow so rapidly as almost to take one's breath away with amazement and delight!

If any individual story ever warmed a Christmas hearth, that was the one; if ever solitary Old-Self was converted by a book, and made to be merry and child-like at that season " when its blessed Founder was himself a child," he surely was by that!

On a former page we spoke of Thackeray's hearty appreciation of Dickens—expressed, too, at a time when the "Vanity Fair" had made its writer's fame. It has been said that a degree of rivalry at one period existed between the two authors; but few readers, we think, will be inclined to characterize by any such term the most friendly competition, after perusing this touching and beautiful tribute* to Mr. Dickens's genius from the pen of the yet unknown Michael Angelo Titmarsh. A box of Christmas books is supposed to have been sent by the editor to Titmarsh, in his retirement in Switzerland, whence the latter writes his notions of their contents. The last book of all is Mr. Dickens's "Christmas Carol"—we mean the story of old Scrooge—the immortal precursor of that long line of Christmas stories which are now so familiar to his readers.

"And now (says the critic) there is but one book left in the box, the smallest one, but oh! how much the best of all. It is the work of the master of all the English humorists now alive; the young man who came and took his place calmly at the head of the whole tribe, and who has kept it. Think of all we owe Mr. Dickens since those half-dozen years; that store of happy hours that he has made us pass; the kindly and pleasant companions whom he has introduced to us; the harmless laughter, the generous wit, the frank, manly, human love which he has taught us to feel! Every month of those years has brought us some kind token from this delightful genius. His books may have lost in art, perhaps, but could we afford to wait? Since the days when the 'Spectator' was produced by a man of kindred mind and temper, what books have appeared that have taken so affectionate a hold of the English public as these?

* * * * * *

"Who can listen to objections regarding such a book as this? It seems to me a national benefit, and, to every man or woman who reads it, a personal kindness. The last two people I heard speak of it were women; neither knew the other or the author, and both said, by way of criticism, 'God bless him!'

"As for Tiny Tim, there is a certain passage in the book regarding that young gentleman about which a man should hardly venture to speak in print or in public, any more than he would of any other affections of his private heart. There is not a reader in England but that little creature will be a bond of union between author and him; and he will say of Charles Dickens, as the women just now, 'God

---

* It appeared in "Fraser's Magazine" for July, 1844.

bless him!' What a feeling is this for a writer to be able to inspire, and what a reward to reap!"

Let the reader call to mind the book itself, and then he will appreciate the warmth and exuberance of good feeling reflected in the following letter to its author by Lord Jeffrey:

"Blessings on your kind heart, my dear Dickens, and may it always be as full and as light as it is kind, and a fountain of kindness to all within reach of its beatings. We are all charmed with your ' Carol;' chiefly, I think, for the genuine goodness which breathes all through it, and is the true inspiring angel by which its genius has been awakened. The whole scene of the Cratchits is like the dream of a beneficent angel, in spite of its broad reality, the little Tiny Tim in life and death almost as sweet and as touching as Nelly. * * * Well, to be sure, you should be happy yourself; for you may be sure you have done more good, and not only fastened more kindly feelings, but prompted more positive acts of benevolence, by this little publication, than can be traced to all the pulpits and confessionals since Christmas, 1842."*

Sydney Smith, too, a few weeks afterwards, wrote: "Many thanks for the ' Christmas Carol,' which I shall immediately proceed upon, in preference to six American pamphlets I found upon my arrival, all promising immediate payment?"†

In a criticism in " Hood's Magazine," a similar sentiment to that contained in Lord Jeffrey's letter occurs: "This book will do more to spread Christian feeling than ten thousand pulpits!"

And in another article the same writer—the kindly Thomas Hood himself—says: "It was a blessed inspiration that put such a book into the head of Charles Dickens—a happy inspiration of the heart, that warms every page. It is impossible to read, without a glowing bosom and burning cheeks, between love and shame for our kind, with perhaps a little touch of misgiving whether we are not personally open, a crack or so, to the reproach of Wordsworth "—

"'The world is too much with us, early and late,
Getting and spending.'"

Men of very different natures to Thomas Hood read of little Nell, and were touched. It is told of Daniel O'Connell, the great Irish agitator, that, riding with a friend one day, and reading the then recently issued book where the death of Little Nell is recorded, the great orator's eyes filled with tears, and he sobbed aloud:

"He should not have killed her!—he should not have killed her! She was too good!" and so he threw the book out of the window, unable to read more, and indignant that the author should have immolated a heroine in death.

The story was dramatized and played at several theatres, the Adelphi, as usual, taking the lead in making the tale popular. It was about this time that Dickens resorted to the Court of Chancery for an injunction against the printer and four publishers of " Parley's Illuminated Library " for piracy.

Mr. Dickens had now two sons—the last being born during the progress of "Martin Chuzzlewit." Early in the new year it was decided upon christening the second boy, and the name *Francis Jeffrey*—after that of a true and tried friend—was determined upon. A letter of the latter, dated 1st February, 1844, in answer to the half-serious, half-jocular proposal of Dickens, says: "About that most flattering, or more probably passing, fancy of that dear Kate (Mrs. Dickens) of yours to associate my name with yours over the baptismal font of your new-come boy, my first impression was that it was a mere piece of kind badinage of hers (or perhaps your own), and not meant to be seriously taken, and, consequently, that it would be foolish to take any notice of it. * * * If such a thing be indeed in your contemplation, it would be more flattering and agreeable to me than most things which have happened to me in my moral pilgrimage; while, if it was but the expression of a happy and confiding playfulness, I shall still feel grateful for the communication, and return you a smile as cordial as your own, with full permission for both of you to smile at the simplicity which could not distinguish jest from earnest. * * * I want amazingly to see you rich and independent of all irksome exertions; and really if you go on having more boys (and naming them after poor Scotch plebeians), you must make good bargains and lucky hits, and, above all accommodate yourself oftener to that deeper and higher tone of human feeling, which, you *now see experimentally,* is more surely and steadily popular than any display of fancy, or magical power of observation and description combined. And so God be with you and yours," etc.

The last part of the letter alludes, no doubt, to the profits of the " Christmas Carol," the sale of which was very large. Jeffrey knew how few authors possessed sufficient worldly wisdom to keep a balance at their bankers', and gave his young friend a delicate hint to "be care-

---

* Edinburgh, December 26, 1843.
† London, February 21, 1844.

ful and save." This was not the only time Lord Jeffrey quietly lectured his correspondent. Three years later, in 1847, we get this piece of practical—shall we say *Northern*—advice?—" I am rather" (he writes in 1847) "disappointed to find your *embankment*" (doubtlessly a fund of future provision) "still so small. But it is a great thing that you have made a beginning and laid a foundation, and you are young enough to think of living yet many years under the proud roof of the completed structure, which even I expect to see ascending in its grandeur. But when I consider that the public has, upon moderate computation, paid at least £100,000 for your work (and had a good bargain, too, for the money), I think it is rather provoking to think that the author should not now have —— in bank, and never have received, I suspect, above ——. There must have been some mismanagement, I think, as well as ill-luck, to have occasioned this result—not extravagance on your part, my dear Dickens, nor even excessive beneficence—but improvident arrangements with publishers, and too careless a control over their proceedings. But you are wiser now, and with Forster's kind and judicious help, will soon redeem the effect of your not ungenerous errors."

It is not generally known that Dickens contributed an article to "Hood's Magazine" and "Comic Miscellany" in May, 1844. Our author had received some kindnesses at the hands of the humorist, and in recognition of them he sent a paper entitled "Threatening Letter to Thomas Hood, from an Ancient Gentleman, *by favor of Charles Dickens*," to his friend's magazine. Speaking of the manner of some complaining old gentlemen, the writer of the letter tried to find fault with every thing modern:

"Mr. Hood. Sir, * * * Ah! governments were governments, and judges were judges, in *my* day, Mr. Hood. There was no nonsense then. Any of your seditious complainings, and we were ready with the military on the shortest notice. We should have charged Covent Garden Theatre, sir, on a Wednesday night, at the point of the bayonet. Then the judges were full of dignity and firmness, and knew how to administer the law.

"There is only one judge who knows how to do his duty now. He tried that revolutionary female the other day, who, though she was in full work (making shirts at three-halfpence apiece), had no pride in her country, but treasonably took it into her head, in the distraction of having been robbed of her easy earnings, to attempt to drown herself and her young child, and the glorious man went out of his way, sir —out of his way—to call her up for instant sentence of death, and to tell her she had no hope of mercy in this world—as you may see yourself if you look in the papers of Wednesday, the 17th of April."

It is curious, after this allusion to Mr. Laing, the notorious police magistrate—said to be the Fang of "Oliver Twist"—and after mentioning the poor distressed needle-woman, with the allusion to Sir Peter Laurie, that the next article immediately following should be the first appearance of Hood's exquisite "Bridge of Sighs." On the same page with Dickens's bitter and telling attack upon the grumblers in power—the grumblers who can only see national prosperity in the increasing misery of the lower orders—there appeared those wonderful lines, commencing—

"One more Unfortunate,
Weary of breath,
Rashly importunate,
Gone to her death!"

as if suggested by the poor female whom Dickens had just described as being brought before the magistrate for an attempt to commit suicide.

In May, 1844, he presided at the Annual Conversazione of the Polytechnic Institution in Birmingham, and made a most telling speech. Writing, soon after, to Jerrold—who was very nervous in addressing an assembly—he said: "Is your modesty a confirmed habit, or could you prevail upon yourself, if you are moderately well, to let me call you up for a word or two at the Sanatorium Dinner? There are some men (excellent men) connected with that institution, who would take the very strongest interest in your doing so; and *do* advise me, one of these odd days, that if I can do it well and unaffectedly, I may." Jerrold overcame his bashfulness, and presided at the next anniversary.

A very kind and graceful act was performed by Dickens this year. Mr. Newby, in July, published, in one volume, "THE EVENINGS OF A WORKING-MAN. *Being the Occupation of his Scanty Leisure, by* JOHN OVERS. *With a Preface, relating to the Author, by Charles Dickens.*" The preface is of the most charming description. It first mentions that Overs was a carpenter, who had employed his evenings in literary compositions, and applied to him, as he was relinquishing the editorship of "Bentley's Miscellany," for help to get his writings into notice. After some correspondence, Dickens trying to dissuade him from the perils of authorship, and a personal interview, " he wrote me," he says, "as manly and straightforward, but, withal, as modest, a letter as ever I read in my life. He explained to me how limited his ambition was, soaring no higher than the establishment of his wife in some light business, and the better education of his children. He set before me the difference of his evening and holiday studies, such as they were, and his having no better resource than an ale-house or a skittle-ground." Dickens accordingly consented to assist him, and got several of his pieces inserted in a magazine. "During this period neither hammer, nor plane, nor chisel had been laid aside for the more enticing service of the pen—literary compositions had neither seduced John Overs into dreams nor lamentations which have damaged his peace of mind.

* * * * * *

"He is very ill; the faintest shadow of the man who came into my little study, for the first time, half a dozen years ago, after the correspondence I have mentioned. He has been very ill for a long period; his disease is a severe and wasting affection of the lungs, which has incapacitated him these many months for every kind of occupation. 'If I could only do a hard day's work,' he said to me, the other day, 'how happy I should be.'

"Having these papers by him, amongst others, he bethought himself that, if he could get a bookseller to purchase them for publication in a volume, they would enable him to make some temporary provision for his sick wife and very young family. We talked the matter over together, and that it might be easier of accomplishment, I promised him that I would write an introduction to his book.

"I would to Heaven that I could do him better service; I would to Heaven it were an introduction to a long, and vigorous, and useful life. But Hope will not trim her lamp the less brightly for him and his because of this impulse to their struggling fortunes; and trust me, reader, they deserve her light, and need it sorely.

."He has inscribed this book to one* whose skill will help him, under Providence, in all that human skill can do—to one who never could have recognized in any potentate on earth a higher claim to constant kindness and attention than he has recognized in him."

The book was eventually published at 5s., and was found to contain some very creditable writing, both prose and verse. Overs did not live long enough to enjoy his popularity, for the malady under which he was laboring terminated fatally the following October. The work and its author are now almost forgotten, but the generous conduct displayed towards him by Dickens is well deserving of remembrance.

---

* Dr. Elliotson.

CHAPTER XII.

VISIT TO ITALY.—"THE CHIMES."

In the summer of this year Dickens went to Italy. He started off with his wife, sister-in-law, five children, courier, nurses, etc, and a carriage, and had a very enjoyable holiday. Previous to his departure, he was entertained at a dinner by his friends, at the "Trafalgar," Greenwich, on the 19th June, 1845, Lord Normanby in the chair. The following extracts from his epistles to Jerrold give us many pleasing bits of an autobiographical character, and at least show us how he enjoyed himself:

"Come, come and see me in Italy—let us smoke a pipe among the vines. I have taken a little house surrounded by them, and no man in the world should be more welcome to it than you."

And in another from Cremona:

"It was very hearty and good of you, Jerrold, to make that affectionate mention of the 'Carol' in 'Punch;' and, I assure you, it was not lost upon the distant object of your manly regard, but touched him as you wished and meant it should. I wish we had not lost so much time in improving our personal knowledge of each other. But I have so steadily read you, and so selfishly gratified myself in always expressing the admiration with which your gallant truths inspired me, that I must not call it lost time either."

From the same place, in November:

"You rather entertained the idea once of coming to see me at Genoa. I shall return straight on the 9th of December, limiting my stay in town to one week. Now, couldn't you come back with me? The journey that way is very cheap, costing little more than £12, and I am quite sure the gratification to you would be high. I am lodged in quite a wonderful place, and would put you in a painted room as big as a church, and much more comfortable. There are pens and ink upon the premises; orange-trees, gardens, battledores and shuttlecocks, rousing wood fires for the evenings, and a welcome worth having. * * * Come! Letter from a gentleman in Italy to Bradbury & Evans in London. Letter from a gentleman in a country gone to sleep, to a gentleman in a country that would go to sleep too, and never wake again, if some people had their way.

You can work in Genoa—the house is used to it: it is exactly a week's post. Have that portmanteau looked to; and when we meet, say, 'I am coming!'"

The visit to Italy often formed a subject for conversation with Dickens, and only a few weeks before his death, he told Mr. Arthur Locker this anecdote of his experiences there: "Mr. Dickens, on one occasion, visited a certain monastery, and was conducted over the building by a young monk, who, though a native of the country, spoke remarkably fluent English. There was, however, one peculiarity about his pronunciation. He frequently misplaced his v's and w's. 'Have you been in England?' asked Mr. Dickens. 'No,' replied the monk, 'I have learnt my English from this book,' producing 'Pickwick;' and it further appeared that he had selected Mr. Samuel Weller as the *beau ideal* of elegant pronunciation."

"The Chimes: a Goblin Story of some Bells that rang an Old Year out and a New Year in," was published at the end of the year, by Messrs. Chapman & Hall, illustrated by Maclise, Doyle, Leech, and Stanfield. It was of the same size and price as the former Christmas book; but, instead of being illustrated by Mr. Leech alone, several Academicians and other artists had now come forward with their pencils. The great success of the "Christmas Carol," in the preceding year, had directed the attention of other authors to this class of literature, and this Christmas there appeared "The Snow-storm," by Mrs. Gore; "The Last of the Fairies," by G. P. R. James; an Irish Story, by Mr. Lever; and others; but we need hardly say Mr. Dickens distanced them all.

Next to the "Christmas Carol," it is one of the most delightful little books he has written. Old Toby Veck, the patient, drudging ticket-porter, plying his vocation near the old church, listening to the voices of the bells, and gathering encouragement from them, is a beautifully drawn character. Meg, his daughter, a hopeful woman, and Richard, her sweetheart, are truthfully portrayed, as also Will Fern, Sir Joshua Bowley, Mr. Filer, and Alderman Cute. The plot is worked out somewhat after the plan of the "Christmas Carol," consisting mainly of a dream by Toby Veck. Every one ought to be well pleased with the *finale*, in which Toby disappears from notice in a country dance to the step he is so accustomed to—a Trot.

Thomas Hood, who had written so beautifully of the "Christmas Carol," could not refrain from expressing in print a like admiration for "The Chimes:"—"This," he wrote, "is another of those seasonable books intended by Boz to stir up and awaken the kindly feelings which are generally diffused among mankind, but too apt, as old Weller says, to lie 'dormouse' in the human bosom. It is similar in plan to the 'Christmas Carol,' but is scarcely so happy in its subject—it could not be—as that famous *Gobbling* Story, with its opulence of good cheer, and all the Gargantuan festivity of that hospitable tide. The hero of the tale is one Toby Veck (we wish that surname had been more English in its sound, it seems to want an outlandish *De* or *Van* before it), a little old London ticket-porter—who does not know the original?—and his humble dwelling down the mews, with his wooden cardboard at the door, with his name and occupation, and the

'*N.B.—Messuages carefully delivered!*'

May 'The Chimes,'" Tom Hood concludes, "be widely and wisely heard, inculcating their wholesome lessons of charity and forbearance, reminding wealth of the claims of want—the feasting of the fasting, and inducing them to spare something for an aching void from their comfortable repletion."

Having alluded to the administration of the law by Mr. Laing, the Clerkenwell magistrate, in "Oliver Twist," under the character of Mr. Fang, likewise to the notorious Sir Peter Laurie, in "The Chimes," as Alderman Cute, the talk about "putting down" various little wants, cares, and troubles of the poor being merely a transcript of what the garrulous old City magistrate had said from the bench, "Particularly well," says one who had heard him, "do we recollect a promise made by that officious personage, 'dressed in a little brief authority,' to a starved and maddened woman, who had attempted to drown herself, that he (Sir Peter Laurie) would *put down suicide!*" The alderman did not forget the attack made upon him, and when he found an opportunity, which he did shortly, ridiculed Mr. Dickens's description of Jacob's Island in "Oliver Twist," and denied in full court the existence, as described, of that locality, and of the Folly Ditch; but the author was again too strong for the alderman, and in his preface to the new edition of the tale he incidentally mentions the fact, and denies, in his turn, the existence of Sir Peter Laurie!

Jerrold, we may remark, under the initial of "Q," often scarified the alderman in the pages of "Punch."

As a drama "The Chimes" became very popular, the Adelphi performing on 19th December a version adapted with some skill by Messrs. Mark Lemon and Gilbert A'Beckett,

Mr. Wright sustaining the part of Alderman Cute, and Paul Bedford Sir Joshua Bowley. The Lyceum had an admirable dramatic version, Mr. Keeley's Toby Veck being a most life-like portrait of Dickens's happy original.

Writing from Milan, in November, 1844, to the Countess of Blessington, we learn how this beautiful little work was composed:

"Since I heard from Count D'Orsay, I have been beset in I don't know how many ways. First of all, I went to Marseilles, and came back to Genoa. Then I went to the Peschiere. Then some people who had been present at the Scientific Congress here, made a sudden inroad on that establishment and overran it. Then they went away, and I shut myself up for one month, close and tight, over my little Christmas book, 'The Chimes.' All my affections and passions got twined and knotted in it, and I became as haggard as a murderer, long before I had wrote ' The End.' When I had done that, like ' *The* man of Thessaly,' who having scratched his eyes out in a quickset hedge, plunged into a bramble-bush to scratch them in again, I fled to Venice, to recover the composure I had disturbed. From thence I went to Verona and to Mantua. And now I am here—just come up from underground, and earthy all over, from seeing that extraordinary tomb in which the Dead Saint lies in an alabaster case, with sparkling jewels all about him to mock his dusty eyes, not to mention the twenty-franc pieces which devout votaries were ringing down upon a sort of skylight in the Cathedral pavement above, as if it were the counter of his Heavenly shop. * * * Old —— is a trifle uglier than when I first arrived. He has periodical parties, at which there are a great many flower-pots and a few ices—no other refreshments. He goes about continually with extemporaneous poetry; and is always ready, like tavern-dinners, on the shortest notice and the most reasonable terms. He keeps a gigantic harp in his bedroom, together with pen, ink, and paper, for fixing his ideas as they flow—a kind of profane King David, truly good-natured and very harmless. Pray say to Count D'Orsay every thing that is cordial and loving from me. The travelling-purse he gave me has been of immense service. It has been constantly opened. All Italy seems to yearn to put its hand into it. I think of hanging it, when I come back to England, on a nail as a trophy, and of gashing the brim like the blade of an old sword, and saying to my son and heir, as they do upon the stage: 'You see this notch, boy? Five hundred francs were laid low on that day for post-horses. Where this gap is, a waiter charged your father treble the correct amount—and got it. This end, worn into teeth like the rasped edge of an old file, is sacred to the Custom Houses, boy, the passports, and the shabby soldiers at town gates, who put an open hand and a dirty coat-cuff into the windows of all Forestieri. Take it, boy. Thy father has nothing else to give!' My desk is cooling itself in a mail-coach, somewhere down at the back of the cathedral, and the pens and ink in this house are so detestable, that I have no hope of your ever getting to this portion of my letter. But I have the less misery in this state of mind, from knowing that it has nothing in it to repay you for the trouble of perusal."

During the early part of the year 1845 Dickens remained on the Continent. He was in London, however, in the summer, making arrangements for new books, and other ventures—amongst them a new daily paper, of the most liberal principles—for the coming autumn season.

CHAPTER XIII.

DICKENS AS AN ACTOR.

It has been very generally stated that it was at the close of this year that our author made his first appearance as an actor upon a public stage. This is not correct. Dickens's extreme fondness for theatricals had tempted him, as far back as the year 1836, when "Pickwick" was publishing, to take a part in "The Strange Gentleman," at St. James's Theatre. The amateur actor was not successful on this occasion, and we believe no further attempt — except drawing-room performances—was made until the autumn of 1845, when he made another appearance on the stage at the St. James's Theatre, on the 19th of September, the play selected being Ben Jonson's "Every Man in his Humor;" the various parts of the amateur performance being taken by literary and artistic celebrities. The triumph achieved was immense. They were induced to repeat the performance for a Charity, at the same theatre, on the 15th of November following, the only alteration being the substitution of a Mr. Eaton for Mr. A'Beckett as William. The playbill itself is a curiosity:

A Strictly Private Amateur Performance
At the St. James's Theatre
(By favor of Mr. Mitchell). Will be performed Ben Jonson's Comedy of

EVERY MAN IN HIS HUMOR.

CHARACTERS:

Knowell.....................Henry Mayhew.
Edward Knowell.............Frederick Dickens.

Brainworm	Mark Lemon.
George Downright	Dudley Costello.
Wellbred	George Cattermole.
Kitely	John Forster.
Captain Bobadil	Charles Dickens.
Master Stephen	Douglas Jerrold.
Master Mathew	John Leech.
Thomas Cash	Augustus Dickens.
Oliver Cob	Percival Leigh.
Justice Clement	Frank Stone.
Roger Formal	Mr. Evans.
William	W. Eaton.
James	W. B. Jerrold.
Dame Kitely	Miss Fortesque.
Mistress Bridget	Miss Hinton.
Tib	Miss Bew.

To conclude with a Farce, in One Act, called

TWO O'CLOCK IN THE MORNING.

CHARACTERS:

Mr. Snobbington	Mr. Charles Dickens.
The Stranger	Mr. Mark Lemon.

Previous to the Play, the Overture to "William Tell." Previous to the Farce, the Overture to "La Gazza Ladra."

His Royal Highness Prince Albert has been pleased to express his intention to honor the performance with his presence.

Ben Jonson, as an acting dramatist, has almost disappeared from the stage he so long adorned, and, probably, no performance of his best comedy was ever more successful than the above. Dickens made such an admirable Captain Bobadil, that Leslie, the Royal Academician, took a most characteristic portrait of him in that character. The moment selected is when the Captain shouts out—

"A gentleman! odds so, I am not within."
Act i., Scene 3.

Mr. Mitchell, of Bond Street, published a fine lithograph of the picture, and collectors of the deceased novelist's portraits will do well to secure a copy. For beauty of portraiture and character there is nothing like it. It is also very interesting, as coming between the beautiful but effeminate portrait of Maclise and the photograph of our own day, because it shows the change that was coming over his features, when deep thought and firmness of purpose were beginning to leave their marks behind them.

But to return to Dickens as an actor, a friend says:

"Analogous to his powers as a reader were his abilities as an actor; and it has been said of him with truth that, with perhaps the exception of Frederick Lemaitre in his best days, there was no one who could excel Charles Dickens in purely dramatic representation. Those who saw the character of the light-house-keeper in Mr. Wilkie Collins's drama, as portrayed first by Mr. Dickens and then by Mr. Robson, were enabled to judge of the wonderful superiority of the rendering given by the former. And not merely as an actor, but as a stage director, were his talents pre-eminent; not merely did he play his own part to perfection, but he taught every one else in his little company how to play theirs; he would devise scenery with Stanfield and Telbin, take a practical share in the stage carpentry, write out the copy for the playbill, and in every way thoroughly earn the title of 'Mr. Crummles,' with which he was always affectionately greeted on these occasions."

At the time of which we are writing, Dickens was full of enthusiasm for the stage, and being appealed to by Jerrold for an opinion on his drama of "Time Works Wonders," he wrote to his friend: "I am greatly struck by the whole idea of the piece. The elopement in the beginning, and the consequences that flow from it, and their delicate and masterly exposition, are of the freshest, truest, and most vigorous kind; especially the characters—especially the governess, among the best I know; and the wit and the wisdom of it are never asunder. I could almost find it in my heart to sit down and write you a long letter on the subject of this play, but I won't. I will only thank you for it heartily, and add that I agree with you in thinking it incomparably the best of your dramatic writings."

During the summer and autumn of this year Mr. Dickens finished his new Christmas book, "The Cricket on the Hearth (a Fairy Tale of Home); printed and published for the Author" by Messrs. Bradbury & Evans, illustrated by Leech, Stanfield, and Maclise, and dedicated to Lord Jeffrey. Next to the "Christmas Carol" and the "Chimes," this is a great favorite.

The quaint way in which it opens, giving an eloquent picture of homely and domestic comfort in the English carrier's house, the construction of the plot, and the glorious *dénouement*, make the book one of his best and heartiest efforts. Tilly Slowboy, the great clumsy nurse-girl, is very charmingly portrayed, her especial *forte* being to hold the baby topsy-turvy, and entertain it with dialogues, consisting mainly of scraps from conversations she hears, with all the nouns turned into plurals.

The Lyceum was first in the field (21st December) with a dramatic adaptation by Mr. Albert Smith, Miss Mary Keeley impersonating Bertha; Mr. Keeley, Caleb; Mrs. Keeley, Mrs. Peerybingle; and Mr. Emery, John, the honest carrier. Under Mrs. Keeley's management it proved an extraordinary success.

On 6th January following, Mr. Webster's version of the story was placed on the Haymarket boards, with this strong cast:

John Peerybingle	Mr. WEBSTER.
Tackleton	Mr. TILBURY.
Caleb	Mr. FARREN.
Mrs. Peerybingle	Miss FORTESQUE.
Bertha	Mrs. SEYMOUR.
Tilly Slowboy	Mr. BUCKSTONE.

At the Adelphi, O'Smith represented Mr. Peerybingle; Wright, Tilly Slowboy; and the celebrated Mrs. Fitzwilliam, Dot. At the City of London Theatre, too, an adaptation was performed with considerable ability. In the beginning of 1862, Mr. Boucicault's adaptation, under the title of "Dot," played at the Adelphi, proved a great triumph, Mr. J. L. Toole sustaining the part of Caleb.

CHAPTER XIV.

DICKENS AS A JOURNALIST.

WE have previously alluded to the fact that Mr. Dickens had for some time past been thinking of connecting himself with a new daily paper which was to appear early in the new year. The idea was well taken up. Money was freely spent by the various shareholders, and many advertisements told the public that a newspaper, which should supply every thing in the first style of newspaper talent, would be published at the price of twopence-halfpenny. The name chosen was the "Daily News," and Mr. Dickens was widely advertised as "the head of the literary department." Expectation was raised to a high pitch by this announcement; and in 1846, on the 21st of January, the first number appeared. The new journal, however, did not prove so successful as was expected. The staffs of other papers had been long organized, their expenses—of course immense—were well and judiciously controlled, and the arrangements complete. All these things were new to the "Daily News," and the expenses entered into did not render it possible, with the circulation it had then reached, to sell the paper at the original price; and it was shortly after raised to threepence, and finally to the same price as the "Times."

Very recently, and only a few days after the death of the great novelist, the paper here alluded to gave this account of his connection with the journal:

"Some of our readers may not be aware that the 'Pictures from Italy,' which are now included in all editions of Charles Dickens's works, were originally contributed to this newspaper, and that its early numbers were brought out under his editorship. In the first number of this journal, in the 'Daily News' of January 21, 1846, appeared No. 1 of 'Travelling Letters, written on the Road, by Charles Dickens.' In the 'Daily News' of February 14th, of the same year, Mr. Dickens wrote the following verses—which will be new to many—elicited by a speech at one of the night meetings of the wives of agricultural laborers in Wiltshire, held to petition for free-trade:

THE HYMN OF THE WILTSHIRE LABORERS.

"Don't you all think that we have a great need to cry to our God to put it in the hearts of our greaseous Queen and her members of Parlerment to grant us free bread!"—LUCY SIMPKINS, *at Brim Hill.*

O God, who by Thy Prophet's hand
  Didst smite the rocky brake,
Whence water came at Thy command,
  Thy people's thirst to slake:
Strike, now, upon this granite wall,
  Stern, obdurate, and high;
And let some drops of pity fall
  For us who starve and die!

The God, who took a little child
  And set him in the midst,
And promised him His mercy mild,
  As, by Thy Son, Thou didst:
Look down upon our children dear,
  So gaunt, so cold, so spare,
And let their images appear
  Where Lords and Gentry are!

O God, teach them to feel how we,
  When our poor infants droop,
Are weakened in our trust in Thee,
  And how our spirits stoop:
For, in Thy rest, so bright and fair,
  All tears and sorrows sleep;
And their young looks, so full of care,
  Would make Thine angels weep!

The God, who with His finger drew
  The Judgment coming on,
Write for these men, what must ensue,
  Ere many years be gone!
O God, whose bow is in the sky,
  Let them not brave and dare,
Until they look (too late) on high
  And see an Arrow there!

O God, remind them, in the bread
  They break upon the knee,
These sacred words may yet be read,
  "In memory of Me!"
O God, remind them of His sweet
  Compassion for the poor,
And how He gave them Bread to eat,
  And went from door to door.
                CHARLES DICKENS.

"There is the true ring in these lines. They have the note which Dickens sounded consistently through life of right against might; the note which found expression in the Anti-Corn Law agitation, in the protests against workhouse enormities, in the raid against those eccentricities in legislation which are anomalies to the rich and bitter hardships to the poor. Let the reader remark how consistently the weekly periodicals which Mr. Dickens has guided have taken this side, and how the many pens employed on them have taken this side whenever political or social subjects have been discussed, and he will understand that the author was not a mere jester and story-teller, but a true philanthropist and reformer."*

Dickens's friends very soon saw that he had taken a false step. The duties of a daily political paper were not suitable to him, and before many months he relinquished the editorship, and retired from participation in the "Daily News"—but not, it is understood, without a considerable loss in money. His place was then filled by Mr. John Forster, the able editor of the "Examiner," and friend—and at that time the champion—of Mr. Macready. For many years previously Dickens had been on the friendliest terms with the author of the delightful "Life of Goldsmith," and this intimacy was maintained to the close of our author's life, and in his will Mr. Forster has been appointed principal executor. After the "Pictures" had appeared in the "Daily News," they were collected and printed and published for the author, in May, 1846, by his new publishers, Messrs. Bradbury & Evans. Both this work and "The Cricket on the Hearth" may be regarded as the speculations of Mr. Dickens in attempting publishing on his own account. No further works written by him have been, we believe, "printed and published for the author." The book did not meet with that hearty applause which had been given to his previous works.

About this time there are evidences that Dickens was planning another novel, to be issued in the old familiar green covers. Two years had elapsed since the completion of "Martin Chuzzlewit," and we now find him writing to his friend, the Countess of Blessington, about a "new book"—which new work must have been "Dombey and Son," that appeared in the following year: "Vague thoughts of a new book are rife within me just now; and I go wandering about at night into the strangest places, according to my usual propensity at such a time, seeking rest, and finding none. As an addition to my composure, I ran over a little dog in the Regent's Park, yesterday (killing him on the spot), and gave his little mistress such exquisite distress as I never saw the like of. I must have some talk with you about those American singers.† They must never go back to their own country without your having heard them sing Hood's 'Bridge of Sighs.' My God! how sorrowful and pitiful it is!"

Writing to Jerrold, also, before his departure to Switzerland, he incidentally speaks of the work he is engaged upon:

"I wish you would seriously consider the expediency and feasibility of coming to Lausanne in the summer or early autumn. I must be at work myself during a certain part of every day almost, and you could do twice as much there as here. It is a wonderful place to see; and what sort of welcome you will find I will say nothing about, for I have vanity enough to believe that you would be willing to feel yourself as much at home in my household as in any man's." Arriving at Lausanne, he writes that he will be ready to accommodate him in June, and goes on: "We are established here, in a perfect doll's house, which could be put bodily into the hall of our Italian palazzo; but it is the most lovely and delicious situation imaginable, and there is a spare bedroom, wherein we could make you as comfortable as need be. Bowers of roses for cigar smoking, arbors for cool punch-drinking, mountain and Tyrolean countries close at hand, piled-up Alps before the windows, etc., etc., etc."

CHAPTER XV.

APPEARANCE OF "DOMBEY AND SON."

On the 1st October, the first number of "Dombey and Son" was issued by Messrs. Bradbury & Evans, illustrated by Phiz. It ran the usual twenty numbers, and on its completion was dedicated to the Marchioness of Normanby.

This is, perhaps, one of his least popular novels. The descriptions of high life are somewhat forced and overdrawn. Dombey is a man thoroughly to be detested—cruel, stern, and unbending. Little Paul and Captain Cuttle are the two best characters in the book, which contains many others excessively diverting. Mr. Toots, with his mania for writing confidential letters to himself from great and eminent men, and his *penchant* for Messrs. Burgess & Co., the celebrated tailors; Perch, the messenger, and father of a large family; the awful Mrs. MacStinger, Susan Nipper, Major Joe Bagstock, Miss Floy, etc.

In "Dombey" Dickens has evidently endeavored to describe a certain phase of "high life," and he has done so with much success. The character of the aristocratic Cousin Feenix is finished and natural.

---

* "The Daily News," 11th June, 1870.
† The Hutchinson family, probably.

It may just be mentioned that Hablot K. Browne (Phiz), with Mr. Dickens's sanction, published some additional designs—full-length portraits of the characters contained in the novel.

While the story was progressing, an enterprising publisher, in January, 1847, started in weekly penny numbers "Dombey and Daughter," coolly announcing its appearance thus:

"This work is from the pen of one of the first Periodical Writers of the day; and is, in literary merit (although so low in price), no way inferior to Mr. Dickens's admirable work, 'Dombey and Son.' Those who are reading 'Dombey and Son' should most assuredly order 'Dombey and Daughter;' it is a production of exalted intellect, written to sustain moral example and virtuous precept—deeply to interest, and sagely to instruct.

"Order of any Bookseller or Newsvender—ONE PENNY will test the truth of this announcement."

The public thought differently, and nothing further was heard of the work.

Early in 1847, in a letter to Lady Blessington, Dickens wrote: "I begin to doubt whether I had any thing to do with a book called 'Dombey,' or ever sat over number five (not finished a fortnight yet), day after day, until I half began, like the monk in poor Wilkie's story, to think it the only reality in life, and to mistake all the realities for short-lived shadows."*

In the preface to the new edition in 1858, is this note: "I began this book by the Lake of Geneva, and went on with it for some months in France. The association between the writing and the place of writing is so curiously strong in my mind, that at this day, although I know every stair in the little midshipman's house, and could swear to every pew in the church in which Florence was married, or to every young gentleman's bedstead in Doctor Blimber's establishment, I yet confusedly imagine Captain Cuttle as secluding himself from Mrs. MacStinger among the mountains of Switzerland. Similarly, when I am reminded by any chance of what it was that the waves were always saying, I wander in my fancy for a whole winter night about the streets of Paris—as I really did, with a heavy heart, on the night when my little friend and I parted company forever."†

---

* It may be remembered how this same beautiful story of Wilkie's was differently applied by Mr. Dickens, in the last speech he ever made at the Royal Academy dinner.

† The Philadelphia "Morning Post" says:—Dickens, while in this city, was very anxious to purchase Mr. James Hamilton's painting entitled "What are the Wild Waves Saying?" But as this beautiful work, one of the artist's best, was already sold, Mr. Dickens requested that he might see the original sketch, with which he was so greatly pleased that he insisted upon buying it. Mr. Hamilton refused to sell the picture, but presented it to Mr. Dickens. The other day the

Lord Cockburn, in a letter under date 31st of January, 1847, wrote to the author:

"Oh, my dear, dear Dickens! What a No. 5 you have given us! I have so cried and sobbed over it last night, and again this morning; and felt my heart purified by those tears, and blessed and loved you for making me shed them; and I never can bless and love you enough. Since that divine Nelly was found in her humble couch, beneath the snow and ivy, there has been nothing like the actual dying of that sweet Paul, in the summershine of that lofty room."

A high medical authority assures us, that in the author's description of the last illness of Mrs. Skewton, he actually anticipated the clinical researches of M. Dax, Broca, and Hughlings Jackson, on the connection of right hemiplegia with asphasia.

The story was cleverly dramatized and well represented at the Marylebone Theatre, in June, 1849, and its success was in proportion to its merits.

In the spring of 1846, on April 6th, the first Anniversary Festival of the General Theatrical Fund Association was held at the London Tavern. Dickens was in the chair, and made some admirable hits in his most effective speech, as when he said, in speaking of the "base uses" to which the two great theatres were then being applied: "Covent Garden is now but a vision of the past. You might play the bottle conjurer with its dramatic company, and put them all into a pint bottle. The human voice is rarely heard within its walls, save in connection with corn, or the ambidextrous prestidigitation of the Wizard of the North. In like manner, Drury Lane is conducted now with almost a sole view to the opera and ballet, insomuch that the statue of Shakspeare over the door serves as emphatically to point out his grave as his bust did in the church of Stratford-upon-Avon."

What, too, can be happier than his pleadings for the poor actor: "Hazlitt has well said that 'There is no class of society whom so many persons regard with affection as actors. We greet them on the stage, we like to meet them in the streets; they almost always recall to us pleasant associations.' When they have strutted and fretted their hour upon the stage, let them not

---

artist received from Mr. Dickens an exquisite edition of his novels, accompanied by the following autograph:—"Gad's-hill Place, Higham by Rochester, Kent, Monday, Twenty-fifth May, 1868, to Mr. James Hamilton, this set of my books, with thanks and regard.—Charles Dickens." It is certain that Charles Dickens's genius never suggested a more imaginative picture than this masterpiece, and his appreciation of Hamilton could not have been more delicately shown.

be heard no more—but let them be heard sometimes to say that they are happy in their old age. When they have passed for the last time from behind that glittering row of lights with which we are all familiar, let them not pass away into gloom and darkness—but let them pass into cheerfulness and light—into a contented and happy home."[*]

Writing to Jerrold from Geneva, in November, 1846, he says: "This day week I finished my little Christmas book (writing towards the close the exact words of a passage in your affectionate letter,[†] received this morning; to wit, 'After all, life has something serious in it'); and ran over here for a week's rest. I can not tell you how much true gratification I have had in your most hearty letter. Forster told me that the same spirit breathed through a notice of 'Dombey' in your paper; and I have been saying since to K. and G., that there is no such good way of testing the worth of a literary friendship as by comparing its influence on one's mind with any that literary animosity can produce. Mr. W. will throw me into a violent fit of anger for the moment, it is true; but his acts and deeds pass into the death of all bad things next day, and rot out of my memory; whereas a generous sympathy like yours is ever present to me, ever fresh and new to me—always stimulating, cheerful, and delightful. The pain of unjust malice is lost in an hour. The pleasure of a generous friendship is the steadiest joy in the world. What a glorious and comfortable thing that is to think of!

"No, I don't get the paper[‡] regularly. To the best of my recollection, I have not had more than three numbers—certainly not more than four. But I knew how busy you must be, and had no expectation of hearing from you until I wrote from Paris (as I intended doing), and implored you to come and make merry with us there. I am truly pleased to receive your good account of that enterprise * * * I have had great success again in magnetism. E——, who has been with us for a week or so, holds my magnetic powers in great veneration, and I really think they are, by some conjunction of

---
[*] Given entire in "The Speeches of Charles Dickens."

[†] Jerrold, in the letter referred to by Dickens, had said (in deprecating Gilbert A'Beckett's "Comic History of England"): "After all, life has something serious in it. It can not be all a comic history of humanity. Some men would, I believe, write the Comic Sermon on the Mount. Think of a Comic History of England; the drollery of Alfred; the fun of Sir Thomas More in the Tower; the farce of his daughter begging the dead head, and clasping it in her coffin, on her bosom. Surely the world will be sick of this blasphemy."

[‡] Douglas Jerrold's "Weekly Newspaper."

---

chances, strong. Let them, or something else, hold you to me by the heart."

"The Battle of Life (a Love Story)" was the Christmas book referred to in the beginning of the foregoing letter. Messrs. Bradbury & Evans were the publishers, and Maclise, Leech, Stanfield, and Doyle the illustrators. It was a great favorite, and enjoyed considerable popularity, on account of its poetical tendency.

Clemency Newcome is a spiritedly drawn and well-conceived character, as are Messrs. Snitchley and Craggs, the solicitors, Dr. Jeddler, his daughters, Heathfield, and Michael Warden, they all displaying considerable care and painstaking in their treatment. Benjamin Britain, sometimes called Little Britain, to distinguish him from Great, is an oddity. He expresses himself in a conversation to this effect: "I don't know any thing, I don't care for any thing, I don't make out any thing, I don't believe any thing, and I don't want any thing."

The Lyceum reopened on the 21st December, with a dramatic version of the story by Albert Smith—*Clemency Newcombe* sustained by Mrs. Keeley; *Benjamin Britain*, by Mr. Keeley; *Alfred Heathfield*, Leigh Murray; and *Doctor Jeddler*, Mr. Frank Matthews. At Astley's Theatre, in March, 1867, a clever adaptation was performed, and ran a considerable time.

CHAPTER XVI.

VICTOR HUGO.—THE HAUNTED MAN.

FROM Paris, early in 1847, our author writes to Lady Blessington, describing his visit to Victor Hugo, then residing in the French capital. Twelve months after this, the great French novelist had to fly. The *coup d'état* brought about a new order of things:

"We were (writes Dickens) at V. H.'s house last Sunday week—a most extraordinary place, something like an old curiosity-shop, or the property-room of some gloomy, vast old theatre. I was much struck by H. himself, who looks like a genius—he is, every inch of him, and is very interesting and satisfactory from head to foot. His wife is a handsome woman, with flashing black eyes. There is also a charming ditto daughter, of fifteen or sixteen, with ditto eyes. Sitting among old armor and old tapestry, and old coffers, and grim old chairs and tables, and old canopies of state from old palaces, and old golden lions going to play at skittles with ponderous old golden balls, that made a most romantic show, and looked like a chapter out of one of his own books."

The letter is most interesting in a double sense. It shows us Victor Hugo's tastes in decoration, and those objects in his house upon which his eye would continually rest, and which would help to form drapery and literary illustration for his fictions; and it shows us in an oblique manner what were Dickens's notions in these matters, and the sympathy—if any—in such surroundings, between the two men.

During this year an announcement appeared that Shakspeare's house at Stratford-upon-Avon was to be sold. A public meeting was held, and a committee organized. By subscriptions, and a grand performance at Covent Garden Theatre, on 7th December—all the principal actors and actresses taking part therein—and readings by Macready, prior to his retirement, a sufficient sum (£3000) was realized.

To provide for the proper care and custody of the house and its relics, a series of amateur entertainments were given. Messrs. Charles Knight, Peter Cunningham, and John Payne Collier were the Directors of the General Management, and Dickens the Stage Manager.

The first performance took place at the Haymarket Theatre on May 15, 1848, the play selected being "The Merry Wives of Windsor," with the following cast:

Sir John Falstaff	Mr. MARK LEMON.
Fenton	Mr. CHARLES ROMER.
Shallow	Mr. CHARLES DICKENS.
Slender	Mr. JOHN LEECH.
Mr. Ford	Mr. FORSTER.
Mr. Page	Mr. FRANK STONE.
Sir Hugh Evans	Mr. G. H. LEWES.
Dr. Caius	Mr. DUDLEY COSTELLO.
Host of the Garter Inn	Mr. FREDK. DICKENS.
Bardolph	Mr. COLE.
Pistol	Mr. GEO. CRUIKSHANK.
Nym	Mr. AUGUSTUS DICKENS.
Robin	Miss ROBINS.
Simple	Mr. AUGUSTUS EGG.
Rugby	Mr. EATON.
Mrs. Ford	Miss FORTESQUE.
Mrs. Page	Miss KENWORTHY.
Mrs. Anne Page	Miss ANNE ROMER.
Mrs. Quickly	Mrs. COWDEN CLARKE.

Towards the close of the year 1847 he was invited by the good people of Leeds to attend a *soirée* at their Mechanics' Institution.* One clause of his speech was in his most characteristic manner. He is speaking of a class of politicians who object to educate the lower orders any more than up to a certain point, because "knowledge is power : '

"I never heard but one tangible position taken against educational establishments for the people, and that was, that in this or that instance, or in these or those instances, education for the people has failed. And I have never traced even this to its source but I have found that the term education, so employed, meant any thing but education—implied the mere imperfect application of old, ignorant, preposterous spelling-book lessons to the meanest purposes—as if you should teach a child that there is no higher end in electricity, for example, than expressly to strike a mutton-pie out of the hand of a greedy boy—and on which it is as unreasonable to found an objection to education in a comprehensive sense, as it would be to object altogether to the combing of youthful hair, because in a certain charity-school they had a practice of combing it into the pupils' eyes."

"Dombey and Son" interfering with his arrangements, the Christmas of 1847 passed without the usual appearance of a separate story, but the ensuing Christmas "The Haunted Man, and the Ghost's Bargain" was published by Messrs. Bradbury & Evans. This is perhaps his least popular little book, although considerable skill and vigorous writing are apparent. Redlaw, the Haunted Man, is a creation of sad and sombre hue. The most genial parts are the accounts of Tetterby, the struggling news-vender, and his family, not forgetting Johnny, and the Moloch baby, Sally.

In a little sketch of Mr. Dickens which appeared many years ago, it is said : "If stories told by booksellers of extraordinary sales be true, this last Christmas volume met with quite as much favor as any of the rest. But somehow, when it was read, it did not please. The 'Haunted Man' did not long haunt our memories. It had a peculiar purpose, opposed to the first part of the old saw, 'Forget and forgive.' This extract will place before us the moral of the tale :

"'I have no learning,' said Milly, 'and you have much ; I am not used to think, and you are always thinking. May I tell you why it seems to me a good thing to remember wrong that has been done us ?'

"'Yes.'

"'That we may forgive it.'

"'Pardon me, great Heaven,' said Redlaw, lifting up his eyes, 'for having thrown away thine own attribute !'

"'And if,' said Milly, 'if your own memory should one day be restored, as we will hope and pray it may be, would it not be a blessing to you to recall at once a wrong and its forgiveness ?'

"Alas for human nature, how few can do this !"

Happy he from whose memory wrong is quickly effaced ; and unfortunate that mind which, in recalling an injury, feels again the poignancy of the wound. We fear that forgiveness, or what

---

* December, 1847.

looks like it, the absence of rancor, often comes through forgetfulness. We fear that it ever must be so; that few will remember vividly, and forgive perfectly. In ordinary minds, then, forgetfulness and forgiveness will be companions, and for them the old motto is a good one; but it is the highest part of the highest creed, to forgive before memory sleeps, and ever to remember how the good overcame the evil.

It has been remarked that the illustrious novelist has curiously mistaken the legend of the old portrait, on which this story is built — "Lord, keep my memory green," which we take to be a wish that the fame of the man shall survive to aftertimes, so as to verify Herrick's sweet lines:

"Only the actions of the just
Smell sweet, *and blossom in the dust*."

While Mr. Dickens makes it mean, "Lord, allow my recollection (mental power of remembrance) to be unimpaired;" like Swift's prayer that he should not die mad, viewing with fear the awful contingency of loss of mind.

"From Marlborough's eyes the tears of dotage flow,
And Swift expires, a driveller and a show."

At the Adelphi and the Polytechnic Institution, this story, by the aid of the patent Pepper's-ghost apparatus, some three or four years since, excited considerable attention, and the satisfactory result, in a monetary sense, was testified by the fact of the numerous audiences at each representation.

The five little Christmas books, which we have separately noticed under the year of their issue, were published in one volume, and entitled "Christmas Books." To this Mr. Dickens contributed a new and admirable preface.

Three days after Christmas-day, 1847, Dickens was in Glasgow, presiding at the opening of the new Athenæum there. The burden of his speech was, "What constituted Real Education?"

"Mere reading and writing is not education," he said; "it would be quite as reasonable to call bricks and mortar architecture—oils and colors art—reeds and catgut music—or the child's spelling-books the works of Shakspeare, Milton, or Bacon—as to call the lowest rudiments of education, education, and to visit on that most abused and slandered word their failure in any instance." These and kindred sentiments were very warmly received, and were acknowledged in a complimentary speech by Sir Archibald (then Mr.) Alison.

CHAPTER XVII.

DICKENS AND THACKERAY.—"DAVID COPPERFIELD."

MR. DICKENS had hitherto met with no competitor in the field of English fiction. He had early won the attention of readers, but no writer had arisen to divide the honor with him. Another novelist, however, was now beginning to be talked of. On the 1st of February, 1847, Mr. Thackeray had issued the first monthly portion of "Vanity Fair," in the yellow wrapper which served to distinguish it from Mr. Dickens's stories, and, after some twelve months had passed, critics began to speak of the work in terms of approbation. The "Edinburgh Review," criticising it in January, 1848, says: "The great charm of this work is its entire freedom from mannerism and affectation both in style and sentiment. * * * His pathos (though not so deep as Mr. Dickens's) is exquisite; the more so, perhaps, because he seems to struggle against it, and to be half ashamed of being caught in the melting mood; but the attempt to be caustic, satirical, ironical, or philosophical on such occasions is uniformly vain; and again and again have we found reason to admire how an originally fine and kind nature remains essentially free from worldliness, and, in the highest pride of intellect, pays homage to the heart."

From this time forward a friendly rivalry ensued between the two representatives of the two schools of English fiction. We say "rivalry," but it never could have existed from Dickens's side; for, when "Vanity Fair" was at its best, finding six thousand purchasers a month, Dickens was taking the shillings from thirty to forty thousand readers; but the gossips of society have always asserted that there *was* a rivalry, and made comparisons so very frequently between the two great men, that we incidentally allude to it here. More than once has Thackeray said to the present writer (or words very similar): "Ah! they talk to me of popularity, with a sale of little more than one half of 10,000! Why, look at that lucky fellow Dickens, with Heaven knows how many readers, and certainly not less than 30,000 buyers!" But the fact is easily explained—only cultivated readers enjoy Thackeray, whereas both cultivated and uncultivated read Dickens with delight.

To return to Mr. Dickens's new book—"David Copperfield," one of the finest and certainly one of the most popular of its author's works. The first number appeared May 1st, 1849, with illustrations by "Phiz." It extended to the usual twenty numbers, and on its completion was issued by Messrs. Bradbury & Evans, with a dedication to the Hon. Mr. and Mrs. Richard Watson, of Rockingham.

The work, as we have previously remarked, is a great favorite, and such it deserves to be, for to our mind it is the happiest of all his fictions. It was the first that we read, and well do we remember the exquisite delight with which we eagerly devoured its pages—a rough seaman's copy of the American edition, which had been lent as an immense favor—and, boy-like, appreciated and sympathized with David in his youthful struggles. At that time we had just quitted the house of a distant relative with whom we had been residing, and who in very many respects—so far as trying to break David's spirit in before going to Salem House—greatly resembled the treatment shown towards ourselves.

The book is written in a delightfully easy, earnest, yet most graceful manner; the plot is well contrived, and never forced. It has often been hinted that in many ways it is partly autobiographical—the hero beginning at the law, turning parliamentary reporter, and finally winding up as a successful novelist, all of which the world knows have been Mr. Dickens's experiences. In fact, it is generally believed to occupy the same position to Dickens as "Pendennis" does to Thackeray.

The peculiar commencement and description of Blunderstone Rookery; the birth of the posthumous child; the second marriage of David's mother to Murdstone; his early days, and the wonderful crocodile book; Peggotty, and the courtship of Barkis the carrier, leaving his offerings behind the door; Mrs. Gummidge, Steerforth, the famous Micawbers, Betsy Trotwood, the kind-hearted aunt, and her aversion to donkeys; Mr. Dick and his memorial, and his inability to keep Charles I. out of it; David's love of darling Dora Spenlow, their marriage, and the dreadful troubles encountered in house-keeping, her death, and his consequent journey to Switzerland, and coming home and marrying Agnes Wickfield; the villainies of Uriah Heep; the eccentricities of Miss Mowcher, the corn extractor; Emily, the poor seduced girl; the magnificent description of the storm at Yarmouth, in which Steerforth the betrayer meets his death, while Ham, seeking to save him, meets the same fate; the love of Daniel Peggotty for his niece, and his patient search after her; Traddles and his ultimate success, and the starting off to the Antipodes of the Micawbers, Peggotty, Martha, Emily, and Mrs. Gummidge, their life in the bush, and how they prospered, are each and all described in such glowing language, destitute of exaggeration, and bearing so strongly the impress of truth and reality, that they can not fail to charm and delight the reader. It would be impertinent further to point out—to our mind—the best points in the book, and one can but thank God that such a writer has penned a work that can never be too much read or admired.

In the latest edition of "David Copperfield" —in the "Charles Dickens Edition"—the author takes us into his confidence and tells us that it was his favorite child. He says: "I remarked, in the original preface to this book, that I did not find it easy to get sufficiently away from it, in the first sensations of having finished, to refer to it with the composure which this formal heading would seem to require. My interest in it was so recent and strong, and my mind so divided between pleasure and regret—pleasure in the achievement of a long design, regret in the separation from many companions—that I was in danger of wearying the reader with personal confidences and private emotions. Besides which, all that I could have said of the story to any purpose I had endeavored to say in it. It would concern the reader little, perhaps, to know how sorrowfully the pen is laid down at the close of a two years' imaginative task; or how an author feels as if he were dismissing some portion of himself into the shadowy world when a crowd of the creatures of his brain are going from him forever. Yet I had nothing else to tell; unless, indeed, I were to confess (which might be of less moment still) that no one can ever believe this narrative in the reading, more than I believed it in the writing. So true are these avowals at the present day, that I can only now take the reader into one confidence more. Of all my books, I like this the best. It will easily be believed that I am a fond parent of every child of my fancy, and that no one can love them as dearly as I love them; but, like many fond parents, I have, in my heart of hearts, a favorite child, and his name is DAVID COPPERFIELD."

At the Strand Theatre, on October 21st, 1850, Almar's adaptation was played under the title of "Born with a Caul." The Surrey Theatre, in the following month, had a much better version; Mr. Thomas Mead as *Peggotty*, and the renowned Mr. Widdicomb combining the characters of *Miss Mowcher* and *Mr. Micawber*. But the most successful representation of all was "The Deal Boatman" at Drury Lane Theatre, two or three years since, in two acts, by Mr. Burnand.

Mr. Dickens was living at this time at No. 1 Devonshire Terrace, in the New Road. In his

"American Notes," in "Martin Chuzzlewit," and elsewhere in his writings, and occasionally in his speeches, he had expressed his disapproval of capital punishment. He now resolved to be a witness at a "hanging match" — as it is frequently called by the lower orders — and afterwards publish his experiences. The trial of the notorious Mannings had recently startled society, and it was thought that the hanging of such notable wretches would at least afford a fair specimen of the riot and demoralization attending a London public execution. For the purpose of seeing the whole ceremony, and giving the institution a fair trial, he left his house with a friend, on the evening previous, determined to make a night of it in the crowd fronting the Southwark scaffold. The following letter to the "Times" was the result:

NO. 1. DEVONSHIRE TERRACE, NEW ROAD (1840-'50).

[After removing from Doughty Street, Mr. Dickens resided in this house, and here were written a large portion of "The Old Curiosity Shop," "Barnaby Rudge," "A Christmas Carol," "The American Notes," and "Chuzzlewit," "The Cricket on the Hearth," "The Battle of Life," "Dombey and Son," "The Haunted Man," and "David Copperfield."]

"I was a witness of the execution at Horsemonger Lane this morning. I went there with the intention of observing the crowd gathered to behold it, and I had excellent opportunities of doing so at intervals all through the night, and continuously from daybreak until after the spectacle was over. I do not address you on the subject with any intention of discussing the abstract question of capital punishment, or any of the arguments of its opponents or advocates. I simply wish to turn this dreadful experience to some account for the general good, by taking the readiest and most public means of adverting to an intimation given by Sir G. Grey, in the last session of Parliament, that the Government might be induced to give its support to a measure making the infliction of capital punishment a private solemnity within the prison-walls (with such guaranties for the last sentence of the law being inexorably and surely administered as should be satisfactory to the public at large), and of most earnestly beseeching Sir G. Grey, as a solemn duty which he owes to society, and a responsibility which he can not forever put away, to originate such a legislative change himself. I believe that a sight so inconceivably awful as the wickedness and levity of the immense crowd collected at that execution this morning could be imagined by no man, and could be presented in no heathen land under the sun. The horrors of the crime which brought the wretched murderers to it faded in my mind before the atrocious bearing, looks, and language of the assembled spectators. When I came upon the scene at midnight, the shrillness of the cries and howls that were raised from time to time, denoting that they came from a concourse of boys and girls assembled in the best places, made my blood run cold. As the night went on, screeching and laughing, and yelling in strong chorus of parodies on negro melodies, with substitutions of 'Mrs. Manning' for 'Susannah,' and the like, were added to these. When the day dawned, thieves, low prostitutes, ruffians, and vagabonds of every kind, flocked on to the ground, with every variety of offensive and foul behavior. Fightings, faintings, whistlings, imitations of Punch, brutal jokes, tumultuous demonstrations of indecent delight when swooning women were dragged out of the crowd by the police with their dresses disordered, gave a new zest to the general entertainment. When the sun rose brightly—as it did—it gilded thousands upon thousands of up-turned faces, so inexpressibly odious in their brutal mirth or callousness, that a man had cause to feel ashamed of the shape he wore, and to shrink from himself, as fashioned in the image of the Devil. When the two miserable creatures who attracted all this ghastly sight about them were turned quivering into the air, there was no more emotion, no more pity, no more thought that two immortal souls had gone to judgment, no more restraint in any of the previous obscenities, than if the name of Christ had never been heard in this world, and there were no belief among men but that they perish like the beasts. I have seen, habitually, some of the worst sources of general contamination and corruption in this country, and I think there are not many phases of London life that could surprise me. I am solemnly convinced that nothing that ingenuity could devise to be done in this city, in the same compass of time, could work such ruin as one public execution, and I stand astounded and appalled by the wickedness it exhibits. I do not believe that any community can prosper where such a scene of horror and demoralization as was enacted this morning outside Horsemonger Lane jail is presented at the very doors of good citizens, and is passed by, unknown or forgotten. And when, in our prayers and thanksgivings for the season, we are humbly expressing before God our desire to remove the moral evils of the land, I would ask your readers to consider whether it is not a time to think of this one, and to root it out.

"Tuesday, November 13th."

The great question of "public hanging" occupied Dickens's attention for some time after. The horrors of that night and the morning preceding the Manning execution he could not readily forget. Some days after he wrote to the "Times," he addressed a long letter to his friend Douglas Jerrold, who was a Conservative on the question of capital punishment, and believed heartily in Tyburn as a public institution. Dickens thus remonstrates with his friend: "In a letter I have received from G. this morning he quotes a recent letter from you, in which you deprecate the 'mystery' of private hanging.

"Will you consider what punishment there is, except death, to which 'mystery' does not attach? Will you consider whether all the improvements in prisons and punishments that have been made within the last twenty years have or have not been all productive of 'mystery?' I can remember very well when the silent system was objected to as mysterious, and opposed to the genius of English society. Yet there is no question that it has been a great benefit. The prison vans are mysterious vehicles; but surely they are better than the old system of marching prisoners through the streets chained to a long chain, like the galley-slaves in 'Don Quixote.' Is there no mystery about transportation, and our manner of sending men away to Norfolk Island, or elsewhere? None in abandoning the use of a man's name, and knowing him only by a number? Is not the whole improved and altered system, from the beginning to end, a mystery? I wish I could induce you to feel justified in leaving that word to the platform people, on the strength of your knowledge of what crime was, and of what its punishments were, in the days when there was no mystery connected with these things, and all was as open as Bridewell when Ned Ward went to see the women whipped."

CHAPTER XVIII.

"HOUSEHOLD WORDS."—THE GUILD OF LITERATURE.

NOTWITHSTANDING past experiences in connection with the "Daily News," Mr. Dickens was still desirous of some periodical in which he could hold frequent and regular intercourse with his readers. Early in 1850 our indefatigable author projected the "Household Words," a name which was more or less familiar to the public through a line in Shakspeare's Henry V.—"Familiar in their mouths as 'Household Words.'" It is just worth while, in passing, to say that this motto was a favorite with Mr. Dickens. He often used it in conversation, long before a periodical of the kind was dreamed of. As far back as his first visit to America, when he was addressing the young men of Boston, and Washington Irving, Holmes, and other celebrities were present, he said: "You have in America great writers—great writers—who will live in all time, and are as familiar to our lips as household words."* And afterwards, in his speeches, the motto was not uncommon.

On Saturday, March 30th, 1850, was issued the first number of "Household Words, price 2d., conducted by Charles Dickens."

No article had the name of its author appended, and when the "Conductor" proposed to Jerrold that he should contribute to its pages, but added that his name could not appear, as the journal was anonymous, the wit replied, "Aye, I see it is, for there's the name of Charles Dickens on every page."

Among the original contributors to "Household Words" may be mentioned John Fors-

---

* February 1, 1842.

ter, W. H. Wills, George Augustus Sala, Moy Thomas, John Hollingshead, Miss Martineau, Professor Morley, Edmund Yates, Dr. Charles Mackay, Andrew Halliday, Edmund Ollier, and many other talented writers. It was the great delight of the "Conductor" to draw around him the rising talent —the new men who gave evidence of literary ability; and many a mark have they made in the pages of "Household Words!"

Connected with "Household Words," at the end of each month, appeared the "Household Narrative," containing a history of the preceding month. It began in April of this year, and involved Mr. Dickens in a dispute with the Stamp Office. An information was laid against the "Narrative," it being contended that, under the Stamp Duty Act, it was a newspaper; but, on appeal to the Court of Exchequer, the barons decided in Mr. Dickens's favor, and thus the first step to the repeal of the newspaper stamp was given. The publication was not a success, people preferring to pay for amusement and information combined, rather than for the latter in a purely statistical form. It stopped at about the 70th number, and sets are now rare.

But to return to "Household Words." A friend who knew Dickens writes: "His editorship of this periodical was no nominal post. Papers sent in for approval invariably went through a preliminary 'testing' by the acting editor (Mr. W. H. Wills); but all those which survived this ordeal were conscientiously read and judged by Mr. Dickens, who again read all the accepted contributions in proof, and made numerous and valuable alterations in them." Besides the ordinary tales and articles upon popular topics, there appeared in "Household Words" in good time for the festive season, and during the first year, a collection of stories, connected entirely with Christmas, viz.: "A Christmas Tree" and "A Christmas Pudding," "Christmas in the Navy, in Lodgings, in India, in the Frozen Regions, in the Bush, and among the Sick and Poor of London," and "Household Christmas Carols."

In the ensuing January, Dickens commenced in this journal the publication of his "Child's History of England." This little work became very popular, and in the following year it was reprinted in a separate form by Messrs.

TAVISTOCK HOUSE, TAVISTOCK SQUARE (1850-'60).

[Before Dickens removed here, the house was occupied by Mr. Perry, the once famous chief of the "Morning Chronicle." Whilst living at Tavistock House, "Bleak House," "A Child's History of England," "Hard Times," "Little Dorrit," "A Tale of Two Cities," portions of "Hunted Down," and the "Uncommercial Traveller" were written. In 1860 our Author finally removed to Gad's Hill.]

Bradbury and Evans, and inscribed as follows:

"TO MY OWN DEAR CHILDREN,
WHOM I HOPE IT MAY HELP, BY-AND-BY, TO READ WITH
INTEREST LARGER AND BETTER BOOKS ON THE
SAME SUBJECT."

The Battle of Hastings is one of the finest and most marvellous pieces of descriptive writing in the "Child's History," which—as has been well remarked—"might be read by many children of larger growth with much profit." This is an extract from his glowing description: "The sun rose high and sank, and the battle still raged. Through all the wild October day the clash and din resounded in the air. In the red sunset, in the white moonlight, heaps upon heaps of dead men lay strewn, a dreadful spectacle, all over the ground. King Harold, wounded with an arrow in the eye, was nearly blind. His brothers were already killed. Twenty Norman knights, whose battered armor had flashed fiery and golden all day long, and now looked silvery in the moonlight, dashed forward to seize the royal banner from the English knights and soldiers, still faithfully collected round their blinded king. The king received a mortal wound and dropped."

If the remainder of the description is turned into blank verse (as Byron did when copying "Werner" from the "Canterbury Tales" of Miss Lee), by adding two words, and expunging some few others, we obtain this glowing and beautiful narration:

> "The English broke and fled.
> The Normans rallied, and the day was lost!
> Oh, what a sight beneath the moon and stars!
> The lights were shining in the victor's tent
> (Pitch'd near the spot where blinded Harold fell);
> He and his knights carousing were within;
> Soldiers with torches, going to and fro,
> Sought for the corpse of Harold 'mongst the dead.
> The Warrior, work'd with stones and golden thread,
> Lay low, all torn, and soil'd with English blood,
> And the three Lions kept watch o'er the field!"

The work has never been reprinted at a lower price than the old three-volume form, and of course it forms no part of the recent "Cheap Editions" and the "Charles Dickens Edition;" but, now that extra attention will be directed to the writings of Mr. Dickens, it is to be hoped that it may be reprinted at a moderate price.

The second Christmas number (1851) of "Household Words" consisted of nine stories about Christmas, and how it was held, and what it was like in different companies and countries —in fact, very similar to the preceding number.

At the Sixth Annual Dinner of the General Theatrical Fund (April 14, 1851), the conductors again begged Mr. Dickens to preside. His speech was short, but exceedingly happy. Speaking of the Theatrical Fund, he said:

"It is a society in which the word exclusiveness is wholly unknown. It is a society which includes every actor, whether he be Benedick or Hamlet, or the Ghost, or the Bandit, or the court-physician, or, in the one person, the whole king's army. He may do the 'light business,' or the 'heavy,' or the comic, or the eccentric. He may be the captain who courts the young lady, whose uncle still unaccountably persists in dressing himself in a costume one hundred years older than his time. Or he may be the young lady's brother in the white gloves and inexpressibles, whose duty in the family appears to be to listen to the female members of it whenever they sing, and to shake hands with every body between all the verses. Or he may be the baron who gives the fête, and who sits uneasily on the sofa under a canopy with the baroness while the fête is going on. Or he may be the peasant at the fête who comes on the stage to swell the drinking chorus, and who, it may be observed, always turns his glass upside down before he begins to drink out of it. Or he may be the clown who takes away the door-step of the house where the evening party is going on. Or he may be the gentleman who issues out of the house on the false alarm, and is precipitated into the area. Or, to come to the actresses, she may be the fairy who resides forever in a revolving star, with an occasional visit to a bower or a palace. Or the actor may be the armed head of the witch's caldron; or even that extraordinary witch, concerning whom I have observed, in country places, that he is much less like the notion formed from the description of Hopkins than the Malcolm or Donalbain of the previous scenes. This society, in short, says, 'Be you what you may, be you actor or actress, be your path in your profession never so high or never so low, never so haughty or never so humble, we offer you the means of doing good to yourselves, and of doing good to your brethren.'"

In June, 1851, a project—which, it is said, Mr. Dickens had long had in contemplation— was brought forward by Sir Edward Bulwer Lytton, namely, the founding of a Guild of Literature and Art; in reality, a provident fund and benefit society for unfortunate literary men and artists. From it the proper persons would receive continual or occasional relief, as the case might be; but the leading feature was the "Provident Fund," to be composed of moneys deposited by the authors themselves, when they were in a position to be able to lay by something. Dickens and Sir Edward Bulwer Lytton (since a peer) were the most active promoters. The precise plan of the "Guild" was discussed at Lord Lytton's seat, at Knebworth, the November previously. There had been three amateur performances, by Dickens and others, of "Every Man in his Humor," for the gratification of his lordship and his neighboring friends, when it was arranged that his lordship should write a comedy, and Dickens and Mark Lemon a farce. The comedy was entitled "Not so Bad as we Seem," and the farce bore the name of "Mrs. Nightingale's Diary." The first performance took place at Devonshire House, before the Queen, the Prince Consort, and the court circles; and afterwards at the Hanover Square Rooms, and at many of the large provincial towns (Bath, Bristol, etc.). At Devonshire House, not the least incident occurred to shade what a late Drury Lane manager might, in his own Titanic way, have called "the blaze of triumph." From the first moment that the scheme was made known to

LIFE OF CHARLES DICKENS.

her Majesty and Prince Albert, both the Queen and the Prince manifested the liveliest interest in its success. The Duke of Devonshire, with a munificence that made the name of his Grace a proverb for liberality, dedicated his mansion to the cause of Literature and Art, and his house was for many days in possession of the amateurs.

The play began at half past nine, Her Majesty, Prince Albert, and the royal family occupying a box erected for the occasion. The seats were filled by the most illustrious for rank and genius. There was the Duchess of Sutherland; there was the "Iron Duke," in his best temper; there was Macaulay, Chevalier Bunsen, Van der Weyer—themselves authors; in fact, all the highest representatives of the rank, beauty, and genius of England, and her foreign ambassadors.

The list of the performers, and the parts taken by them, is a curiosity in its way:

MEN.

The Duke of Middlesex, } Peers attached to the son of James II., commonly called the First Pretender............. Mr. FRANK STONE.
The Earl of Loftus, } .... Mr. DUDLEY COSTELLO.
Lord Wilmot, a young man at the head of the *mode* more than a century ago, son to Lord Loftus.. Mr. CHARLES DICKENS.
Mr. Shadowly Softhead, a young gentleman from the city, friend and double to Lord Wilmot.. Mr. DOUGLAS JERROLD.
Mr. Hardman, a rising Member of Parliament, and adherent to Sir Robert Walpole.. Mr. JOHN FORSTER.
Sir Geoffrey Thornside, a gentleman of good family and estate................... Mr. MARK LEMON.
Mr. Goodenough Easy, in business, highly respectable, and a friend to Sir Geoffrey.. Mr. E. W. TOPHAM.
Lord Le Trimmer, ... Mr. PETER CUNNINGHAM.
Sir Thomas Timid, } Frequenters of Will's Coffee-house............... Mr. WESTLAND MARSTON.
Colonel Flint, ... Mr. R. H. HORNE.
Mr. Jacob Tonson, a bookseller.. Mr. CHARLES KNIGHT.
Smart, valet to Lord Wilmot.. Mr. WILKIE COLLINS.
Hodge, servant to Sir Geoffrey Thornside.. Mr. JOHN TENNIEL.
Paddy O'Sullivan, Mr. Fallen's landlord.. Mr. ROBERT BELL.
Mr. David Fallen, Grub Street, author and pamphleteer.. Mr. AUGUSTUS EGG, A.R.A.
Lord Strongbow, Sir John Bruin, Coffee-house Loungers, Drawers, Newsmen, Watchmen, etc., etc.

WOMEN.

Lucy, daughter to Sir Geoffrey Thornside.. Mrs. COMPTON.
Barbara, daughter to Mr. Easy.. Miss ELLEN CHAPLIN.

The Silent Lady of Deadman's Lane.

The royal party paid the deepest attention to the progress of the play, Her Majesty frequently leading the applause. And when the curtain fell upon the three hours' triumph, Her Majesty rose in her box, and, by the most cordial demonstration of approval, "commanded" (for such may be the word) the reappearance of all the actors, again to receive the royal approval of their efforts. Nor did the Queen and Prince merely bestow applause. Her Majesty took seventeen places for herself, visitors, and suite; and, further, as a joint contribution of herself and the Prince, headed the list of subscriptions with £150, making the sum total of £225. It is said that the receipts of the night exceeded £1000. Another representation at Devonshire House took place on the following Tuesday, the admission being £2. The farce written for the occasion, called "Mrs. Nightingale's Diary," was performed, and Charles Dickens and Mark Lemon sustained the principal characters. A critic at the time remarked: "Both these gentlemen are admirable actors. It is by no means amateur playing with them. Dickens seizes the strong points of a character, bringing them out as effectively upon the stage as his pen undyingly marks them upon paper. Lemon has all the ease of a finished performer, with a capital relish for comedy and broad farce."

For the representations in the provinces a portable theatre was constructed, Messrs. Clarkson Stanfield, David Roberts, Grieve, and others, painting the scenes, etc., which are said to have been very beautiful. The funds raised were unfortunately, by a flaw in the act of Parliament, unintentionally tied up for a number of years; but on Saturday, July 29th, 1865, the surviving members of the Fund proceeded to the neighborhood of Stevenage, near the magnificent seat of the President, Lord Lytton, to inspect three houses built in the Gothic style on the ground given by him for that purpose. An enterprising publican in the vicinity had just previously opened his establishment, which bore the very appropriate sign of "Our Mutual Friend"—Mr. Dickens's then latest work—and caused considerable merriment.

So popular had Mr. Dickens become in the character of President or Chairman at the anniversaries of benevolent societies, that the gardeners begged him to officiate for them at their dinner and meeting of the "Gardeners' Benevolent Institution." The affair came off on the

14th June, 1852, at the London Tavern. The splendid display of flowers was the result of a very hearty combination of the very best efforts of the best gardeners, and Mr. Dickens (to use his own phrase) "burst into bloom" upon the culture of flowers and fruits in such a way as to astonish his auditory.

The "Household Words" Christmas number for 1852 was entitled "A Round of Stories by the Christmas Fire," told by A Poor Relation—A Child—Somebody—An Old Nurse—The "Boots"—A Grandfather—A Char-woman—A Deaf Playmate—A Guest, and A Mother.

CHAPTER XIX.

"BLEAK HOUSE."—LEIGH HUNT.

Two years had now elapsed since the completion of "David Copperfield," and a new novel was announced, to appear in the old familiar serial form, under the title of "Bleak House." It is not generally known, we believe, that the name "Bleak House" was taken from that tall, solitary brick house which stands away from the others, and rising far above them, at Broadstairs—the house where for one, if not for two seasons, Mr. Dickens resided. This charming little town was for many years Mr. Dickens's favorite sea-side resort—in fact, "Our Watering-place," as he called it in an article in "Household Words" some years since. The house in question is a square, sullen structure—hard and bleak, and of course it is now one of the lions of the place, the guide-books and local photographers setting great store by it. Just below Bleak House, on the point that runs out to form the harbor, is the Tartar Frigate, the cosiest little sailor's inn, selling the strongest of tobacco, and the strongest-smelling rum that is to be met with around the coast. Close by is a rope-house, decorated with wonderful figure-heads, each having a wild story of shipwreck to tell. As you pass the little Tartar Frigate, with its red blinds and little door, you know what are the sounds that are to be heard there any night during the winter. The very walls must have long ago learnt "Tom Bowling" and the "Bay of Biscay" by heart, and would now be very thankful for a fresh song. Dickens knew the little inn very well, and, under the title of "The Tartar Frigate," he gave in "Household Words," some years since, an admirable description of this little town with a tiny harbor. The great novelist was fond of genuine sailors—the hardy, good-tempered fellows of Deal and Broadstairs—brave as lions, and guileless as children; and it was to his being so much in their company that he doubtless owed his sailor look. Mr. Arthur Locker, whose recollections we have before quoted, saw him only a few weeks before his death, when he was "struck by his sailor-like aspect—a peculiarity observed by many other persons. Yet, except his two voyages to America, he had not been much on the sea, and was not, I believe, a particularly good sailor. But we all know his sympathy for seamen, and I think, without being fanciful, that his nautical air may in part be attributed to early Portsmouth associations."

"Bleak House" ran through its course of numbers, and appeared in a complete form in August of the following year:

"DEDICATED,
AS A REMEMBRANCE OF OUR
FRIENDLY UNION,
TO MY COMPANIONS
IN THE
GUILD OF LITERATURE AND ART."

The work was directed with considerable effect against the Court of Chancery. Lawyers and others were loud in their complaints at the way in which their favorite court had been assailed; but the majority of legal readers, whether then or even now practising, or connected in any shape or way with the court in question—or even *only* as unfortunate suitors—can testify as to the enormous waste of time, and the costly procedure therein. Matters have of late years somewhat improved, but a great deal yet remains to be remedied.

The author, in his preface, took the opportunity of defending himself from the remarks made upon the supposititious suit of Jarndyce *vs.* Jarndyce,* and Krook's death by spontaneous combustion. The latter incident excited much controversy at the time, Mr. G. H. Lewes opposing the idea strongly; but Dickens maintained his ground, and referred to several well-authenticated cases in support of the theory.

One of the characters in the book, Harold Skimpole, an incarnation of a canting and hypocritical scoundrel, whom one longs to kick, was fastened upon as the impersonation of that kind and genial writer, the late Leigh Hunt. Those who had the good fortune to know him personally indignantly refuted the calumny, and, like

---

* Suggested, it is believed, by the celebrated case of the Jennings property. Dickens had previously brought an antagonist upon himself in the person of Sir Edward Sugden (now Lord St. Leonards), in consequence of an article in "Household Words," headed "Martyrs in Chancery," on the offense of Contempt of Court, and replied to by the above eminent lawyer, in a letter to the "Times" (7th January, 1851), giving a true version of the case therein referred to.

other unfounded rumors, the matter died out, until, after his death, the idea was again bruited forth.

Mr. Thornton Hunt (his eldest son), in preparing a new edition of his father's famous "Autobiography," prefixed an introductory chapter, in which the following passages occur:

"His animation, his sympathy with what was gay and pleasurable, his avowed doctrine of cultivating cheerfulness, were manifest on the surface, and could be appreciated by those who knew him in society, most probably even exaggerated as salient traits, on which he himself insisted *with a sort of gay and ostentatious willfulness.*

"The anxiety to recognize the right of others, the tendency to 'refine,' which was noted by an early school companion, and the propensity to elaborate every thought, made him, along with the direct argument by which he sustained his own conviction, recognize and almost admit all that might be said on the opposite side.

"It is most desirable that his qualities should be known as they were; for such deficiencies as he had are the honest explanation of his mistakes; while, as the reader may see from his writing and his conduct, they are not, as the faults of which he was accused would be, incompatible with the noblest faculties both of head and heart. To know Leigh Hunt as he was, was to hold him in reverence and love."

Dickens immediately, in a number of "All the Year Round," under the head of "Leigh Hunt—a Remonstrance," made this statement:

"Four or five years ago, the writer of these lines was much pained by accidentally encountering a printed statement, 'that Mr. Leigh Hunt was the original of Harold Skimpole in Bleak House.' The writer of these lines is the author of that book. The statement came from America. It is no disrespect to that country, in which the writer has, perhaps, as many friends and as true an interest as any man that lives, good-humoredly to state the fact that he has now and then been the subject of paragraphs in transatlantic newspapers more surprisingly destitute of all foundation in truth than the wildest delusions of the wildest lunatics. For reasons born of this experience, he let the thing go by.

"But since Mr. Leigh Hunt's death the statement has been revived in England. The delicacy and generosity evinced in its revival are for the rather late consideration of its revivers. The fact is this: Exactly those graces and charms of manner which are remembered in the words we have quoted were remembered by the author of the work of fiction in question when he drew the character in question. Above all other things, that 'sort of gay and ostentatious willfulness' in the humoring of a subject, which had many times delighted him, and impressed him as being unspeakably whimsical and attractive, was the airy quality he wanted for the man he invented. Partly for this reason, and partly (he has since often grieved to think) for the pleasure it afforded him to find that delightful manner reproducing itself under his hand, he yielded to the temptation of too often making the character *speak* like his old friend. He no more thought, God forgive him! that the admired original would ever be charged with the imaginary vices of the fictitious creature than he has himself ever thought of charging the blood of Desdemona and Othello on the innocent Academy model who sat for Iago's leg in the picture. Even as to the mere occasional manner, he meant to be so cautious and conscientious that he privately referred the proof-sheets of the first number of that book to two intimate literary friends of Leigh Hunt (both still living), and altered the whole of that part of the text on their discovering too strong a resemblance to his 'way.'

"He can not see the son lay this wreath on the father's tomb, and leave him to the possibility of ever thinking that the present words might have righted the father's memory and were left unwritten. He can not know that his own son may have to explain his father when folly or malice can wound his heart no more, and leave this task undone."

Mr. Thornton Hunt, alluding to his father's incapacity to understand figures, frankly admitted, "His so-called improvidence resulted partly from actual disappointment in professional undertakings, partly from a real incapacity to understand any objects when they were reduced to figures,* and partly from a readiness of self-sacrifice, which was the less to be guessed by any one who knew him, since he seldom alluded to it, and never, except in the vaguest and most unintelligible terms, hinted at its real nature or extent."

Very recently, and since the decease of the great novelist, a similar statement about Skimpole and Leigh Hunt, made in the columns of a daily journal,† was thus replied to by Mr. Edmund Ollier, an old friend of the deceased essayist: "Dickens himself corrected the misapprehension in a paper in 'All the Year Round,'

---

* Several anecdotes have been circulated relative to the late Lord Macaulay's dislike to mathematics, and, acting on this distaste, he declined to compete for honors, but was, in consideration of his great proficiency in other studies, elected a fellow of his college (Trinity, Cambridge).

† "Daily News," 10th June, 1870.

towards the close of 1859, after Hunt's death; and during Hunt's life, and after the publication of 'Bleak House,' he wrote a most genial paper about him in 'Household Words.' It is also within my knowledge that he expressed to Leigh Hunt personally his regret at the Skimpole mistake."

Leigh Hunt himself, in confessing his inability at school to master the multiplication-table, naïvely adds, "Nor do I know it to this day!" And again: "I equally disliked Dr. Franklin, author of 'Poor Richard's Almanac,' a heap, as it appeared to me, of 'scoundrel maxims.'* I think I now appreciate Dr. Franklin as I ought; but, although I can see the utility of such publications as his almanac for a rising commercial state, and hold it useful as a memorandum to uncalculating persons like myself, who happen to live in an old one, I think there is no necessity for it in commercial nations long established, and that it has no business in others who do not found their happiness in that sort of power. Franklin, with all his abilities, is but at the head of those who think that man lives 'by bread alone.'"

And again, in his "Journal," a few years ago, that gentleman, after narrating several agreeable hardships inflicted upon him, says: "A little before this, a friend in a manufacturing town was informed that I was a terrible speculator in the money markets! I who was never in a market of any kind but to buy an apple or a flower, and who could not dabble in money business if I would, from sheer ignorance of their language!"

Just at this time other characters in Mr. Dickens's novel were selected by gossips as representing this or that distinguished individual. Thus Boythorne was affirmed to be the energetic Mr. Walter Savage Landor. Miss Martineau came forward in her own person to take the cap of Mrs. Jellaby, and to scold Mr. Dickens for his allusions to "blue-stockingism" and "Borioboola Gha." Whether there was any foundation for these parallels between living individuals and the characters in "Bleak House," it is not now likely the world will ever know, but there can be no doubt about one of the characters in that book—the French lady's maid. Mr. Dickens made no secret about her representing Mrs. Manning the murderess. Indeed he attended at her examination at the Police Court, and was present both at her trial and her execution. Her broken English, her impatient gestures, and her volubility, are imitated in the novel with marvellous exactness.

The character of Turveydrop, we may mention, was always believed to portray "the first gentleman in Europe," his Sacred Majesty King George the Fourth.

CHAPTER XX.

AMERICAN PUBLISHERS.—THE FIRST READING.

As many statements have recently been made in this country and in the United States respecting Mr. Dickens's relations to the American publishers of his works, we may say that "Bleak House" was his first novel issued there in profits arising from the sale of which he participated.

Up to the publication of "Dombey and Son" he had received nothing from America. It was understood that he was rather more angry with Messrs. Harper & Brothers — subsequently his recognized publishers—than with any other transatlantic house. They had just begun publishing their "New Monthly Magazine," and the publishers of the "International Magazine" were contesting with the Harpers the first place in American periodical literature. After a severe and indecisive struggle of a year, one of the conductors of the "International" conceived an idea which, if successfully carried out, would have given the victory to that Magazine: one of its publishers was going abroad, and was authorized to secure from Mr. Dickens "advanced sheets" of his next novel for publication in the "International."

The steamer on which he sailed had hardly got out of sight before Dr. Griswold, of the "International," had given to the "Evening Post" a sensational paragraph, stating that Mr. Dickens had been engaged to write for the "International Magazine" a new novel, for which he was to be paid $2000—a sum considerably larger in 1850 than in 1867—and then considered enormous for the favor demanded. The watchful Harpers sent out in the next steamer a messenger who went directly to Mr. Dickens, and found him ready for any reasonable offer. The "Post" with Dr. Griswold's paragraph being shown him, he at once decided to hold the Yankees to the terms therein set forth, and agreed for the $2000 to furnish Harper & Brothers with "advanced sheets" of the next novel, which was the present one of "Bleak House." The messenger of the "International" had

---

* Thomson's phrase in his "Castle of Indolence," speaking of a miserly money-getter:

"'A penny savèd is a penny got;'
Firm to this scoundrel maxim keepeth he,
Nor of its rigor will he bate a jot,
Till he hath quench'd his fire and banished his pot."

made the very great blunder of going to Mr. Dickens's publisher instead of to Mr. Dickens himself. The publisher had told him that Mr. Dickens was busy about private theatricals, which would probably absorb his attention for an indefinite period, and that no new novel was in contemplation. In fact, it is not improbable that, on account of the bargain with the Harpers, "Bleak House" was written, or at least published, before it otherwise would have been. It is said that Mr. Dickens has received upwards of $100,000 on the sale of his works in America.

Early in the new year Mr. Dickens paid a visit to the Midland counties. Birmingham has always been very partial to our great novelist, and he in turn has been equally partial to Birmingham. One of his earliest speeches was delivered here, and for services rendered to the town a public presentation of a diamond ring and a silver salver was made to him, in the rooms of the society of Artists there, on January 6, 1853. A banquet was subsequently given to him, and Mr. Dickens made three speeches on the occasion.

In May of this year Dickens was the guest of the Lord Mayor. His lordship had invited a number of literary celebrities to dine with him, including Mrs. Beecher Stowe and her husband, and Dickens was called upon to respond to Mr. Justice Talfourd's toast, "Anglo-Saxon Literature."

Mrs. Stowe, in her "Sunny Memories of Foreign Lands," alludes to the occasion, and to the author of 'Bleak House," remarking: "Directly opposite me was Mr. Dickens, whom I now beheld for the first time, and was surprised to see looking so young. Mr. Justice Talfourd made allusion to the author of 'Uncle Tom's Cabin' and Mr. Dickens, speaking of both as having employed fiction as a means of awakening the attention of the respective countries to the condition of the oppressed and suffering classes. We rose from table between eleven and twelve o'clock—that is, we ladies—and went into the drawing-room, where I was presented to Mrs. Dickens and several other ladies. Mrs. Dickens is a good specimen of a truly English woman; tall, large, and well-developed, with fine, healthy color, and an air of frankness, cheerfulness, and reliability. A friend whispered to me that she was as observing and fond of humor as her husband. After a while the gentlemen came back to the drawing-room, and I had a few moments of very pleasant friendly conversation with Mr. Dickens. They are both people that one could not know a little of without desiring to know more."

In her adieus she said: "I have omitted, however, that I went with Lady Hatherton to call on Mr. and Mrs. Dickens, and was sorry to find him too unwell to be able to see me. Mrs. Dickens, who was busy in attending him, also excused herself, and we saw her sister."

We now come to an important event in Mr. Dickens's career—his first public "reading." Various towns claim the honor of being the first to invite the great novelist to read to its inhabitants; but we believe Peterborough was the real scene of his first appearance in the capacity of a public reader. Reading aloud, however, to the circle of his household, and at those Hampstead dinners, had often been a source of gratification to his friends. The first allusion to reading his works in public was made at Birmingham, 6th January, 1853, when he returned thanks for a present that had been made to him. He then promised to come next December to give two or three readings, from his own books, on behalf of the Midland Institute; suggesting that the novelty of such a proceeding might produce something towards the funds of that admirable institution. A daily journal* with which Mr. Dickens was formerly connected has, however, recently asserted that it was at Chatham that our author made his first public appearance; but we believe that in the quiet little city of Peterborough, some few months before the time for the Birmingham reading had arrived, Mr. Dickens essayed his first public reading, he himself going down a day or two before to superintend the stage, and those "effects" which, however small, he never neglected.

Whether Birmingham, Peterborough, or Chatham can claim the honor, there can be no question about the result of Mr. Dickens's efforts in this new line. It was an undoubted success, and was soon repeated for other charitable institutions in various parts of England. At Birmingham over £300 were collected. Mr. Dickens used to tell some amusing stories of his "reading" experiences in the provinces. At one town in the North, a door-keeper's opinion was invited by a gentleman who was entering the room to hear the second "reading" of the course.

"Very fair, sir," was the reply; "very fair; he does not read amiss; but his attitudes are poor, sir. I think nothing of his attitudes."

It is tolerably well known that our author never experienced those bashful sensations which most persons experience when they come before the public for the first time. The reader's own recollections of rising to respond to toasts, even

---

* "The Daily News," 11th June, 1870.

in a private circle, will suggest the feeling which Mr. Dickens never knew. Mr. George Hodder says: "I once asked Mr. Dickens if he ever felt nervous in public.

"'Not in the least,' was the answer. 'The first time I took the chair, I felt as much confidence as if I had done the thing a hundred times.'

"At a dinner to his eldest son, who was going out to China, the young man became warmed with the wine; and Dickens, in returning thanks when his own health was drunk, said that after so good a dinner 'a little transaction in tea would do his son a world of good.'"

It was always this happy readiness at response, this being able to reply on the moment, that made him, as he certainly was, the best after-dinner speaker in England. There is an exquisite delicacy in his treatment of an ordinary subject, and in the selection of words, which, if possessed by any other speaker in this country—Mr. Bright, perhaps, excepted—is certainly not shown in any recent efforts of their oratory. As has been remarked, some of his speeches are equal to the finest pages of his printed works.

CHAPTER XXI.

"HARD TIMES."—"SEVEN POOR TRAVELLERS." —"HOLLY-TREE INN."

In August, 1854, Mr. Dickens published his "Hard Times," which had previously appeared in the weekly pages of "Household Words." It was "*Inscribed to Thomas Carlyle*," for whom Mr. Dickens ever felt the warmest admiration. This work is treated differently to any of his other books, and hardly sustains his reputation, being the least read and admired of his numerous fictions. The plot is meagre and aimless. The personages are too often exaggerated and overdrawn; the design, apparently, being to place facts, figures, science, and political economy in any thing but a favorable or correct light. The education received by the Gradgrinds is preposterous. Mr. Charles Knight, in his "Passages of a Working Life," said: "Before I published, in 1854, my volume of 'Knowledge is Power,' I sent a copy to my eminent friend (Mr. Charles Dickens), with somewhat of apprehension, for he was then publishing his 'Hard Times.' I said that I was afraid that he would set me down as a cold-hearted political economist. His reply, of the 30th of January, 1854, was very characteristic; and I venture to extract it, as it may not only correct some erroneous notions as to his opinions on such subjects, but proclaim a great truth, which has perhaps not been sufficiently attended to by some of the dreary and dogmatic professors of what has been called the *dismal science:* 'My satire is against those who see figures and averages, and nothing else—the representatives of the wickedest and most enormous vice of this time—the men who, through long years to come, will do more to damage the really useful truths of political economy than I could do (if I tried) in my whole life—the addled heads who would take the average of cold in the Crimea during twelve months as a reason for clothing a soldier in nankeen on a night when he would be frozen to death in fur—and who would comfort the laborer, in travelling twelve miles a day to and from his work, by telling him that the average distance of one inhabited place from another on the whole area of England is not more than four miles. Bah! what have you to do with these?'"

An amusing parody or skit on the tale by the late Robert Brough appeared in "Our Miscellany," a work the joint production of that lamented writer and Mr. Edmund Yates. At the Strand Theatre, in the August following, a version was placed on the stage, and was well received, all the melancholy parts being cut out, and all the humor heightened as much as possible! the *dénouement* being somewhat different to Mr. Dickens's! The new bill for closing the public-houses creating great excitement and discussion at the time, Mr. Gradgrind was made to exhibit strong animosity and hostility to the proposed measure. It may be mentioned that an adaptation was performed at Astley's Theatre, with the title of "Under the Earth; or, the Sons of Toil," as recently as April and May, 1867.

It was in this year, on the 13th of March, that Dickens lost his dear friend, Sir Thomas Noon Talfourd—better known as Serjeant Talfourd, the friend of Charles Lamb, and of many other eminent men of letters in his day. That Dickens keenly felt the loss, we know from various passages in the life of his deceased friend. How beautiful is this description of the dead man's virtues—how delicately are his graces dwelt upon!

"The chief delight of his life was to give delight to others. His nature was so exquisitely kind, that to be kind was his highest happiness. Those who had the privilege of seeing him in his own home, when his public successes were greatest—so modest, so contented with little things, so interested in humble persons and humble efforts, so surrounded by children and young people, so adored in remembrance of a domestic generosity and greatness of heart too sacred to be unveiled here, can never forget the pleasure of that sight."

"The Seven Poor Travellers" formed the title of the Christmas number for 1854. It was one of the most popular of the series of Christmas stories. The idea was that Dickens had staid one Christmas-eve at the Poor Traveller's House at Rochester (founded by good old Richard Watts*) in company with six poor travellers, and entertained them with roast beef, turkey, and punch from the neighboring inn, when each in turn told a story. His own, the history of Richard Doubledick, is one of the most impressive and beautiful stories ever written.

On January 15th following, he presided, at the London Tavern, at the Annual Dinner of the Commercial Travellers' School at Wanstead. This was the occasion when he made a most amusing and sprightly speech upon "Commercials." On 27th June, in the same year, he delivered a telling speech upon "Reform" at Drury Lane Theatre.

It was during this year, in July, that the much-talked-of private theatricals at Campden House were set on foot by Dickens, for the benefit of the Brompton Consumption Hospital. The piece performed was the "Light-house," a thrilling melodrama, written by Mr. Wilkie Collins. Dickens took the part of *Aaron Gur-*

---

* The house appointed for the reception of the poor travellers is situated on the north side of the High Street, adjoining to the custom-house, and is probably the original building. A very considerable sum was expended by the mayor and citizens on its repair in 1771. Agreeably to the benevolent design of the donor, poor travellers have lodging and four-pence each; and that this charity may be more generally known, the following inscription is fixed over the door:

"RICHARD WATTS, ESQ.,
BY HIS WILL DATED 22 AUG., 1579,
FOUNDED THIS CHARITY,
FOR SIX POOR TRAVELLERS,
WHO, NOT BEING ROGUES, OR PROCTORS,
MAY RECEIVE GRATIS, FOR ONE NIGHT,
LODGING, ENTERTAINMENT,
AND FOUR-PENCE EACH.
IN TESTIMONY OF HIS MUNIFICENCE,
IN HONOR OF HIS MEMORY,
AND INDUCEMENT TO HIS EXAMPLE,
NATH^{L.} HOOD, ESQ., THE PRESENT MAYOR,
HAS CAUSED THIS STONE,
GRATEFULLY TO BE RENEWED
AND INSCRIBED,
A.D. 1771."
The History of Rochester, 1772.

By direction of the Court of Chancery, the large income derived from the property bequeathed for the support of the house (being now £3500 per annum) was, in pursuance of a scheme settled in 1855, applied in building of almshouses for ten men and ten women. The result has been the erection of a splendid edifice, in the Elizabethan style, with two magnificent gateways.

---

nock, the old light-house-keeper, to perfection; Miss Dickens representing *Phœbe;* Mr. Egg, a rough *Sailor;* and Mr. Mark Lemon, *Jacob Bell.*

In October, 1855—prior to his departure to America—a dinner was given to Mr. Thackeray at the London Tavern, of which one who was present gave the following account: "The Thackeray dinner was a triumph. Covers, we are assured, were laid for sixty; and sixty and no more sat down precisely at the minute named to do honor to the great novelist. Sixty very hearty shakes of the hand did Thackeray receive from sixty friends on that occasion; and hearty cheers from sixty vociferous and friendly tongues followed the Chairman's (Mr. Charles Dickens's) proposal of his health, and of wishes for his speedy and successful return among us. Dickens was never happier. He spoke as if he was fully conscious that it was a great occasion, and that the absence of even one reporter was a matter of congratulation, affording ampler room to unbend. The table was in the shape of a horse-shoe, having two Vice-Chairmen; and this circumstance was wrought up and played with by Dickens in the true Sam Weller and Charles Dickens manner. Thackeray, who is far from what is called a good speaker, outdid himself. There was his usual hesitation; but this hesitation becomes his manner of speaking and his matter, and is never unpleasant to his hearers, though it is, we are assured, most irksome to himself. This speech was full of pathos, and humor, and oddity, with bits of prepared parts imperfectly recollected, but most happily made good by the felicities of the passing moment. Like the 'Last Minstrel'—

'Each blank in faithless memory void,
The poet's glowing thought supplied.'

It was a speech to remember for its earnestness of purpose and its undoubted originality. Then the Chairman quitted, and many near and at a distance quitted with him. Thackeray was on the move with the Chairman, when, inspired by the moment, Jerrold took the chair, and Thackeray remained. Who is to chronicle what now passed?—what passages of wit—what neat and pleasant sarcastic speeches in proposing healths—what varied and pleasant, aye, and at times, sarcastic acknowledgments? Up to the time when Dickens left, a good reporter might have given all, and with ease, to future ages; but there could be no reporting what followed. There were words too nimble and too full of flame for a dozen Gurneys, all ears, to catch and preserve. Few will forget that night. There was an 'air of wit' about the room for three days after. Enough to make the two next companies, though downright fools, right witty."

The ensuing month an appeal was made on behalf of Johnson's god-daughter, signed by nineteen eminent literary men, including Dickens, Hallam, Disraeli, Carlyle, Thackeray, Milman, and Macaulay. A large sum of money was raised, but the recipient did not live many years to enjoy the annuity secured for her, and this quaint advertisement appeared in the "Times" of the 18th of January, 1860:

"On the 15th inst., at No. 5 Minerva Place, Hatcham, S.E., Ann Elizabeth, eldest daughter of the late Mauritius Lowe, Esq., of the Royal Academy, Gold Medallist, and god-daughter of the late Samuel Johnson, LL.D., aged 82."

"*The Late Samuel Johnson, LL.D.*," sounds strange in these days!

Another appeal to aid in a philanthropic cause was made to our author in the Christmas week, and again he expressed his readiness to assist.

He read his "Christmas Carol" to an immense audience at the Mechanics' Institute, Sheffield, in aid of its funds, and we are told in the papers of the time that at the termination the Mayor presented him with a very handsome table service of cutlery, including, we are further told, with a circumstantiality which is amusing—"a pair of fish-carvers, and a couple of razors," in the name of the inhabitants, for his generous help and assistance. In thanking him, Dickens said that, in an earnest desire to leave imaginative and popular literature something more closely associated than he found it, at once with the private homes and the public rights of the English people, "he should be faithful to death."*

This Christmas the celebrated number, entitled "The Holly-Tree Inn," came out. The best story in it—of course by Dickens—was "The Boots," a charming sketch, the writing delightfully fresh and vivid. It recorded the droll adventures of a young gentleman of the tender age of eight running off with his sweetheart, aged seven, to Gretna Green.

Mr. Johnstone dramatized it for the Strand Theatre, and, we may mention, it was the means of introducing the now celebrated Miss Herbert to the London boards. A much better version was produced at the Adelphi, Mr. Benjamin Webster playing, with all those peculiar and delicate touches of nature he is capable of, the rôle of Cobbs, "the Boots."

CHAPTER XXII.

"LITTLE DORRIT."—TAVISTOCK HOUSE THEATRICALS.

THE leading events in our author's career from the time we now begin to approach will be fresh in the memories of most readers. In the Christmas week of this year the first number of "Little Dorrit" appeared, and on its completion, twenty months later, was issued by Messrs. Bradbury & Evans, with illustrations by "Phiz," and dedicated to Clarkson Stanfield, R.A., the eminent landscape-painter. This work was written with the express intention of showing the procrastination and formal routine of the Government administration of business, happily designated as "The Circumlocution Office," and the Tite Barnacle's family, who impede the machinery by their inefficiency and supercilious know-nothing propensities.

Soon after it was published, Lord Lytton unwittingly furnished a specimen of the mode in which the dispatch of public business is conducted. Receiving an important deputation at the Colonial Office (when he was Minister), it appeared that, though a memorial had been sent in, and due notice given, he had heard nothing of the matter till five minutes before, if indeed he had heard of it at all; in explanation of which he somewhat naïvely remarked that in such offices "papers of importance passed through several departments, and required time for inspection—first they were sent to the Emigration Board, then to *another* office, and then to the Secretary of State, who might refer it to some other department." One can not fail to observe the extreme vagueness of the final resting-place of the unfortunate document: "*some other* department." What other department? This is what Mr. Clennam and his mechanical partner were always "wanting to know."

The work met with an immense sale in the serial form, but it is not now so popular as some of the other works of Mr. Dickens. The story was dramatized, and well represented at the Strand Theatre.

We come now to note Dickens's change of residence from Tavistock House, Tavistock Square, to Gad's Hill Place, Kent, or, as the great man himself always wrote it, with that amplitude

---

* Dickens, in a letter to Charles Knight, in 1844, alluding to the appearance of "Knight's Weekly Volumes," wrote him:

"If I can ever be of the feeblest use in advancing a project so intimately connected with an end on which my heart is set—the liberal education of the people—I shall be sincerely glad. All good wishes and success attend you."

and unmistakable clearness which made him write, not only the day of the month, but the day of the week, in full at the head of his letters—*Gad's Hill Place, Higham by Rochester, Kent.* How he came to live here is pleasantly told by a friend.*

"Though not born at Rochester, Mr. Dickens spent some portion of his boyhood there; and was wont to tell how his father the late Mr. John Dickens, in the course of a country ramble, pointed out to him as a child the house at Gad's Hill Place, saying, 'There, my boy; if you work and mind your book, you will, perhaps, one day live in a house like that.' This speech sunk deep, and in after years, and in the course of his many long pedestrian rambles through the lanes and roads of the pleasant Kentish country, Mr. Dickens came to regard this Gad's Hill House lovingly, and to wish himself its possessor. This seemed an impossibility. The property was so held that there was no likelihood of its ever coming into the market; and so Gad's Hill came to be alluded to jocularly, as representing a fancy which was pleasant enough in dream-land, but would never be realized.

"Meanwhile the years rolled on, and Gad's Hill became almost forgotten. Then a further lapse of time, and Mr. Dickens felt a strong wish to settle in the country, and determined to let Tavistock House. About this time, and by the strangest coincidences, his intimate friend and close ally, Mr. W. H. Wills, chanced to sit next to a lady at a London dinner-party, who remarked, in the course of conversation, that a house and grounds had come into her possession of which she wanted to dispose. The reader will guess the rest. The house was in Kent, was not far from Rochester, had this and that distinguishing feature which made it like Gad's Hill and like no other place; and the upshot of Mr. Wills's dinner-table chitchat with a lady whom he had never met before was, that Charles Dickens realized the dream of his youth, and became the possessor of Gad's Hill." The purchase was made in the spring of 1856.

In the "Uncommercial Traveller," under the head of "Travelling Abroad," No. VII., Dickens makes this mention of it:

"So smooth was the old high-road, and so fresh were the horses, and so fast went I, that it was midway between Gravesend and Rochester, and the widening river was bearing the ships, white-sailed, or black-smoked, out to sea, when I noticed by the way-side a very queer small boy.

---

* "Daily News," 15th June, 1870.

"'Hallo!' said I to the very queer small boy, 'where do you live?'

"'At Chatham,' says he.

"'What do you do there?' says I.

"'I go to school,' says he.

"I took him up in a moment, and we went on.

"Presently the very queer small boy says, 'This is Gad's Hill we are coming to, where Falstaff went out to rob those travellers and ran away.'

"'You know something about Falstaff, eh?' said I.

"'All about him,' said the very queer small boy.

"'I am old (I am nine) and I read all sorts of books. But *do* let us stop at the top of the hill and look at the house there, if you please!'

"'You admire that house?' said I.

"'Bless you, sir!' said the very queer small boy, 'when I was not more than half as old as nine, it used to be a treat for me to be brought to look at it. And now I am nine, I come by myself to look at it. And ever since I can recollect, my father, seeing me so fond of it, has often said to me, "If you were to be very persevering and were to work hard, you might some day come to live in it." Though that's impossible!' said the very queer small boy, drawing a low breath, and now staring at the house out of window with all his might.

"I was rather amazed to be told this by the very queer small boy, for that house happens to be *my* house, and I have reason to believe that what he said was true."

Of "Gad's Hill's haunted greenness," a modern poet well says:

"There is a subtle spirit in its air;
   The very soul of humor homes it there;
So is it now: of old so has it been;
Shakspeare from off it caught the rarest scene
   That ever shook with laughs the sides of Care;
   Falstaff's fine instinct for a Prince grew where
That hill—what years since!—show'd its Kentish
   green.
Fit home for England's world-loved Dickens."

Before Dickens left Tavistock House, where he had resided for many years, and where "Bleak House" and "Little Dorrit" were written, he gave some dramatic performances which elicited the warmest praise from those who had the good fortune to be present. A large room had been fitted up with stage, scenery, and foot-lights, and his friend Wilkie Collins had written an entirely new drama of the most romantic character for the occasion. The title was "The Frozen Deep," and the rigors of the Arctic regions were scenically portrayed by Clarkson Stanfield, R.A., and Mr. Danson. The following rough outline will give some idea of the piece as then performed. First, there was a beautiful scene in Kent, painted by Mr. Telbin, in which the members of the family of Captain Ebsworth and Lieutenants Crayford and Steventon, who are on board certain vessels engaged in an expedition at the North Pole, are assembled, and disclose the sufferings and the suspense by which they are agonized during the absence of their relatives. These consist of five young ladies—Mrs. Steventon (*Miss Helen*), Rose Ebsworth (*Miss Kate*), Lucy Crayford (*Miss Hogarth*), Clara Burnham (*Miss Mary*), and the Nurse Esther (*Mrs. Wills*), with their Maid (*Miss Martha*). Clara Burnham has two lovers—one Richard Wardour, performed by *Mr. Charles Dickens* himself, and the other Frank Aldersley (*Mr. Wilkie Collins*), to whom she is engaged. The former has vowed a terrible vengeance against his rival. And now that they are both on the Polar Seas together, Clara's fears are awakened, and haunt her imagination continually. To deepen the impression still more, Nurse Esther pretends to second-sight, and predicts the most fatal catastrophe.

Doubts are entertained of the character of Wardour from his strange conduct. This arises from "the pangs of despised love," with which his heart still wrestles. As yet he knows not who his rival may be, and does not suspect that he dwells in the same hut with him. Lieutenant Crayford, a bluff, hearty sailor (*Mark Lemon*), takes a strong interest in him, and believes in him, and believes in his inherent goodness. But at length his faith gives way; for, in a well-managed conversation, he penetrates the state of Wardour's soul, and forms of his tendencies the most awful judgment. Soon after Wardour makes the discovery that Aldersley is his rival, and his resolution is formed to accomplish the vengeance on which he had so long brooded. We next find all the party, with the young ladies, on the shore of Newfoundland. But Wardour and Aldersley are for a while missing, and Crayford is haunted with a horrible suspicion that the latter has been made the victim of the former. Wardour in rags, wild as a maniac, rushes into the cave. He claims food and drink, part of which he takes, and carefully preserves the rest in a wallet. Crayford at last recognizes him—endeavors to seize him—but the madman dashes away, soon to return with poor exhausted Aldersley in his arms. He had become the preserver of the man whom he had seduced to the most desolate spots on the Arctic snows for the purpose of destroying. He makes full reparation for his intended crime; and, ere his death, blesses the union of Clara Burnham and Frank Aldersley. Dickens's personation of Wardour required the best acting of a well-practised performer. His acting surprised all who witnessed it. The character was a fervid, powerful, and distinct individuality; not unlike, in some respects, Mr. B. Webster's tragic impersonations. Mrs. Inchbald's farce of "Animal Magnetism" concluded the evening's amusements, Mr. Dickens acting the *Doctor*, and Mr. Mark Lemon *Pedrillo*.

On the Wednesday following, Buckstone's well-known farce of "Uncle John" was performed, Mr. Dickens acting the vigorous old gentleman of seventy to perfection. Representations subsequently took place at the Gallery of Illustration, and at the Free Trade Hall, Manchester, for charitable purposes. On the 27th October, 1864, it was publicly produced at the Olympic Theatre, and met with a very enthusiastic reception.

The death of Douglas Jerrold, in June, 1867, was keenly felt by Dickens. The two friends had been on the most intimate terms for many years, as the few extracts we have already given from pleasant letters will show. The funeral was at Norwood Cemetery. The coffin was of plain oak, and on each side were the initials " D. J." The pall-bearers were Charles Dickens, W. M. Thackeray, Charles Knight, Horace Mayhew, Mark Lemon, Monckton Milnes (Lord Houghton), and Mr. Bradbury. A great gathering of artists and literary men surrounded the grave.

With his usual thoughtfulness and practical kindness, he soon ascertained the position in which poor Mrs. Jerrold, the widow, had been left. He found, as he had really suspected—for few men of letters were such good business men as Dickens—that a helping hand would be necessary, and he then, in conjunction with Mark Lemon, Albert Smith, Arthur Smith, and other friends, formed a committee to raise a fund, which was to be known as the "Jerrold Fund."

"Dickens entered warmly into the matter," remarks one who knew him; "and on the day of Jerrold's funeral, after dining with two or three friends, of whom the informant was one, at the Garrick Club, drew up the programme of a series of entertainments, which was that same night taken round to the editors of the various newspapers for insertion." Arthur Smith was the honorary secretary, and an entertainment, including the performance of "The Frozen Deep," was given at the Egyptian Hall, on 4th July, at which the Queen, Prince Albert, and the royal family were present. Other performances took place elsewhere, and readings were given by Thackeray and Dickens at St. Martin's Hall, and a large sum of money was the result.

The occasion for these charitable performances excited considerable outcry and disapprobation in literary circles, Jerrold being esteemed to be a prosperous man, as he received a very large salary as editor of "Lloyd's Weekly Newspaper." Dickens and Arthur Smith at once communicated to the papers the result of their labors, viz., the purchase of an annuity for the widow and her unmarried daughter, and added that they had considered their personal responsibility a sufficient refutation to any untrue or preposterous statements that had obtained circulation as to property asserted to have been left by Mr. Jerrold, and that unless they had thoroughly known, *and beyond all doubt* assured themselves, that their exertions were needed by the dearest objects of Mr. Jerrold's love, those exertions would never have been heard of. Lord Palmerston, it may be added, granted to the widow an annual pension of £100 out of the Civil List.

It was at the anniversary dinner of the Warehousemen and Clerks' Schools, held in November of this year, that Dickens made his well-known speech upon "Schools," when he told his hearers of all the schools he did not like, and, after a long enumeration of these, he described to them the one he did like.

The Christmas number of "Household Words" was entitled "Perils of certain English Prisoners," and was founded on the Indian Mutiny. It was in three chapters, "The Island of Silver Store," "The Prison in the Woods," and "The Rafts on the River," supposed to be narrated by Gilbert Davis, private in the Royal Marines. It is, as may be remembered, full of the most exciting adventures.

CHAPTER XXIII.

WORKS TRANSLATED INTO FRENCH.—DICKENS AND THACKERAY.

DURING this year a complete and authorized edition of Dickens's novels was published in France, beginning with "Vie et Aventures de Nicholas Nickleby." To this the author added this introductory address to the French public:

"For a long time I have wished to see a uniform and complete translation of my works into French. Hitherto, less fortunate in France than in Germany, I have not been made known to French readers who are not familiar with the English language, except by isolated and partial translations, published without my authority and control, and from which I have derived no personal advantage. The present publication has been proposed to me by MM. Hachette & Co., and by M. Charles Lahure, in terms which do honor to their elevated, liberal, and generous character. It has been executed with great care; and the numerous difficulties it presents have been vanquished with uncommon ability, intelligence, and perseverance. I am proud of being thus presented to the French people, whom I sincerely love and honor."

It must have been a great source of satisfaction to him to have known that not only in Western Europe and America were his books, with their kindly teachings and influences for good, widely read by the common people, but that as far away as Russia there existed a translation of Dickens's works, all of which are very popular.

"Who among us"—exclaims a writer in "Vedomoste," one of the leading journals of St. Petersburg—"does not know the genius—who has not read the novels of Dickens? There was a time when the Russian translators of foreign novels did almost nothing else than translate the charming productions of Boz! The journals and newspapers rivalled each other in being the first to communicate his last work. Every word he wrote was offered to the Russian reading community in five or six different periodicals, and as soon as the concluding part of each of his novels appeared in England a variety of St. Petersburg and Moscow editions bore the fame of Dickens over all the East of Europe. Every scrap of Dickens"—exclaims the Northern critic with the keen appetite of his climate—"has been devoured. With the sole exception of Walter Scott, none among the English novelists has enjoyed such an enormous and prolonged success as Dickens."

And since his death long obituary notices of him have been given in the Italian papers. The "Diritto" thinks that Sam Weller and the "modern Tartuffe," in "Martin Chuzzlewit," will be immortal, like Perpetua and Don Abbondio in Manzoni's "Promessi Sposi," which have become popular types of character. The "Nazione" speaks of the deceased as the greatest of modern English novelists. "He was," it adds, "for five-and-thirty years, at once the most esteemed novelist and the greatest social reformer of his fellow-countrymen. There will be monuments to him in marble and bronze, but his finest monument will be the good he did for the poorer classes."

In March of this year Dickens visited Edinburgh to read his "Christmas Carol" to upwards of two thousand members of the Philosophical Institute there. After the reading was over, the Lord Provost presented him with a splendid silver wassail bowl. Dickens, in replying said: "The first great public recognition and encouragement I ever received was bestowed on me by your generous and magnificent city. To come to Edinburgh is to me like coming home."

And in a recent letter to the writer of an article in "All the Year Round"—entitled "Dr. Johnson from a Scottish Point of View"—Dickens said: "By all means let me have the paper proposed; *but, in handling Johnson, be pleasant with the Scottish people, because I love them.*"

A STUDY OF DICKENS'S CHARACTERS DRAWN BY "PHIZ"—HABLOT K. BROWNE,
The original delineator of Charles Dickens's principal characters.

A few days after, on the 29th of March, Thackeray, supported by Dickens and other literary men, presided at the Royal General Theatrical Fund Dinner at the Freemasons'

Tavern; and, in proposing the health of the Chairman, Dickens took occasion to bear his testimony to the goodness, the self-denial, and the self-respect of the actors of England, and passed a very flattering encomium upon the Chairman's works: "It is not for me, at this time and in this place," he said, "to take on myself to flutter before you the well-thumbed pages of Mr. Thackeray's books, and to tell you to observe how full they are of wit and wisdom, how out-speaking, and how devoid of fear or favor they are. * * * The bright and airy pages of 'Vanity Fair.' * * * To this skillful showman, who has so often delighted us, and who has charmed us again to-night, we have now to wish God-speed, and that he may continue for many years to exercise his potent art. To him fill a bumper toast, and fervently utter God bless him!"

Alas! the "many years" were to be barely six! In 1864 the speaker himself wrote some memorial pages commemorative of his illustrious friend in the deceased author's own "Cornhill Magazine."

So much interest had been shown by the public in Mr. Dickens's performance of his part of the "Jerrold Fund" programme, that he now determined to give his readings professionally, and as an avowed source of income. It was on the evening of Thursday, the 29th of April, 1858, that he appeared in St. Martin's Hall (now converted into the New Queen's Theatre) for the first time, as a source of personal profit to himself.

We may mention that on the 25th of the following month one of the assistants in the Library at the British Museum, M. Louis Augistin Prévost, a great linguist, died. It was he who imparted instruction in the French tongue to Dickens.

We come now to a painful matter, which occasioned a great talk at the time, and led Mr. Dickens's warmest friends to marvel at the course he had thought fit to pursue.

It appears that some domestic unhappiness in the great novelist's family had occasioned the usual gossip out of doors, and these "rumors and slanders"—as he energetically termed the whisperings that were so repugnant to him—led to his inserting a manifesto on the front page of "Household Words."*

All the newspapers and journals copied it, with various comments—in some cases exceedingly rancorous and spiteful—and various long letters and documents from friends on both sides appeared in the public journals. The simple explanation was, that a misunderstanding had arisen between Mr. and Mrs. Dickens, of a purely domestic character—so domestic—almost trivial, indeed—that neither law nor friendly arbitration could define or fix the difficulty sufficiently clear to adjudicate upon it. All we can say is, that it was a very great pity that a purely family dispute should have been brought before the public, and, saying thus much, we trust the reader will think we act wisely in dropping any further mention of it.

That Mr. Dickens loves his home, and that his domestic tastes were very strong, there is abundant proof. Hawthorne, in his "English Diary," has a passage *apropos* of this: "Mr. Dickens mentioned how he preferred home enjoyments to all others, and did not willingly go much into society. Mrs. Dickens, too, the other day told us of his taking on himself all possible trouble as regards their domestic affairs."

It is somewhat singular that on the very day when Mr. Dickens's personal explanation appeared in "Household Words," on that very day (12th June, 1858) a paper, also of a personal character, but concerning our author's distinguished contemporary, Mr. W. M. Thackeray, appeared in a little journal called "Town Talk;" both articles eventually acquiring a painful notoriety, and the latter occasioning an unhappy difference between the two great men. The article which occasioned so much pain to Mr. Thackeray professed to give an account of the author of "Vanity Fair"—his appearance, his career, and his success. The article was coarse and offensive in tone, but it was notorious that the periodical was edited by a clever writer of the day, well known to Mr. Thackeray as a brother member of a club to which he belonged. As such, the subject of the attack felt himself compelled to take notice of it. This is a specimen of the article:

"HIS APPEARANCE.

"Mr. Thackeray is forty-six years old, though, from the silvery whiteness of his hair, he appears somewhat older. He is very tall, standing upwards of six feet two inches. His face is bloodless, and not particularly expressive, but remarkable for the fracture of the bridge of the nose, the result of an accident in youth. His bearing is cold and uninviting, his style of conversation either openly cynical or affectedly good-natured and benevolent; his *bonhomie* is forced, his wit biting, his pride easily touched.

"HIS SUCCESS.

"No one succeeds better than Mr. Thackeray in cutting his coat according to his cloth. * * * Our own opinion is, that his success is on the wane."

Two days later Mr. Thackeray addressed the assumed writer of this article in a manly but indignant letter.

Subsequently Mr. Thackeray, "rather (he

---

* June 12th.

said) than have any further correspondence with the writer of the character," determined to submit the letters which had passed between them to the committee of the club. The committee accordingly met, and decided that the writer of the attack complained of was bound to make an ample apology, or to retire from the club. The latter contested the right of the committee to interfere. Suits at law and proceedings in Chancery against the committee were threatened, when Mr. Dickens, who was also a member of the club, interfered, with the following letter:

"Tavistock House, Tavistock Square, London, W.C., Wednesday, 24th November, 1858.

"MY DEAR THACKERAY,—Without a word of prelude, I wish this note to revert to a subject on which I said six words to you at the Athenæum when I last saw you.

"Coming home from my country work, I find Mr. Edwin James's opinion taken on this painful question of the Garrick and Mr. Edmund Yates. I find it strong on the illegality of the Garrick proceeding. Not to complicate this note, or give it a formal appearance, I forbear from copying the opinion; but I have asked to see it, and I have it, and I want to make no secret from you of a word of it.

"I find Mr. Edwin James retained on the one side; I hear and read of the Attorney-General being retained on the other. Let me, in this state of things, ask you a plain question:

"Can any conference be held between me, as representing Mr. Yates, and an appointed friend of yours, as representing you, with the hope and purpose of some quiet accommodation of this deplorable matter, which will satisfy the feelings of all concerned?

"It is right that, in putting this to you, I should tell you that Mr. Yates, when you first wrote to him, brought your letter to me. He had recently done me a manly service I can never forget, in some private distress of mine (generally within your knowledge), and he naturally thought of me as his friend in an emergency. I told him that his article was not to be defended; but I confirmed him in his opinion that it was not reasonably possible for him to set right what was amiss, on the receipt of a letter couched in the very strong terms you had employed. When you appealed to the Garrick committee and they called their general meeting, I said at that meeting that you and I had been on good terms for many years, and that I was very sorry to find myself opposed to you; but that I was clear that the committee had nothing on earth to do with it, and that in the strength of my conviction I should go against them.

"If this mediation that I have suggested can take place, I shall be heartily glad to do my best in it—and, God knows, in no hostile spirit towards any one, least of all to you. If it can not take place, the thing is at least no worse than it was; and you will burn this letter, and I will burn your answer.

"Yours faithfully, CHARLES DICKENS.
"W. M. THACKERAY, Esq."

To this Mr. Thackeray replied:

"36 Onslow Square, 26th November, 1858.

"DEAR DICKENS,—I grieve to gather from your letter that you were Mr. Yates's adviser in the dispute between me and him. His letter was the cause of my appeal to the Garrick Club for protection from insults against which I had no other remedy.

"I placed my grievance before the committee of the club as the only place where I have been accustomed to meet Mr. Yates. They gave their opinion of his conduct, and of the reparation which lay in his power. Not satisfied with their sentence, Mr. Yates called for a general meeting; and, the meeting which he had called having declared against him, he declines the jurisdiction which he had asked for, and says he will have recourse to lawyers.

"You say that Mr. Edwin James is strongly of opinion that the conduct of the club is illegal. On this point I can give no sort of judgment; nor can I conceive that the club will be frightened, by the opinion of any lawyer, out of their own sense of the justice and honor which ought to obtain among gentlemen.

"Ever since I submitted my case to the club, I have had, and can have, no part in the dispute. It is for them to judge if any reconcilement is possible with your friend. I subjoin the copy of a letter* which I wrote to

---

* The inclosure referred to was as follows:

"Onslow Square, November 28, 1858.

"GENTLEMEN,—I have this day received a communication from Mr. Charles Dickens relative to the dispute which has been so long pending, in which he says:

"'Can any conference be held between me, as representing Mr. Yates, and any appointed friend of yours, as representing you, in the hope and purpose of some quiet accommodation of this deplorable matter, which will satisfy the feelings of all parties?'

"I have written to Mr. Dickens to say that, since the commencement of this business, I have placed myself entirely in the hands of the committee of the Garrick, and am still, as ever, prepared to abide by any decision at which they may arrive on the subject. I conceive I can not, if I would, make the dispute once more personal, or remove it out of the court to which I submitted it for arbitration.

"If you can devise any peaceful means for ending it, no one will be better pleased than

"Your obliged faithful servant,
"W. M. THACKERAY.
"THE COMMITTEE OF THE GARRICK CLUB."

the committee, and refer you to them for the issue.

"Yours, etc., W. M. THACKERAY.
"C. DICKENS, Esq."

It would be in vain to attempt to conceal that this painful affair left a coolness between Mr. Thackeray and his brother novelist. Mr. Thackeray, smarting under the elaborate and unjust attack, portions of which were copied and widely circulated in other journals, could not but regard the friend and adviser of his critic as in some degree associated with it; and Mr. Dickens, on the other hand, naturally hurt at finding his offer of arbitration rejected, gave the letters to the original author of the trouble for publication, with the remark—"As the receiver of my letter did not respect the confidence in which it addressed him, there can be none left for you to violate. I send you what I wrote to Mr. Thackeray, and what he wrote to me, and you are at perfect liberty to print the two." Thus, for a while, ended this painful affair. Readers of Disraeli's "Quarrels of Authors" will miss in it those sterner features of the dissensions between literary men as they were conducted in the old times; but none can contemplate this difference between the two great masters of fiction of our day with other than feelings of regret for the causes which led to it.

It is pleasing, however, to learn that the differences between them were ended before Mr. Thackeray's death. Singularly enough, this happy circumstance occurred only a few days before the time when it would have been too late. The two great authors met by accident in the lobby of a club. They suddenly turned and saw each other, and the unrestrained impulse of both was to hold out the hand of forgiveness and fellowship. With that hearty grasp the difference which estranged them ceased forever. This must have been a great consolation to Mr. Dickens when he saw his great brother laid in the earth at Kensal Green; and ho one who read the beautiful and affecting article on Thackeray, from the hand of Mr. Dickens, which appeared in the "Cornhill Magazine," can doubt that all trace of this painful affair had then vanished.

CHAPTER XXIV.

ROYAL DRAMATIC COLLEGE.—"ALL THE YEAR ROUND."

WE turn now to a more pleasant theme. On the 21st July, 1858, a public meeting was held at the Princess's Theatre, for the purpose of establishing the now famous Royal Dramatic College. Mr. Charles Kean was the Chairman, and Dickens delivered one of his excellent speeches on a topic ever dear to him—the theatrical profession. Charles Kean was then conducting his Shakspearian revivals—those splendid pageantries and archæological displays which we all remember at this theatre twelve years ago —and Dickens, with his usual tact, turned the circumstance to account in his speech. The play then being performed was the "Merchant of Venice," and, in concluding, the speaker remarked, "I could not but reflect, while Mr. Kean was speaking, that in an hour or two from this time, the spot upon which we are now assembled will be transformed into the scene of a crafty and a cruel bond. I know that a few hours hence the Grand Canal of Venice will flow, with picturesque fidelity, on the very spot where I now stand dryshod, and that the 'quality of mercy' will be beautifully stated to the Venetian Council by a learned young doctor from Padua, on these very boards on which we now enlarge upon the quality of charity and sympathy. Knowing this, it came into my mind to consider how different the real bond of to-day from the ideal bond of to-night. *Now* all generosity, all forbearance, all forgetfulness of little jealousies and unworthy divisions, all united action for the general good. *Then* all selfishness, all malignity, all cruelty, all revenge, and all evil; *now* all good. *Then* a bond to be broken within the compass of a few—three or four—swiftly passing hours; *now* a bond to be valid and of good effect generations hence."

The committee's labors were successful, and an elegant building, in the Elizabethan style, at Maybury, was the result. On June 1st, 1860, the late prince consort, in laying the foundation-stone, spoke of the Dramatic College as conferring "a benefit upon the public as well as upon the stage, by aiding a profession from which the community at large derived national entertainment." Five years after, on 5th June, the Prince of Wales inaugurated the Central Hall of the College. The annual Fancy Fair at the Crystal Palace, and the junketings thereat, it is needless to say, are the means of adding a large accession to the funds.

During the autumn months of this year, the readings were continued in London, and at various large towns in England and Ireland, the novelist receiving both applause and money to a greater extent than ever.

It was in November, 1858, that he allowed his name to be put in nomination for the high office of Lord Rector of Glasgow University. His rivals were Lord Lytton (who was chosen to the office) and Lord Shaftesbury. The result of the poll was: Lord Lytton, 216; Lord Shaftesbury, 203; Dickens, 68. The cause of this large minority is now not remembered, but it is more than probable that Dickens took no special pains to secure votes in his own behalf.

During the following month he was entertained at a public dinner by the citizens of Coventry, and received from them a very handsome gold watch, as a testimony of their gratitude for his reading, in aid of the Coventry Institute, twelve months before. The day previously he had presided at Manchester, in aid of an Institute there.

Early in 1859 a dispute arose between Mr. Dickens and his publishers, originating mainly in the unfortunate family disagreement to which we alluded on a former page; and in consequence of this the conductor of "Household Words" resolved that the journal should cease, and he would close business relations with Messrs. Bradbury & Evans. Mr. Dickens advertised that the discontinuance of "Household Words" would take place on March 28th. Messrs. Bradbury & Evans filed a Bill in Chancery, and the matter was heard by the Master of the Rolls. Both parties refusing to sell their interest, the winding up of the publication was directed. Dickens owned five-eighths, and had command over another eighth. At the sale, on 16th May, by Mr. Hodgson of Chancery Lane, the property, after a spirited contest, was knocked down to Dickens (represented by Mr. Arthur Smith) for £3550. In the last number of "Household Words," introducing the forthcoming periodical, he wrote:

"He knew perfectly well, knowing his own rights, and his means of attaining them, that *it could not* be but that this work must stop, if he chose to stop it. He therefore announced, many weeks ago, that it would be discontinued on the day on which this final number bears date. The public have read a great deal to the contrary, and will observe that it has not in the least affected the result."

Messrs. Bradbury & Evans, to justify their proceedings, published a statement, affirming—

"That 'Household Words' stopped against their will, and mentioned the appearance of 'Once a Week'—remarking, at the same time, that their business relations with Dickens had commenced in 1836; that in 1844 they acquired an interest in all works he might write, or in any periodical he might originate, during a term of seven years, and that under this agreement they became possessed of a joint though unequal share of 'Household Words,' which started in 1850; that on the publication of his manifesto as to his conjugal differences, they understood from a friend that he had resolved to break off his connections with them by reason of its non-insertion in 'Punch,' in which they had not thought fit to do so, 'Punch' being entirely a comic publication; that in the November he summoned a meeting of the proprietors, and in consequence of the advertisement announcing the cessation of the work, they had no alternative but to apply to the Master of the Rolls for protection."

It was a most unfortunate affair, as Mr. Evans's son had married Miss Dickens, and thus a family, as well as a business, disagreement came about. Mr. Dickens's next step was to return to his original publishers, Messrs. Chapman & Hall, who now issue all his works.

"All the Year Round" was the title of Mr. Dickens's new venture, taking its motto, like "Household Words," from Shakspeare—

"The story of our lives from year to year."

In its first number was contained the commencement of "A Tale of Two Cities," subsequently published by Messrs. Chapman & Hall, illustrated by Mr. Marcus Stone (a rising young artist), and dedicated to Earl Russell.

In the preface the author mentions that he first thought of the story while acting with his children and friends in Mr. Wilkie Collins's drama of "The Frozen Deep." "As the idea became familiar to me, it gradually shaped itself into its present form. Throughout its execution, it has had complete possession of me; I have so far verified what is done and suffered in these pages, as that I have certainly done and suffered it all myself. * * * It has been one of my hopes to add something to the popular and picturesque means of understanding that terrible time, though no one can hope to add any thing to the philosophy of Mr. Carlyle's wonderful book."

Dickens had the greatest respect for the works of that eminent writer, and it would be difficult to say which of the two distinguished authors, Tennyson or Carlyle, he was most fond of quoting. Only a few weeks before his death, Mr. Arthur Locker was discussing some literary topics with him: "On this occasion," that gentleman writes, "Mr. Dickens conversed with me chiefly about Mr. Carlyle's writings, for whose 'French Revolution' he expressed the strongest admiration, as he had practically shown in his 'Tale of Two Cities.'"

The story holds the reader perfectly spellbound. The power and awful grandeur exhibited in the descriptive scenes of bloodshed and carnage enacted in the dreadful reign of Terror are almost beyond conception. It has, however, occasional passages of humor—as, for instance, where Mr. Jeremiah Cruncher determines not to let his wife say her prayers, being of opinion that such a course of procedure, described by him as "flopping," is injurious to his business!

Tom Taylor dramatized the story for the Lyceum, where it was produced the January following, but it met with an indifferent reception, although the principal character was undertaken by Madame Celeste.

During October, Dickens gave readings at the Town Hall, Oxford, and attracted large audiences. On one occasion the Prince of Wales, then entering on his career as an Oxonian, was present, and expressed considerable satisfaction at the pleasure he had experienced in hearing him read.

The reader may remember that on an earlier page we gave an account of the handsome present which Mr. Dickens once received from his many Birmingham friends—more especially his artist friends there. On that occasion an address was presented to him expressing the great admiration all Birmingham people felt for his genius. Mr. W. P. Frith, in his portrait of Dickens, exhibited at the Royal Academy in 1858, made the address form a portion of the picture; but a Mr. Walker, an artist of Birmingham, could scarcely believe that the great novelist had troubled himself to remember the address, so he wrote to know the truth of the matter, when Mr. Dickens immediately replied: "I have great pleasure in assuring you that the framed address in Mr. Frith's portrait is the address presented to me by my Birmingham friends, and to which you refer. It has stood at my elbow, in that one place, ever since I received it, and, please God, it will remain at my side as long as I live and work."*

It was the Christmas number for this year, "The Haunted House," which at the time provoked so much discussion on the subject of ghosts and supernatural visitors. The idea of the number may have been suggested by the appearance of a work, published a few months previously, entitled "A Night in a Haunted House: a Tale of Facts. By the Author of 'Kazan,' and dedicated to Charles Dickens." Howitt took the matter up warmly, and Dickens, in a letter to Howitt, said that he had always taken great interest in these matters, but required evidence such as he had not yet met with; and that when he thinks of the amount of misery and injustice that constantly obtains in this world, which a word from the departed dead person in question could set right,* he would not believe—could not believe—in the War Office ghost without overwhelming evidence.

Howitt sent a letter to one of the weekly papers, stating that "Mr. Dickens wrote me some time ago, to request that I would point out to him some house said to be haunted. I named to him two—that at Cheshunt, formerly inhabited by the Chapmans, and one at Wellington, near Newcastle. Never seen former, but had the latter." Dickens went to Cheshunt and visited the house, and communicated to Howitt that "the house in which the Chapmans lived has been greatly enlarged, and commands a high rent, and is no more disturbed than this house of mine."

If any one of a nervous and superstitious temperament will read all the seven ghost stories contained in "The Haunted House" at a late hour, alone, and in a dull and gloomy room, a very quiet and comfortable night's rest may be safely calculated on!

About this time the Americans tried very hard to persuade Dickens to visit them and give his readings, and many of their newspapers were jubilant at the idea, and reported that his services had been secured. To dissipate all doubts, he wrote to Lieutenant-colonel Foster, of Boston, U. S. A.:

"I beg to assure you, in reply to your obliging letter, that you are misinformed, and that I have no intention of visiting America in the ensuing autumn."†

In the numbers for the 4th and 11th August, 1860, of "All the Year Round," the two portions of "Hunted Down" appeared. It was supposed to be a reminiscence supplied by a Mr. Sampson, chief manager of a life assurance office, relating the history of an assurance effected on the life of Mr. Alfred Beckwith by Mr. Julius Slinkton, whom he (Slinkton) attempts to poison to get the money; but, foiled in his object, destroys himself. The story was of a most melodramatic and sensational character. Before it appeared in this country, it had a six months' run in the "New York Ledger," and the American publisher paid £1000 for the privilege. Dickens was loath to undertake its composition, but finally his objections were overcome. "I thought," he wrote to the American publisher, "that I could not be tempted at

---

* Tuesday, July 20th, 1859.

* "Oh that it were possible, for one short hour, to see
The souls we loved, that they might tell us
What and where they be!"—TENNYSON.
† Wednesday night, 7th September, 1859.

this time to engage in any undertaking, however short, but the literary project which will come into active existence next month. But your proposal is so handsome that it changes my resolution, and I can not refuse it. * * * I will endeavor to be at work upon the tale while this note is on its way to you across the water." The "project" referred to here as coming into active existence next month was "A Tale of Two Cities."

CHAPTER XXV.

"THE UNCOMMERCIAL TRAVELLER."

IT was at the end of this year that a series of quaint and descriptive papers, which had appeared in "All the Year Round," was published by Messrs. Chapman & Hall, under the title of "The Uncommercial Traveller." They were originally seventeen in number, but in a subsequent edition they were increased to twenty-eight papers, bearing such titles as "City Churches," "Sly Neighborhoods," "Night Walks," "Chambers," "Birthdays," "Funerals," "Tramps." We need scarcely remark that they are all admirably written, and abound in delicate touches. In "Nurse's Stories," Mr. Dickens says, "Brobingnag (which has the curious fate of being usually misspelt when written)." Here the illustrious author actually falls into the very error he is speaking of. The proper spelling of the word is *Brobvingnag*.

It was in the autumn of this year that Mr. Dickens finally removed from Tavistock House to Gad's Hill, a place which he had purchased four years before. Some arrangement, we believe, in connection with the lease of the London house prevented his removing earlier. Tavistock House thenceforward became the residence of Mr. Phineas Davis, a gentleman well known in aristocratic circles. The house next to Tavistock House was occupied by the late Mr. Frank Stone, the eminent artist, and for a long time Mr. Dickens's neighbor.

The Christmas number for 1860 was "A Message from the Sea." It was here that we became acquainted with Captain Jorgan, the American captain, and his faithful steward, Tom Pettifer. The Captain's task satisfactorily terminated, he shakes hands with the entire population of the fishing village, inviting the whole, without exception, to come and stay with him for several months at Salem, United States.

"The Sea-faring Man," narrating the shipwreck, and the island on fire, in vividness of description are wonderful pieces of writing.

The manager of the Britannia Theatre, Hoxton, having announced for representation a dramatic adaptation of the tale, Dickens, in a letter to the "Times," gave his reasons for interfering with its production. Subsequently, Mr. Charles Reade tried the question in his action against Mr. Conquest for representing "Never too Late to Mend," and was unsuccessful.

It was towards the close of this year that "Great Expectations," which had been published in "All the Year Round," came out in the (for Mr. Dickens) somewhat unusual form—the old lending-library form—of three volumes, and was published by Messrs. Chapman & Hall, illustrated by Marcus Stone, and inscribed to Mr. C. H. Townshend. It is a novel of the most peculiar and fantastic construction, the plot of an extraordinary description, and the characters often grotesque, and sometimes impossible. Here we meet with Abel Magwitch, the convict, a powerfully-drawn character; with Pip, a selfish, and oftentimes a pitiful fellow, but good in the end, when his expectations have entirely faded; with Joe Gargery, the blacksmith, the finest character of all—kind, patient, and true to Pip, from his infancy to manhood, shielding him in all his shortcomings when a child, and liberally spooning gravy into his plate when he gets talked at by Pumblechook at dinner; with Miss Havisham, the broken-hearted woman, existing with the one idea of training her adopted child; with Estella, a beautiful conception (Pip's love for her, and his grief when he finds her married to Bentley Drummle, the man without a heart to break, are masterpieces of description); with Pumblechook, that frightful impostor. Perhaps the most entertaining portions are those connected with Wemmick, the lawyer's clerk, his "Castle" at Walworth, and his peculiar ideas of portable property, his post-office mouth, and Mr. Jaggers, the criminal lawyer of Little Britain, his employer.

We may here mention that "Satis House," the residence of Miss Havisham, lies a little to the west of Boley Hill, near Rochester, and derived its peculiar name from the fact of Richard Watts (founder of the Poor Travellers' House previously referred to) entertaining Queen Elizabeth in it—when on her journey round the coasts of Sussex and Kent—in 1573. Here she staid some days, and, on her leaving, Watts apologized for the smallness of the house for so great a Queen; she merely replied "*Satis*," signifying she was well content with her accommodation.

CHAPTER XXVI.

MR. DICKENS AND THE ELECTORS OF FINSBURY.—"TOM TIDDLER'S GROUND."—"SOMEBODY'S LUGGAGE."—"MRS. LIRRIPER'S LODGINGS."

In November of this year, some admirers in Finsbury formed the idea that Mr. Dickens would have no objections to represent that borough in Parliament, and his name was brought prominently forward as a candidate. He was then at Newcastle-upon-Tyne, and on the 21st of November he wrote to the "Daily News:" "Being here for a day or two, I have observed, in your paper of yesterday, an account of a meeting of Finsbury electors, in which it was discussed whether I should be invited to become a candidate for the borough.* It may save some trouble if you will kindly confirm a sensible gentleman, who doubted at that meeting whether I was quite the sort of man for Finsbury. I am not at all the sort of man, for I believe nothing would induce me to offer myself as a parliamentary representative of that place, or any other under the sun."

In the early part of this winter he resumed his readings in the provinces, and met with considerable success, especially in Lancashire, where there was great enthusiasm shown to see and hear the author of "Pickwick," and latterly of "Hard Times," which had found thousands of readers in the cotton districts.

The Christmas number for this year, "Tom Tiddler's Ground," excited considerable curiosity, and one of the stories became a subject of general discussion—that of "Mr. Mopes," the hermit. "Picking up Soot and Cinders" gives the history and description of the hermit —a dirty, lazy, slothful fellow, dressed up in a blanket fastened by a skewer, and revelling in soot and grease. There is one story in the number, called "Picking up Terrible Company," of the most intense sensational character. It is told by François Thierry, a French convict, under the head of "Picking up a Pocket-book."

The "hermit" was a living reality—a person of property and education, who, to mortify his friends, we believe, withdrew from the world, and lived in rags and filth. Soon after a letter, signed "A County Down Lady," was inserted in the "Downpatrick Recorder," in which the writer related the particulars of a visit she had paid to "Mr. Mopes," the hermit, and concluded by saying: "Charles Dickens offended him terribly. He pretended he was a Highlander, and Mr. Lucas at once began to question him about the country, and then spoke to him in Gaelic, which he couldn't reply to. Mr. Lucas said to him, 'Sir, you are an impostor; you are no gentleman.'"

A copy of the newspaper was at once forwarded to Mr. Dickens by a friend, who asked if there was any truth in the statement. The reply was: "As you sent me the paper with that very cool account of myself in it, perhaps you want to know whether or not it is true. There is not a syllable of truth in it. I have never seen the person in question but once in my life, and then I was accompanied by Lord Orford, Mr. Arthur Helps, the clerk of the privy council, my eldest daughter, and my sister-in-law, all of whom know perfectly well that nothing of the sort passed. It is a sheer invention of the wildest kind."* Lucas, the papers reported, was terribly cut up by the inclement winter of 1866–'7, and was hardly expected to get over it.

In March, 1862, Dickens commenced a new series of readings at St. James's Hall, which proved a very advantageous speculation. He officiated as Chairman at the Annual Festival of the Dramatic Equestrian and Musical Association, on the 5th of the same month, at Willis's Rooms, and delivered an eloquent address; he fulfilled the same duty at the annual dinner of the Artists' General Benevolent Fund, at the Freemasons' Tavern, on the 29th of this month, and the result was a large accession to its treasury. Acting in the same capacity at the Annual Festival of the News-venders' and Provident Institution, at the last-named tavern, on the 20th May following, in proposing the toast of the evening, "Prosperity to the News-venders' Benevolent Institution,"† he delivered a very amusing speech on "The Newsman's Calling." In the course of his remarks he "started off with the newsman on a fine May morning, to take a view of the wonderful broad-sheets which every day he scatters broadcast over the country. Well, the first thing that occurs to me, following the newsman, is, that every day we are born, that every day we are married—some of us—and that every day we are dead; consequently, the first thing the news-vender's column informs me is, that Atkins has been born, that Catkins has been married, and that Datkins is dead. But the most remarkable thing I immediately discover in the next column is, that Atkins has grown to be

---

* Consequent on the death of Mr. Thomas S. Duncombe—the "Tom Duncombe" of Finsbury—the late representative.

* London, 27th March, 1862.
† He was elected President of the Institution in May, 1854.

seventeen years old, and that he has run away, for at last my eye lights on the fact that William A., who is seventeen years old, is adjured immediately to return to his disconsolate parents, and every thing will be arranged to the satisfaction of every one. I am afraid he will never return, simply because, if he had meant to come back, he would never have gone away. Immediately below, I find a mysterious character in such a mysterious difficulty, that it is only to be expressed by several disjointed letters, by several figures, and several stars; and then I find the explanation in the intimation that the writer has given his property over to his uncle, and that the elephant is on the wing. * * * I learn, to my intense gratification, that I need never grow old, that I may always preserve the juvenile bloom of my complexion; that if ever I turn ill it is entirely my own fault; that if I have any complaint, and want brown cod-liver oil or Turkish baths, I am told where to get them; and that if I want an income of £7 a week, I may have it by sending half a crown in postage-stamps. Then I look to the police intelligence, and I can discover that I may bite off a human living nose cheaply; but if I take off the dead nose of a pig or a calf from a shop-window, it will cost me exceedingly dear. I also find that if I allow myself to be betrayed into the folly of killing an inoffensive tradesman on his own door-step, that little incident will not affect the testimonials to my character, but that I shall be described as a most amiable young man, and, as above all things, remarkable for the singular inoffensiveness of my character and disposition."

But the entire speech is much too long for our space.

We have now reached another winter—that of 1862—and this time our novelist devoted his Christmas number, "Somebody's Luggage," to that peculiar class of individuals known as "Waiters." Mr. Arthur Locker truly says of it: "We rise from the little story with kindlier feelings towards the whole race of waiters; we know more of their struggles and trials, and so we sympathize with them more." Most of our readers will remember the description of Christopher, the head-waiter, with his amusing revelations of his profession—the mysterious luggage left in Room 24 B, with a lien on it for £2 12s. 6d., his purchasing the whole of it, and finding all the articles crammed full of MSS.—his subsequently selling them, and, on the arrival of *the proofs*, his horror at the appearance of the owner—his placing them before him, and the joy of the unknown at finding his stories in print, and sitting down, with several new pens and all the inkstands well filled, to correct, in a high state of excitement, and being discovered in the morning, himself and the proofs, so smeared with ink, that it would have been difficult to have said which was him, and which was them, and which was blots—is sufficient to keep the reader in one continual roar of laughter.

In the preceding year several imitation Christmas numbers had appeared, but this season they swarmed. The newspapers and the boardings were filled with advertisements of them, and Mr. Dickens expressed great annoyance at the manner in which he was being copied.

In the March following (1863) he presided at the eighteenth anniversary of the Royal General Theatrical Fund, and made a most excellent speech.

About this time Mr. Charles Reade's "Very Hard Cash" was appearing in the pages of "All the Year Round," and that gentleman having attacked with virulence the Commissioners in Lunacy, Dickens, in a foot-note to Chapter XLVI., wrote:

"The conductor of this journal desires to take this opportunity of expressing his personal belief that no public servants do their duty with greater ability, humanity, and independence than the Commissioners in Lunacy."

When the story was concluded, to further show that the sentiments expressed in it were not those of Mr. Dickens—or that at least he had not controlled them—he wrote:

"The statements and opinions of this journal generally are, of course, to be received as the statements and opinions of its conductor. But this is not so in the case of a work of fiction first published in these pages as a serial story, with the name of an eminent writer attached to it. When one of my literary brothers does me the honor to undertake such a task, I hold that he executes it on his own personal responsibility, and for the sustainment of his own reputation; and I do not consider myself at liberty to exercise that control over his text which I claim as to other contributions.

"CHARLES DICKENS."

He was justified in making this statement, as Mr. Forster, an old and true friend—and who has since been appointed by Mr. Dickens his principal executor—is one of the commissioners.

Another Christmas has come round—the Christmas of 1863. "Mrs. Lirriper's Lodgings" was the title of the number for this season, and it created an immense *furore*. The quaint manners and ideas of Mrs. Lirriper, lodging-house keeper, of 81 Norfolk Street, Strand —her troubles with the domestics, willing Sophy, Mary Anne—the fiery Carolina fighting with the lodgers, and being sent off to prison—the odious Miss Wozenham, an opposition lodging-house keeper—the adoption of poor little Jemmy, under the joint guardianship of her eccentric but good-hearted lodger, Major Jackman, his education at home, and then his being sent off to a boarding-school, are inimitably sketched.

Thackeray died on Christmas-eve, 1863. In the February number of the "Cornhill Magazine," for the ensuing year, Dickens wrote a most beautiful and touching "In Memoriam;" which shows in what estimation he was held by his surviving friend:

"We had our differences of opinion. I thought that he too much feigned a want of earnestness, and that he made a pretense of undervaluing his art, which was not good for the art that he held in trust. But when we fell upon these topics, it was never very gravely, and I have a lively image of him in my mind, twisting both his hands in his hair, and stamping about, laughing, to make an end of the discussion. When we were associated in remembrance of the late Mr. Douglas Jerrold, he delivered a public lecture in London, in the course of which he read his very last contribution to 'Punch,' describing the grown-up cares of a poor family of young children. No one hearing him could have doubted his natural gentleness, or his thoroughly unaffected manly sympathy with the weak and lowly. He read the paper most pathetically, and with a simplicity of tenderness that certainly moved one of his audience to tears. This was presently after his standing for Oxford, from which place he had dispatched his agent to me, with a droll note (to which he afterwards added a verbal postcript), urging me to 'come down and make a speech, and tell them who he was, for he doubted whether more than two of the electors had ever heard of him,* and he thought there might be as many as six or eight who had heard of me.' He introduced

---

* This anecdote from "Thackeray; the Humorist and the Man of Letters," by Theodore Taylor, may be fittingly appended:

"Pray, what can I do to serve you, sir?" inquired the vice-chancellor.—"My name is Thackeray."—"So I see by this card."—"I seek permission to lecture within the precincts."—"Ah! you are a lecturer; what subjects do you undertake, religious or political?"—"Neither; I am a literary man."—"Have you written any thing?"—"Yes; I am the author of 'Vanity Fair.'"—"I presume a Dissenter; has that any thing to do with John Bunyan's book?"—"Not exactly; I have also written 'Pendennis.'"—"Never heard of these works; but no doubt they are proper books."—"I have also contributed to 'Punch.'"—"'Punch!' I have heard of that; is it not a ribald publication?"

the lecture just mentioned with a reference to his late electioneering failure, which was full of good sense, good spirits, and good humor. He had a particular delight in boys, and an excellent way with them. I remember his once asking me, with a fantastic gravity, when he had been to Eton, where my eldest son then was, whether I felt as he did in regard of never seeing a boy without wanting instantly to give him a sovereign? I thought of this when I looked down into his grave, after he was laid there, for I looked down into it over the shoulder of a boy to whom he had been kind."

Frequently, in the numbers of "Household Words," and in "All the Year Round," has Mr. Dickens given us an anecdote, a biographical scrap concerning himself, or an article which could only be considered as "personal;" and no future biographer of the great man can tell the complete story of his life without having recourse to the pages of these magazines.

The anecdotes we have already given of Dickens's ravens show his fondness for animals. Mr. Collam, Secretary of the Society for the Prevention of Cruelty to Animals, now kindly directs our attention to the great novelist's admirable paper in "All the Year Round,"* entitled "Pincher Astray: an account of the Home for Lost and Starving Dogs," at Holloway. The paper records the adventures of a favorite dog, Pincher:

"He was not handsome—at least, in the common acceptation of the term. * * * He was a morose beast, and of most uncertain temper. * * * He was the terror of the trades-people: he loathed the butcher; he had a deadly hatred for the fishmonger's boy; and when I complained to the post-office of the non-receipt in due course of a letter from my aunt's legal adviser, advising me to repair at once to the old lady's death-bed (owing to which non-receipt I was cut out of my aunt's will), I was answered that 'the savage character of my dog—a circumstance with which the department could not interfere—prevented the letter-carrier from the due performance of his functions after nightfall.' Still I love him! What though my trowser-ends were frayed into hanging strips by his teeth; what though my slippers are a mass of chewed pulp; what though he has towzled all the corners of the manuscript of my work on Logarithms—shall I reproach him now that he is lost to me? Never!"

Pincher strayed away—was lost. Application was made at the "Home," which afforded Mr. Dickens an opportunity to describe that in-

---

* January 30, 1864.

stitution, but he was not there. After some days he returned "with a ruffled coat, a torn ear, a fierceness of eye which bespoke recent trouble. I afterwards learned that he had been a principal in a combat held in the adjoining parish, where he acquitted himself with a certain amount of honor, and was pinning his adversary, when a rustic person from a farm broke in upon the ring, and kicked both the combatants out of it. This ignominy was more than Pincher could bear; he flung himself upon the rustic's leg, and brought him to the ground; then fled, and remained hidden in a wood until hunger compelled him to come home. We have interchanged no communication since, but regard each other with sulky dignity. I perceive that he intends to remain obdurate until I make the first advances."

Early in the new year Mr. Dickens received intelligence of the death of his son, Walter Landor Dickens, in the Officers' Hospital at Calcutta. He was a lieutenant of the 26th Native Infantry Regiment, and had been doing duty with the 42d Highlanders. His decease occurred on the last day of the old year.

During this spring* he was requested by the Working-men's Shakspeare Memorial Committee to take the chief direction in planting the "Shakspeare Oak" on Primrose Hill. Mr. F. G. Tomlins, a well-known *littérateur*, and at one time editor of the "Leader" newspaper, wrote to him, stating the working-men's wishes, and Mr. Dickens at once replied: "I am truly honored by the feeling of the working-men towards me, as expressed in your note, and would far rather take part in their interesting proceedings than in any other ceremonial held on that day.

"But I am not free. The request, unfortunately, comes too late. I have declined several public invitations on the ground that I had resolved to take part in none, and had bound myself to a few personal friends for a quiet, private remembrance of the occasion. From this conclusion I can not now depart. Do me the kindness to assure the delegates, with whom you are in communication, of my cordial sympathy and respect."

CHAPTER XXVII.

"OUR MUTUAL FRIEND." — "DOCTOR MARIGOLD'S PRESCRIPTIONS." — "MUGBY JUNCTION."

DICKENS was a guest at the Anniversary Banquet at the Royal Academy, on 1st May,

---
* Wednesday, 12th April, 1864.

1864; and Mr. John Forster, responding to the toast, "The Interests of Literature," gracefully remarked: "In fiction, I see not only the great master of character and humor (Mr. Dickens) who has held sway over both now for more than a quarter of a century, and this very day starts after new laurels with as much vigor and freshness as when he first began the race."

"Our Mutual Friend" was the work alluded to by Mr. Forster, and Number I. was published on the 1st of May, by Messrs. Chapman & Hall, with illustrations by Mr. Marcus Stone.

The plot is most ingeniously constructed, and each character an elaborate and highly executed portrait, although, perhaps, occasionally verging on caricature.

Miss Jenny Wren, the entertaining Doll's dressmaker; her drunken father, "Fascination" Fledgeby; Riah, the patient and kind-hearted Jew; Silas Wegg, the wooden-legged individual, a parasite and selfish impostor, "literary man" to Boffin, employed at the rate of twopence-halfpenny an hour to read and expound the "Decline and Fall of the Rooshian Empire," otherwise "Roman Empire;" John Harman; Lizzie Hexam; Venus, the anatomical artist; Bradley Headstone; Mr. and Mrs. Boffin; and Bella Wilfer, daughter of the Cherub; are the best-remembered characters in the book. The story is somewhat improbable, and contains many scenes of horror and crime. Taken as a specimen of literary workmanship, it is his best production since "David Copperfield," but it is not popular with readers.

Mr. Crabb Robinson has preserved in his Diary some playful lines by Southey; but his editor has omitted to add a circumstance which would have increased their interest. They were written in the album of Mrs. S. C. Hall, and the opposite page contained the autographs of Joseph Bonaparte and Daniel O'Connell, a circumstance which suggested what the Laureate wrote:

"Birds of a feather flock together,
But *vide* the opposite page;
And thence you may gather I'm not of a feather
With some of the birds in this cage."
ROBERT SOUTHEY, 22d *October*, 1836.

Some years afterwards, Charles Dickens, good-humoredly referring to Southey's change of opinion, wrote in the album, immediately under Southey's lines, the following:

. "Now, if I don't make
The completest mistake
That ever put man in a rage,
This bird of two weathers
Has moulted his feathers,
And left them in some other cage."—Boz.

When these last lines first appeared in the

"Art Journal," a friend of Southey's, resenting Boz's remark, retaliated by "good-humoredly referring" to the change of style between "Pickwick" and "Our Mutual Friend," and wrote in the margin of the periodical:

"Put his *first* work and *last* work together,
And learn from the groans of all men,
That if he's not alter'd his feather,
He's certainly alter'd his pen."

"Our Mutual Friend" was dramatized as "The Golden Dustman," and was acted on June 16th, 1866, with great ability, at the Sadler's Wells, and afterwards at Astley's and the Britannia Theatres.

Dickens, on the 11th of May, 1864, presided at the Adelphi Theatre, at a public meeting for the purpose of founding the Shakspeare Foundation Schools, in connection with the Royal Dramatic College. On this occasion he made, as usual, an admirable speech, and a large sum of money was collected.

During the summer of this year, and while on a trip to Paris, Mr. Dickens met with a sunstroke, which greatly alarmed his friends. For many hours he was in a state of complete insensibility, but at length recovered, and in due course returned home.

The interest taken in "Mrs. Lirriper and her Lodgings," the preceding Christmas, induced Dickens to give a sequel to the old lady's experiences. Accordingly, in the Christmas of 1864, we had "Mrs. Lirriper's Legacy." This narrated the death, in France, of Mr. Edson, the father of Jemmy; the journey of Mrs. Lirriper, the Major, and Master Jem, to the deathbed of the repentant man; their adventures going and returning; the revelations of the extraordinary conduct of her brother-in-law, Doctor Joshua Lirriper; the vagaries of Mr. Buffle, the collector of the assessed taxes; her meritorious conduct towards him and his family on the night of the fire, and also, when Miss Wozenham was in danger of being sold up, lending her money to pay the execution out, and becoming intimate friends — are all very charmingly and amusingly described.

A little matter occurred in the following March, to which we may just allude in passing. Mr. Dickens had nominated, and Mr. Wilkie Collins seconded, a very intimate friend as a member of the Garrick Club, to which they both belonged. The committee, for some unaccountable reason, blackballed the gentleman; Dickens and Collins, disgusted at this treatment, resigned their membership, and the affair for the moment created some considerable stir in the literary world.

On the 9th May he presided at the annual festival of the News-venders' Benevolent and Provident Association, and delivered another admirable speech.

Ten days afterwards, on the 20th of the same month, he fulfilled a similar post at the second anniversary of the Newspaper Press Fund (being a vice-president of that useful association). His speech was that well-known one in which he gave us his early reporting experiences. In defending the profession he said: "I would venture to remind you, if I delicately may, in the august presence of members of Parliament, how much we, the public, owe to the reporters, if it were only for their skill in the two great sciences of condensation and rejection. Conceive what our sufferings under an Imperial Parliament, however popularly constituted, under however glorious a constitution, would be, if the reporters could not skip!" And it was on this occasion that he exclaimed, in the midst of the warmest applause, "I am not here advocating the case of a mere ordinary client of whom I have little or no knowledge. I hold a brief to-night for my brothers!" Since his death this passage has been often quoted in proof of the love he bore to the literary profession and all connected with it.

We come now to a very sad occurrence, from the effects of which Mr. Dickens never entirely recovered. On the 9th of June he was unfortunate enough to be a passenger in the train that met with the lamentable accident at Staplehurst, in consequence of the plate-layer's negligence. The carriage in which he was sitting toppled over the edge of the precipice, and hung suspended sufficiently long to allow him to escape by scrambling out of the window, uninjured in body, and without even a bruise, but his nerves receiving a shock from which he often afterwards complained. The News-venders' Benevolent and Provident Institution, at a special meeting, a few days after, passed a resolution congratulating him on his miraculous and providential escape, and concluded by expressing "their sincere hope that a life so publicly and privately valuable may be spared for many, many years, further to adorn English literature with imperishable works, and to grace with apt eloquence, and promote by strenuous practical example and advocacy efforts made to ameliorate distress and provide for the sad contingencies of sickness and old age."

Dickens always considered the regular contributors to "Household Words" and to "All the Year Round" as connected with him in a manner much more closely than as ordinary professional or purely business connections. "My brothers" was his favorite phrase; and when Miss Adelaide Anne Procter died he wrote for the beautiful "Legends and Lyrics,"* which her family published as an "In Memoriam" volume, a most touching preface. This passage explains how he came to know the daughter of "Barry Cornwall:"

"In the spring of the year 1853, I observed, as conductor of the weekly journal, 'Household Words,' a short poem among the proffered contributions, very different, as I thought, from the shoal of verses perpetually passing through the office of such a periodical, and possessing much more merit. Its authoress was quite unknown to me. She was one Miss Mary Berwick, whom I had never heard of; and she was to be addressed by letter, if addressed at all, at a circulating library in the western district of London. Through this channel Miss Berwick was informed that her poem was accepted, and was invited to send another. She complied, and became a regular and frequent contributor. Many letters passed between the journal and Miss Berwick, but Miss Berwick herself was never seen. How we came gradually to establish, at the office of 'Household Words,' that we knew all about Miss Berwick, I have never discovered. But we settled somehow, to our complete satisfaction, that she was governess in a family; that she went to Italy in that capacity, and returned; and that she had long been in the same family. We really knew nothing whatever of her, except that she was remarkably business-like, punctual, self-reliant, and reliable: so I suppose we insensibly invented the rest. For myself, my mother was not a more real personage to me than Miss Berwick the governess became. This went on until December, 1854, when the Christmas number, entitled 'The Seven Poor Travellers,' was sent to press. Happening to be going to dine that day with an old and dear friend, distinguished in literature as Barry Cornwall, I took with me an early proof of that number, and remarked, as I laid it on the drawing-room table, that it contained a very pretty poem, written by a certain Miss Berwick. Next day brought me the disclosure that I had so spoken of the poem to the mother of its writer, in its writer's presence; that I had no such correspondent in existence as Miss Berwick; that the name had been assumed by Barry Cornwall's eldest daughter, Miss Adelaide Anne Procter."

And, after describing her cheerfulness, her modesty, her conviction that life "must not be dreamed away," her unceasing efforts to do good, he thus describes the final ending. She had then lain an invalid upon her bed through fifteen months: "In all that time her old cheerfulness never quitted her. In all that time not an impatient or querulous minute can be remembered. At length, at midnight on the 2d of February, 1864, she turned down a leaf of a little book she was reading, and shut it up. The ministering hand that had copied the verses into the tiny album was soon round her neck, and she quietly asked, as the clock was on the stroke of one: 'Do you think I am dying, mamma?' —'I think you are very, very ill to-night, my dear.'—'Send for my sister. My feet are so cold. Lift me up!' Her sister entering as they raised her, she said: 'It has come at last!' And with a bright and happy smile, looked upward, and departed."

We are now approaching the last of those Christmas numbers which for so many years have formed a friendly tie between author and reader at the festive season. "Doctor Marigold's Prescriptions" was the number for Christmas, 1865. It gave the history of an itinerant "Cheap Jack," named "Doctor," in remembrance of a kind-hearted medical man who officiated at his birth, and who would only accept a tea-tray in payment for his services. The "Doctor's" peculiar talents in his line of business, and the happy contrast to the political Cheap Jack, making rash promises never intended to be kept; the giant Pickleson, otherwise Rinaldo di Velasco, with his small head, weak eyes, and weak knees; his master, Mr. Mim, the proprietor of the caravan; the death of little Sophy in her father's arms, while he convulses his rustic audience with his witticisms and funny speeches; the suicide of his wife; the peculiarities of his old horse; and the intelligent dog, who "taught himself out of his own head to growl at any person in the crowd that bid as low as sixpence;" the purchase of the poor little deaf and dumb girl for a pair of braces; his kindness to her, then sending her to an institution to be educated; her subsequent marriage with one similarly afflicted as herself; their coming home, after a long absence, with their little girl; and Marigold's intense excitement in finding the child can speak, is all a delightful reality, and thoroughly true to nature.

Dickens was a guest at the Mansion House, on January 16th following, on the occasion of a magnificent banquet. He proposed the "Health of the Lady Mayoress." The next month we find him taking the chair (for the second time) at the annual dinner of the Dramatic, Equestrian, and Musical Fund at Willis's rooms.*

The following month Dickens took a promi-

---

* It was published by Messrs. Bell & Daldy as a Christmas gift-book.

* February 14, 1866.

nent part in another public meeting—the annual festival of the Royal General Theatrical Fund. It came off on March 28th, and Sir Benjamin Phillips, the Lord Mayor, in replying to his "health"—which our author had proposed—told this interesting anecdote: "My acquaintance with Mr. Dickens dates from my boyhood. I recollect being in Hamburg, some thirty years ago, upon a commercial errand, when my mind and time were engaged in those pursuits, and, meeting with a gentleman with whom I had some very large transactions, he invited me to breakfast with him the following morning. I went to him, we passed a pleasant hour, and after he rose from his table he looked at his watch and said, 'Let us take a walk.' 'Well,' I said, 'I have no objection to that,' and we walked together. He seemed very restless. We went to a *café* and read a newspaper, and I could get him to do any thing but attend to business. At last out he took his watch and said:

"'My dear friend, you must excuse me, this is the day on which the fifth number of a work written by one of your countrymen, and called "Boz," comes to Hamburg, and until I get that number and read it I can neither talk of business nor any thing else.'

"I take shame to myself," continued the Lord Mayor on this occasion, "that I at that moment should have been in utter ignorance of the brilliant talent of my illustrious friend, of whom I can say, as was said by another distinguished poet, that the price of his literary labors is immortality, and that posterity will generously and proudly pay it. * * * I never contemplated in my philosophy that I should have the honor of what Mr. Dickens has been pleased to call a personal friendship with the man whom, I do not hesitate to say, any crowned head in Europe would be proud to shake by the hand and call by the name—the man who has added, in this generation, honor and dignity to his profession—who has penetrated and dug from the hearts of men their virtues and their qualities, and to whom the whole world owes a deep and a lasting debt of gratitude; and I unhesitatingly say, and say most proudly, that it is to me, representing, as I do, the largest commercial city in the world—that I consider it to be a great honor to be permitted, in the name of humanity, to offer my grateful and graceful tribute to Mr. Charles Dickens."

The members of the Metropolitan Rowing-clubs, dining together at the London Tavern, on the 7th May following, Dickens, as President of the Nautilus Rowing-club (of which his eldest son was captain), occupied the chair: his speech on this occasion was full of humor.

The last number but one of the old familiar Christmas Numbers was now at hand. "Mugby Junction" was the title of that issued in December, 1866, and it contained a larger amount of writing by Dickens than usual. "Barbox Brothers and Co.," "The Boy at Mugby," and "The Signalman," were his contributions.

The description of the Mugby Junction Station at three in the morning, in tempestuous weather; the arrival of the express train, the guard "glistening with drops of wet, and looking at the tearful face of his watch by the light of his lantern;" the alighting of Barbox Brothers; the appearance of "Lamps," the velveteen individual; his daughter Phœbe, who kept a school; the episode of Polly going astray, and being found by Barbox Brothers; and the relating of Barbox Brothers' past life and adventures, are told in a manner the reader will not easily forget.

"The Boy at Mugby" was intended to show the abominable system of our railway refreshment rooms, with their stale pastry, saw-dust sandwiches, scalding tea and coffee, and unpalatable butter-scotch, in comparison with the excellent arrangements for the comfort and accommodation of railway travellers in France.

As some indication of the sale of these "Christmas Numbers," we may state that the sale of "Mugby Junction" exceeded a quarter of a million copies.

During the first three months of the year 1867 he gave readings at St. James's Hall to crowded audiences, having in the previous April, May, and June (1866) appeared at Manchester, Greenwich, the Crystal Palace, St. James's Hall, and other places, delighting and amusing many thousands of people.

On the 5th of June we find him presiding at the ninth anniversary festival of the Railway Benevolent Society, at Willis's Rooms; and it was in his speech on this occasion that he gave the amusing story of "The Ten Suitors."

In May his old and dear friend, Clarkson Stanfield, the Royal Academician, died, and the reader may remember the beautiful and touching obituary notice which Dickens penned on the occasion—the affectionate appreciation of the delicate shades of the great maritime artist's character which that notice evinced, and the noble peroration with which it closed. A friend of the late illustrious author, to whom we are already indebted for some interesting facts, remarks: "The recent earnest wish displayed by the Queen to confer upon Dickens some title of honor, and the womanly refinement shown by Her Majesty in seeking to make that honor one which he could accept without derogating from his social principles, gives his parting words on Stanfield a not unkindly significance. It was after enumerating the artist's many claims to public distinction, after specifying several of his works by name, and after pointing to the recognition he would have received had he belonged to a foreign state, that Dickens said: 'It is superfluous to add that he died Mr. Stanfield— he was an Englishman.'"

On the 17th September following, he took the chair at a public meeting of the Printers' Readers. A corrector of the press, and at that time a member of the "Association," who was present with the other working-men, has forwarded to us this account of the meeting. Coming from one of the men themselves, it is of interest, as showing their appreciation of that respect and sympathy which Charles Dickens ever expressed for honest and intelligent working-men:

"I well remember, on the evening when Dickens so readily consented to preside at a meeting of the London Association of Correctors of the Press, following the immortal novelist up the steps of the Salisbury Hotel, Fleet Street, where the meeting was to be held. The great master, on that occasion, met the assemblage of literary drudges with the open-hearted frankness of a brother. As he threw aside his large light cloak, he shook hands with all who sought that honor with the utmost warmth. Even now I fancy I can feel the firm grip, and see his cheery smile. He was dressed with the greatest care and elegance, as if for an evening party or state ball. His florid complexion, dark glittering eye, and grizzled beard, were very striking; but above all, the loftiness of his massive brow—denoting 'the mighty brain within'—inspired the beholder with reverence. In his speech he expressed the warmest friendship for the intelligent body of men before him, to whom he said, 'he was indebted for many kindly hints, and judicious corrections and queries in his proofs, which in the hurry of business had escaped his notice while preparing "copy," or revising sheets for press.' He said that he had other engagements for that evening, but had at once put them aside when he had been invited to spend an hour with the *practical* correctors of the Press, for the advancement of their interests."

CHAPTER XXVIII.

SECOND VISIT TO AMERICA.—PEDESTRIAN TASTES.

PRESSING invitations from American friends, and the desire to carry out a long-nursed project, induced Mr. Dickens early in the year to make preparations for a visit to the United States in the autumn. The fact soon became known to the American journalists, and from that time until he landed, paragraphs, poems of welcome, and scraps of so-called intelligence —scraps which surprised even Mr. Dickens himself—were continually appearing in the papers there. The "New York Tribune" said: "Charles Dickens is coming to the United States to give a series of readings in the principal cities of the republic. The announcement will be received with pleasure throughout the country. Our people do, indeed, remember the 'American Notes,' and the satirical chapters in 'Martin Chuzzlewit,' and are no doubt of opinion that, as a matter of taste, Mr. Dickens might well have been more gracious. But, on the other hand, our people like free speech and appreciate frankness—not forgetting that truth should be the North Star of authorship; and there is a good deal of truth in what Mr. Dickens said about us on returning from his first visit to this country." In England, the great novelist's friends arranged for a Farewell Banquet on the most sumptuous scale. It took place on Saturday evening, November 2d, at the Freemasons' Tavern. The new hall was specially decorated for the occasion, the panels being adorned with laurel leaves, and each inscribed with the name of one of Dickens's works in splendid letters of gold. The company numbered between four hundred and five hundred gentlemen, including nearly all the eminent men in art, literature, science, law, and medicine.

Lord Lytton presided, and in the course of a magnificent eulogium upon the illustrious novelist, said: "We are about to intrust our honored countryman to the hospitality of those kindred shores in which his writings are as much household words as they are in the homes of England.

"If I may speak as a politician, I should say that no time for his visit could be more happily chosen. For our American kinsfolk have conceived, rightly or wrongly, that they have some recent cause of complaint against ourselves, and out of all England we could not have selected an envoy—speaking not on behalf of our Government, but of our people—more calculated to allay irritation and propitiate good-will.

* * * * *

"How many hours in which pain and sickness have changed into cheerfulness and mirth beneath the wand of that enchanter! How many a hardy combatant, beaten down in the battle of life—and nowhere on this earth is the battle of life sharper than in the commonwealth of America — has taken new hope, and new courage, and new force from the manly lessons of that unobtrusive teacher."

He concluded by proposing "A prosperous voyage, health, and long life to our illustrious guest and countryman, Charles Dickens;" and, if we remember the reports given of the banquet rightly, the company rose as one man to do honor to the toast, and drank it with such expressions of enthusiasm and good-will as are rarely to be seen in any public assembly. Again and again the cheers burst forth, and it was some minutes before silence was restored.

Mr. Dickens replied in a speech such as no one else could have delivered, and towards its conclusion he said: "The story of my going to America is very easily and briefly told. Since I was there before a vast and entirely new generation has arisen in the United States. Since that time, too, most of the best known of my books have been written and published. The new generation and the books have come together and have kept together, until at length numbers of those who have so widely and constantly read me, naturally desiring a little variety in the relations between us, have expressed a strong wish that I should read myself. This wish, at first conveyed to me through public as well as through business channels, has gradually become enforced by an immense accumulation of letters from private individuals and associations of individuals, all expressing in the same hearty, homely, cordial, unaffected way a kind of personal affection for me, which I am sure you will agree with me that it would be downright insensibility on my part not to prize. Little by little this pressure has become so great that, although, as Charles Lamb says, 'My household gods strike a terribly deep root,' I have driven them from their places, and this day week, at this hour, shall be upon the sea. You will readily conceive that I am inspired besides by a natural desire to see for myself the astonishing progress of a quarter of a century over there—to grasp the hands of many faithful friends whom I left there—to see the faces of a multitude of new friends upon whom I have never looked — and, though last, not least, to use my best endeavors to lay down a third cable of intercommunication and alliance between the Old World and the New.

"Twelve years ago, when, Heaven knows, I little thought I should ever be bound upon the voyage which now lies before me, I wrote in that form of my writings which obtains by far the most extensive circulation, these words about the American nation: 'I know full well that whatever little motes my beamy eyes may have descried in theirs, that they are a kind, large-hearted, generous, and great people.' In that faith I am going to see them again. In that faith I shall, please God, return from them in the spring, in that same faith to live and to die. My lords, ladies, and gentlemen, I told you in the beginning that I could not thank you enough, and Heaven knows I have most thoroughly kept my word. If I may quote one other short sentence from myself, let it imply all that I have left unsaid and yet deeply feel; let it, putting a girdle round the earth, comprehend both sides of the Atlantic at once in this moment. As Tiny Tim observed, 'God bless us, every one.'"

The great novelist left London on the following Friday for Liverpool, being accompanied to the station by a host of friends desirous of bidding him "God speed" and *au revoir*. The directors of the London and North-western Company paid Mr. Dickens and party the compliment of placing at their disposal one of the Royal saloon carriages, the appearance of which excited great interest at the various stations at which the train stopped. On Saturday morning Mr. Dickens was on board the Cunard mail-steamer "Cuba," commanded by Capt. Stone. A second officer's cabin was set aside for his exclusive use, and every thing done that could insure his personal comfort. He was accompanied by his machinist, Mr. Kelly, and a manservant; and—like a true showman—carried with him the arrangements of his own platform, with the gas apparatus required for his readings.

On Friday, the 23d of the same month, a telegram, "Safe and well," was received in London, announcing his arrival at Boston. He arrived there on the 19th, and was received with acclamations. Mr. Dolby, his agent, who preceded him, had disposed of an immense number of tickets. The first reading took place on December 2d, at Tremont Temple. After a few readings in Boston, he proceeded to New York, Washington, and Philadelphia, and read to immense audiences, being everywhere received with the greatest enthusiasm.

One of the papers* there said: "No literary man except Thackeray ever had such a welcome from Philadelphia as Charles Dickens received last night at Concert Hall. The selling of the tickets two weeks ago almost amounted to a disturbance of the peace. Five hundred people in line, standing from midnight till noon, poorly represented the general desire to hear the great novelist on his first night. Everywhere that I looked in the crowded hall I saw some

---

* "New York Tribune," 14th January, 1868.

one not unknown to fame—some one representing either the intelligence or the beauty, the wealth or the fashion of Philadelphia. It was an audience which, in the words of Sergeant Buzfuz, I might declare an enlightened, a high-minded, a right-feeling, a dispassionate, a conscientious, a sympathizing, a contemplative, and a poetical jury, to judge Charles Dickens without fear or favor. The novelist stepped upon the stage, his book in his hand, his bouquet in his coat; but I will not describe to readers the face and form many of them know so well. Mr. Dickens was received coldly. Here was an Englishman who had pulled us to pieces and tweaked the national nose by writing 'Martin Chuzzlewit' and 'American Notes.' Philadelphia held out as long as she could. The first smile came in when Bob Cratchit warmed himself with a candle, but before Scrooge had got through with the first ghost the laughter was universal and uproarious. The Christmas dinner of the Cratchits was a tremendous success, as was Scrooge's Niece by marriage. There was a young lady in white fur and blue ribbons, name unknown to the writer, upon whose sympathies Mr. Dickens played as if she had been a piano. A deaf man could have followed his story by looking at her face. The goose convulsed her. The pudding threw her into hysterics; and when the story came to the sad death of Tiny Tim, 'my little, little child,' tears were streaming down her cheeks. This young lady was as good as Mr. Dickens, and all the more attractive because she couldn't help it. Then, as a joke began to be dimly foreseen, it was great to see the faint smile dawning on long lines of faces, growing brighter and brighter till it passed from sight to sound, and thundered to the roof in vast and inextinguishable laughter."

During his visit to America, the great men of the land travelled from far and near to be present at the readings; the poet Longfellow went three nights in succession, and he afterwards declared to a friend that they were "the most delightful evenings of his life."

On Saturday, the 18th April, he was entertained at a farewell dinner at Delmonico's Hotel, New York. Two hundred gentlemen sat down to it, and Mr. Horace Greeley presided. Dickens was somewhat indisposed; but in reply to the toast of his health, he gave this interesting experience of his second visit to America: "It has been said in your newspapers that for months past I have been collecting materials for and hammering away at a new book on America. This has much astonished me, seeing that all that time it has been perfectly well known to my publishers, on both sides of the Atlantic, that I positively declared that no consideration on earth should induce me to write one. But what I have intended, what I have resolved upon (and this is the confidence I seek to place in you), is, on my return to England, in my own person, to bear, for the behoof of my countrymen, such testimony to the gigantic changes in this country as I have hinted at to-night. Also, to record that, wherever I have been, in the smallest places equally with the largest, I have been received with unsurpassable politeness, delicacy, sweet temper, hospitality, consideration, and with unsurpassable respect for the privacy daily enforced upon me by the nature of my avocation here, and the state of my health. This testimony, so long as I live, and so long as my descendants have any legal right in my books, I shall cause to be republished as an appendix to every copy of those two books of mine in which I have referred to America. And this I will do and cause to be done, not in mere love and thankfulness, but because I regard it as an act of plain justice and honor."

The time for Mr. Dickens's departure was now close at hand. His last reading was given at Steinway Hall on the ensuing Monday evening. The task finished, he was about to retire, but a tremendous burst of applause stopped him. He knew what his audience wanted—a few words—a parting greeting before saying good-bye. Their illustrious visitor did not disappoint them: "The shadow of one word has impended over me this evening," said Mr. Dickens, "and the time has come at length when the shadow must fall. It is but a very short one, but the weight of such things is not measured by their length, and two much shorter words express the round of our human existence. When I was reading 'David Copperfield,' a few evenings since, I felt there was more than usual significance in the words of Peggotty, 'My future life lies over the sea.' * * * The relations which have been set up between us must now be broken forever. Be assured, however, that you will not pass from my mind. I shall often realize you as I see you now, equally by my winter fire and in the green English summer weather. I shall never recall you as a mere public audience, but rather as a host of personal friends, and ever with the greatest gratitude, tenderness, and consideration. Ladies and gentlemen, I beg to bid you farewell. God bless you, and God bless the land in which I leave you!"

He left America on the 22d of April, and the following extract from the "New York Tribune" of the day after will convey the best impression of the great respect paid to him, and the general regret expressed at his departure:

"The 'Russia' left her wharf early yesterday morning, and steamed down the bay. When near Staten Island, she rounded to and waited for mails and passengers to arrive by the tug-boat from Jersey City. When the boat came alongside, bearing, among others, M. Paul du Chaillu and Mr. G. W. Childs, the passengers crowded to the side to catch a glimpse of Mr. Dickens, who, leaning over the rail on the quarter-deck of the 'Russia,' smiled and nodded to his friends below. Two hours before he had left the Westminster Hotel, amidst the cheers of those who had gathered to bid him farewell, and, as he entered his carriage, bouquets tossed by fair hands from windows fell at his feet. In order to avoid a crowd of spectators, he left the city from the foot of Spring Street, in the private tug-boat of his friend Mr. Morgan. On board the tug were Mr. James T. Fields, of Boston; Mr. Anthony and Mr. Eytinge, artists; Mr. William Winter, Mr. Osgood, of Ticknor & Fields (this gentleman has accompanied Mr. Dickens throughout his American campaign); Mr. H. D. Palmer and his associate, Mr. H. C. Jarrett, of Niblo's; and Mr. Marshall B. Wild, of Boston. The last-named gentleman was Mr. Dickens's ticket agent. Before he bade his farewell, Mr. Dickens acknowledged the value of his agent's services by making him a present of a check for $150. They steamed down the bay, followed by the police boat, having on board Mr. Thurlow Weed, the Superintendent of Police, and a number of ladies bearing beautiful bouquets for Mr. Dickens. They reached the 'Russia,' and were soon on board. The state-room prepared for Mr. Dickens was laden with flowers.

"A basket, elegantly arranged, was presented to him by Mr. Childs. In the centre, in white carnations, upon a ground of red roses, was the word 'Farewell,' and below, the initials 'C. D.'

"It was a lovely day—a clear blue sky overhead. As he stood resting on the rail, chatting with this friend and writing an autograph for that one, the genial face all aglow with delight, it was seemingly hard to say the word 'Farewell,' yet the tug-boat screamed the note of warning, and those who must return to the city went down the side.

"All had left save Mr. Fields. 'Boz' held the hand of the publisher within his own. There was an unmistakable look on both faces. The lame foot came down from the rail, and the friends were locked in each other's arms.

"Mr. Fields then hastened down the side, not daring to look behind. The lines were 'cast off.'

"A cheer was given for Mr. Dolby, when Mr. Dickens patted him approvingly upon the shoulder, saying, 'Good boy.'

"Another cheer for Mr. Dickens, and the tug steamed away.

"'Good-bye, "Boz!"'

"'Good-bye!' from Mr. Fields, who stood the central figure of a group of three, Messrs. Du Chaillu and Childs upon each side.

"Then 'Boz' put his hat upon his cane and waved it, and the answer came, 'Good-bye!' and 'God bless you, every one!'"

After a pleasant homeward voyage, he arrived at Liverpool on 1st May, 1868.

During his stay, he was besieged to such an extent with applications for his autograph that he was obliged to have a printed form in reply:

"*To comply with your modest request would not be reasonably possible.*"

To envelop, direct, and post these replies, the services of three secretaries were required.

Applications of another kind, however, were personally attended to. Thus it was told there that a lady of Charleston, a great admirer of Mr. Dickens's writings, but unfortunately paralyzed in her limbs from an accident, so that she could not walk, wrote to ask if the doors of the "Temple" could be opened to her earlier than the usual hour, that she might be lifted into the hall unobserved. Mr. Dickens immediately acknowledged the note, gave the requisite order for the lady's accommodation, and claimed the honor of presenting her, besides, with complimentary tickets of admission.

It is a curious fact that the smallest house which welcomed Mr. Dickens anywhere in America was Rochester, New York, where the reading "netted" only $2500. The largest receipts, on several occasions exceeded $6000.

Mr. Dickens's capabilities as a pedestrian had been discussed in America long before he arrived there, and our transatlantic friends were not satisfied until a "match" had been brought about. This was arranged at Boston, between Mr. Dolby (Mr. Dickens's English agent) and Mr. Osgood (the American publisher). The distance was to be twelve miles, and the contest was to take place on the Mill-dam Road, towards Newton. Mr. Dickens and Mr. Fields (the publisher) were to be umpires, and had to walk the whole twelve miles with their respective men. Immediately the match was made known, the papers teemed with particulars concerning it. "Dickens," one journal said, "was a superb pedestrian, good for thirty miles 'on end' any day." The articles were drawn up by the great author, and subscribed to by all four gentlemen. The public were, however, not made acquainted with the place or the time until after the contest was over. The affair came off on the following Saturday, at twelve o'clock. The pedestrians were all, it is said, "appropriately costumed, and they went at a tremendous pace. The first six miles were accomplished in one hour and twenty-three minutes, and the return six miles were finished by Mr. Osgood (the American) in one hour and twenty-five minutes, he winning the match by exactly seven minutes. An elegant dinner was given by Mr. Dickens at the Parker House, the same evening, to signalize the occasion." This anecdote shows the heartiness with which he entered into any healthy out-door sport he cared to join in, and his gameness and youthful vigor in keeping up with men not more than half his age.

While we are upon the subject of our author's pedestrian tastes, we may mention that, like Dr.

Johnson, Dickens was singularly fond of the old city streets and alleys when emptied of the busy throng that filled them in the day-time. Lord Jeffrey, writing to him once, remarked: "How funny that *besoin* of yours for midnight rambling in city streets; and how curious that Macaulay should have the same taste or fancy! If I thought there was any such inspiration as yours to be caught by the practice, I should expose my poor irritable *trachea*, I think, to a nocturnal pilgrimage, without scruple. But, I fear, I should have my venture for my pains."

The reader may remember our extract from his letter to the Countess of Blessington, where he says—in allusion to his habit of walking at nights while planning out a new novel—"I go wandering about at night into the strangest places, according to my usual propensity at such times, seeking rest and finding none."

A story is told that on one pedestrian occasion he was taken for a "smasher." He had retired to rest at Gad's Hill, but found he could not sleep, when he determined to turn out, dress, and walk up to London—some thirty miles. He reached the suburbs in the gray morning, and applied at an "early" coffee-house for some refreshment, tendering for the same a sovereign, the smallest coin he happened to have about him.

"It's a bad 'un," said the man, biting at it, and trying to twist it in all directions, "and I shall give you in charge." Sure enough the coin did have a suspicious look. Mr. Dickens had carried some substance in his pocket which had oxydized it. Seeing that matters looked awkward, he at once said, "But I am Charles Dickens!"

"Come, that won't do; any man could say he was 'Charles Dickens.' How do I know?" The man had been victimized only the week previously, and at length, at Mr. Dickens's suggestion, it was arranged that they should go to a chemist, to have the coin tested with *aquafortis*. In due course, when the shops opened, a chemist was found, who immediately recognized the great novelist—notwithstanding his dusty appearance—and the coffee-house keeper was satisfactorily convinced that he had not been entertaining a "smasher."

It is pleasant to know that, upon the great novelist's return to England, the farmers and neighbors around Gad's Hill draped their houses with flags to receive him. "He was extremely popular in the place where he lived," says our informant; "he was a man of practical charity at home and abroad, and gave away large sums judiciously every year. Indeed he would get up in the night and go ten miles to aid any one who was suffering."

"No Thoroughfare" was the title of the Christmas number of "All the Year Round," which appeared during Dickens's absence in the Christmas of 1867. It consisted of a sensational story, the joint production of Dickens and Wilkie Collins.

It was dramatized by the authors, and had a most successful run at the Adelphi Theatre for one hundred and fifty-one nights, and was then produced at the Royal Standard by the same company, which consisted of the following distinguished actors and actresses: Messrs. Benjamin Webster, Fechter, Belmore, and Neville; Mesdames Mellon and Billington, and Miss Carlotta Leclercq.

"Holiday Romance" and "George Silverman's Explanation," both by Dickens, and published in "All the Year Round," in the months of January to March, 1868, attracted some slight attention, but did not add very much to his fame as an author.

CHAPTER XXIX.

THE FAREWELL READINGS.—FAILING HEALTH.

The "Farewell Readings," which commenced towards the close of 1868, will be too familiar to most readers to require other than a passing mention of them. The Messrs. Chappell, the well-known music publishers of Bond Street, had contracted with Mr. Dickens for a given number of final readings, to take place in the principal towns of England, Ireland, and Scotland; and the enormous crowds who thronged to hear them showed the unabated interest all classes took in the great novelist and his books.

In the month of November, 1868, a new series of "All the Year Round" appeared, the first series having reached twenty volumes. It was marked by the disappearance of his popular Christmas number, by reason—Mr. Dickens said —that had it been so extensively and regularly and often imitated, that it was in very great danger of becoming tiresome—a statement which was not at all well received by the press, which said, very truly, that to the great body of readers the absence of the Christmas number would be a national disappointment.

Continuing the readings in London and the provinces, Dickens at last reached Liverpool, where it was forthwith resolved to entertain him at a grand banquet. This took place on Saturday evening, the 10th April, 1869, at St. George's Hall, the Mayor presiding. At the time it was spoken of as being one of the most sumptuous gatherings of the kind ever seen in this country. The number of ladies and gentlemen who sat down to dinner was about seven hundred. The invited guests, in addition to the guests of the evening, were Lord Dufferin, M. Alphonse Esquiros, Lord Houghton, A. Trollope, Palgrave Simpson, W. Hepworth Dixon, Andrew Halliday, Joseph Mayer, F.S.A., G. A. Sala, A. Trollope, Jun., and Charles Dickens, Jun. Next to Mr. Dickens, Lord Dufferin made the best speech, and some of his allusions to the good effects which the writings of their guest were destined to exercise over all English-speaking peoples were admirable. Concerning the friendly hint which Lord Houghton gave our author, that, had he sought parliamentary honors, he might have done his country good service, and have been rewarded by titles of honor, this extract from his speech has a biographical significance : " When I first took literature as my profession in England, I calmly resolved within myself that, whether I succeeded or whether I failed, literature should be my sole profession. It appeared to me at that time that it was not so well understood in England as it was in other countries that literature was a dignified profession, by which any man might stand or fall. I made a compact with myself that in my person literature should stand, and by itself, of itself, and for itself ; and there is no consideration on earth which would induce me to break that bargain."

Continuing the "Farewell Readings" with unvaried success, he reached Preston a fortnight after, but became so ill there that he was forbidden by his medical advisers to read again until the following year. A personal friend, who was with him on this journey, thus describes his indisposition. The friend had gone down to Leeds at Mr. Dickens's request:

"After the business of the evening was over we supped together at the Queen's Hotel, and I noticed that he (Dickens) looked jaded and worn, and had to a certain extent lost that marvellous elasticity of spirits which was his great characteristic. He was suffering, too, from an inflammation of the ball of the foot, which had previously occasioned him some annoyance, and the origin and cause of which could never be rightly settled by his medical attendants, although among those whom he had consulted about it were Sir Henry Thompson and Professor Syme.

"He relieved himself of his boot immediately on gaining the room, and while he remained sat with his foot swathed in lotioned bandages; but he was evidently fatigued and depressed, and retired early. The next morning at breakfast his ordinary cheerfulness had returned, and he rallied the writer, who was about to visit Sheffield in the rain which was then pouring down, about his probable chances of pleasure, remarking that 'it was just the kind of day in which the loveliness of the locality would be seen to the highest advantage.' On the Thursday in the next week Mr. Dickens was to read at Preston ; but, still feeling ill, had summoned his friend and usual medical attendant, Mr. Frank Beard, of Welbeck Street, to meet him there. On Mr. Beard's arrival he at once saw the gravity of the case, and instantly ordered Mr. Dickens then and there to give up all bodily and mental exertion for the time. In vain it was urged that an enormous number of tickets had been sold for that evening's reading. Mr. Beard would hear of no excuse, but carried off Mr. Dickens with him to London by the five o'clock train.

"The precaution thus seasonably taken seemed to have due effect. Mr. Dickens retired to his residence at Gad's Hill, and, implicitly obeying the orders of his physicians, appeared soon to regain his normal state of physical health and strength. Indeed, a very few weeks afterwards, replying to an inquiry made by a friend as to his condition, he wrote, 'After all that has been said, I feel almost like an impostor ; I am so unconscionably well.' "*

This illness served to bring him under the notice of several bigots and fanatics, who pestered him with tracts, and preached at him. But soon after, in his own periodical and in his own earnest manner, he showed them how distasteful these pertinacious attentions were to him, and how very unnecessary he considered them. It is believed now that these were the first symptoms of the malady which finally carried him off.

The great International University Boat-race between Oxford and Harvard having taken place on the 27th August, the London Rowing-club invited the crews to dinner at the Crystal Palace on the following Monday. Desirous of showing his American friends the love he bore their country, and of expressing his sympathy with a healthy and manly exercise, he at once accepted the invitation to be present, and on the occasion delivered one of his very best speeches, notwithstanding that he was in the doctor's hands at the time.

His health continuing to improve, he was, on the 27th of September, enabled to deliver the annual address at the commencement of the winter session of the Birmingham and Midland

---

* "Observer," June 12th, 1870.

Institute, of which Mr. Dickens was President. This was his longest effort in public speaking, and although somewhat severe and didactic when compared with former speeches, it is an admirable example of his inimitable style. It was delivered—one who was present during the delivery informs us—without note of any kind, except the quotation from Sydney Smith, and without a single pause. Respecting Mr. Dickens's concluding words, when acknowledging the vote of thanks: "My faith in the people governing is, on the whole, infinitesimal; my faith in the People governed is, on the whole, illimitable," considerable discussion arose in the public prints as to the precise meaning the speaker desired to convey. But in the following January (1870), when he attended at the Institution to distribute the prizes and certificates to the most successful students, he gave this explanation:

"When I was here last autumn, I made, in reference to some remarks of your respected member, Mr. Dixon, a short confession of my political faith—or perhaps I should better say, want of faith. It imported that I have very little confidence in the people who govern us—please to observe 'people' there will be with a small 'p'—but that I have great confidence in the People whom they govern—please to observe 'People' there with a large 'P.' This was shortly and elliptically stated, and was with no evil intention, I am absolutely sure, in some quarters inversely explained. Perhaps, as the inventor of a certain extravagant fiction, but one which I do see rather frequently quoted as if there were grains of truth at the bottom of it—a fiction called the 'Circumlocution Office' —and perhaps also as the writer of an idle book or two, whose public opinions are not obscurely stated—perhaps in these respects I do not sufficiently bear in mind Hamlet's caution to speak by the card, lest equivocation should undo me.

"Now I complain of nobody; but simply in order that there may be no mistake as to what I did mean, and as to what I do mean, I will restate my meaning, and I will do so in the words of a great thinker, a great writer, and a great scholar,* whose death, unfortunately for mankind, cut short his 'History of Civilization in England:' 'They may talk as they will about reforms which Government has introduced and improvements to be expected from legislation, but whoever will take a wider and more commanding view of human affairs will soon discover that such hopes are chimerical. They will learn that lawgivers are nearly always the obstructers of society instead of its helpers, and that in the extremely few cases where their measures have turned out well, their success has been owing to the fact that, contrary to their usual custom, they have implicitly obeyed the spirit of their time, and have been—as they always should be—the mere servants of the people, to whose wishes they are bound to give a public and legal sanction.'"

During the past winter Dickens resumed his readings at St. James's Hall, and, to avoid the necessity of frequent journeyings to and from Gad's Hill, he rented for six months the town

NO. 5 HYDE PARK PLACE (1869–'70).

[Mr. Milner Gibson's house, which Dickens rented during the winter months. It was the temporary home where much of his last unfinished work, "Edwin Drood," was written. He only lived a few weeks after his return to Gad's Hill.]

house of his old friend, Mr. Milner Gibson, in Hyde Park Place, which he continued to occupy up to the end of May last. This house in future will have a special interest, from the fact that here, in his bedroom on the first floor, with the roar of Oxford Street beneath him—his studies suffered no interruption from street noises—a large part of his unfinished work, "Edwin Drood," was written.

---

* Henry Thomas Buckle.

We may mention that Mr. Dickens's father-in-law, Mr. George Hogarth, died on the 12th February, in his 87th year. In his earlier days he was Sir Walter Scott's law agent, and was personally acquainted with most of the literary characters of the day. Christopher North, in "Noctes Ambrosianæ," makes mention of him. He was musical critic on the staff of the "Daily News," from the time of its starting until 1866, when failing health compelled him to resign his post.

On the 15th of March, Dickens gave his "Farewell reading" at St. James's Hall. It was his favorite selection—the "Christmas Carol," and "The Trial from Pickwick." Long before the hour appointed the thoroughfare leading to the hall was blocked up, and when the doors were opened every seat was instantly taken, and many thousands of people were unable to obtain admittance. As if to assure his auditors that his powers were undiminished, he read with more than usual spirit and energy, and his voice was clear to the last. At the conclusion, and after the "Trial from Pickwick," in which the speeches of the opposing counsel, and the owlish gravity of the judge, seemed to be delivered and depicted with greater dramatic power than ever, the applause of the audience rang for several minutes through the hall; and when it had subsided, Mr. Dickens, with evidently strong emotion, but in his usual distinct and impressive manner, spoke as follows:

"LADIES AND GENTLEMEN,— It would be worse than idle—for it would be hypocritical and unfeeling—if I were to disguise that I close this episode in my life with feelings of very considerable pain. For some fifteen years, in this hall and in many kindred places, I have had the honor of presenting my own cherished ideas before you for your recognition, and, in closely observing your reception of them, have enjoyed an amount of artistic delight and instruction which, perhaps, is given to few men to know. In this task, and in every other I have ever undertaken, as a faithful servant of the public, always imbued with a sense of duty to them, and always striving to do his best, I have been uniformly cheered by the readiest response, the most generous sympathy, and the most stimulating support. Nevertheless, I have thought it well, at the full flood-tide of your favor, to retire upon those older associations between us which date from much farther back than these, and henceforth to devote myself exclusively to the art that first brought us together. Ladies and gentlemen, in but two short weeks from this time I hope that you may enter, in your own homes, on a new series of readings, at which my assistance will be indispensable;* but from these garish lights I vanish now for evermore, with a heartfelt, grateful, respectful, and affectionate farewell."

The speaker then retired, amidst acclamations of the most enthusiastic description, hats and handkerchiefs being waved in every part of the hall.

Since the illustrious author's decease, this address has acquired a peculiar significance by reason of that almost prophetic line: "From these garish lights I vanish now for evermore."

Shortly after, on April 5, he was with his friends the News-venders, presiding at the annual dinner of their Benevolent and Provident Institution. He was in excellent spirits, and his speech upon the occasion was a most humorous one. Those who were present will remember with what inimitable gravity he told this story:

"I was once present at a social discussion, which originated by chance. The subject was, 'What was the most absorbing and longest-lived passion in the human breast? What was the passion so powerful that it would almost induce the generous to be mean, the careless to be cautious, the guileless to be deeply designing, and the dove to emulate the serpent?' A daily editor of vast experience and great acuteness, who was one of the company, considerably surprised us by saying with the greatest confidence that the passion in question was the passion of getting orders for the play.

"There had recently been a terrible shipwreck, and very few of the surviving sailors had escaped in an open boat. One of these, on making land, came straight to London, and straight to the newspaper office, with his story of how he had seen the ship go down before his eyes. That young man had witnessed the most terrible contention between the powers of fire and water for the destruction of that ship and of every one on board. He had rowed away among the floating, dying, and the sinking dead. He had floated by day, and he had frozen by night, with no shelter and no food, and, as he told this dismal tale, he rolled his haggard eyes about the room. When he had finished, and the tale had been noted down from his lips, he was cheered, and refreshed, and soothed, and asked if any thing could be done for him. Even within him that master-passion was so strong that he immediately replied he should like an order for the play."

"One of his latest acts in the way of busi-

---

* Alluding to the forthcoming serial story of "Edwin Drood."

ness," Mr. Hingston writes to us, "was in relation to Miss Glyn, and her then approaching reading at St. James's Hall, with her departure for Australia. I persuaded Miss Glyn, some five weeks since, to take a trip to Australia, and I drew out a form of agreement. Dickens took great interest in her welfare; the agreement had to be submitted to him. It was sent back with his annotations and suggestions, all of which were eminently practical, and very illustrative of his keen business abilities. He acted as a lawyer would for a client."

Towards the end of the month he again became indisposed. A promise that he had made to dine at the annual dinner of the General Theatrical Fund he found himself unable to keep, and at the last moment he telegraphed that he was too unwell to attend. Two days later he sent a short note to one of his intimates, postponing a little expedition which had been arranged, and stating that the old enemy in his foot was again causing him annoyance.

On 2d May he was better—sufficiently well, indeed, to accept the invitation of his artist friends, and to dine with them at the opening of the Royal Academy.

Mr. Arthur Locker writes: "The last time I saw him was a few weeks since, when I had the pleasure of meeting him at dinner. To all outward appearance he then looked like a man who would live and work until he was fourscore. I was especially struck by the brilliancy and vivacity of his eyes. There seemed as much life and animation in them as in twenty ordinary pair of eyes."

It was at the Academy dinner that he made his last public speech, and his concluding words upon this occasion were a tribute to the memory of his dear friend, Daniel Maclise, then recently deceased: "Since," he said, "I first entered the public lists, a very young man indeed, it has been my constant fortune to number among my nearest and dearest friends members of the Royal Academy who have been its grace and pride. They have so dropped from my side, one by one, that I already begin to feel like the Spanish monk of whom Wilkie tells, who had grown to believe that the only realities around him were the pictures which he loved, and that all the moving life he saw, or ever had seen, was a shadow and a dream.

"For many years I was one of the two most intimate friends and most constant companions of the late Mr. Maclise. Of his genius in his chosen art I will venture to say nothing here, but of his prodigious fertility of mind and wonderful wealth of intellect, I may confidently assert that they would have made him, if he had been so minded, at least as great a writer as he was a painter. The gentlest and most modest of men, the freshest as to his generous appreciation of young aspirants, and the frankest and largest-hearted as to his peers, incapable of a sordid or ignoble thought, gallantly sustaining the true dignity of his vocation, without one grain of self-ambition, wholesomely natural at the last as at the first, 'in wit a man, simplicity a child,' no artist, of whatever denomination, I make bold to say, ever went to his rest leaving a golden memory more pure from dross, or having devoted himself with a truer chivalry to the art goddess whom he worshipped."

CHAPTER XXX.

INTERVIEW WITH THE QUEEN.—LAST ILLNESS.—DEATH.—BURIAL IN WESTMINSTER ABBEY.

ONLY *since* the death of Mr. Dickens is it that the high respect in which Her Majesty has always held the great novelist and his writings has become generally known, but for many years past our Queen has taken the liveliest interest in his literary labors, and has frequently expressed a desire for an interview with him. And here it may not be uninteresting to mention a circumstance in illustration of Her Majesty's regard for her late distinguished subject which came under the writer's personal notice. Six years ago, just before the library of Mr. Thackeray was sold off at Palace Green, Kensington, a catalogue of the books was sent to Her Majesty—in all probability by her request. She desired some memorial of the great man, and preferred to make her own selection by purchase rather than ask the family for any memento by way of gift. There were books with odd drawings from Thackeray's pen and pencil; there were others crammed with MS. notes, but there was one lot thus described in the catalogue:

DICKENS (C.) A CHRISTMAS CAROL, in prose, 1843;
Presentation Copy.
INSCRIBED
" W. M. Thackeray, from Charles Dickens (whom he made very happy once a long way from home)."

Her Majesty expressed the strongest desire to possess this, and sent an *unlimited commission* to buy it. The original published price of the book was 5s. It became Her Majesty's property for £25 10s., and was at once taken to the palace.

The personal interview Her Majesty had long expressed a desire to have with Mr. Dickens took place on the 9th April, 1870, when he received her commands to attend her at Buckingham Palace, and accordingly did so, being introduced by his friend, Mr. Arthur Helps, the clerk of the Privy Council.

The interview was a lengthened one, and most satisfactory to both. In the course of it Her Majesty expressed to him her warm interest in, and admiration of his works; and, on parting, presented him with a copy of her own book, "Our Life in the Highlands," with an autograph inscription, "Victoria R. to Charles Dickens," on the fly-leaf; at the same time making a charmingly modest and graceful remark as to the relative positions occupied in the world of letters by the donor and the recipient of the book.

Soon after his return home, he sent to Her Majesty an edition of his collected works; and when the clerk of the Council recently went to Balmoral, the Queen, knowing the friendship that existed between Mr. Dickens and Mr. Helps, showed the latter where she had placed the gift of the great novelist. This was in her own private library, in order that she might always see the books; and Her Majesty expressed her desire that Mr. Helps should inform the great novelist of this arrangement.*

Since our author's decease the journal with which he was formerly connected has said :

"We were not at liberty at that time to make known that the Queen was then personally occupied with the consideration of some means by which she might, in her public capacity, express her sense of the value of Mr. Dickens's services to his country and to literature. It may now be stated that the Queen was ready to confer any distinction which Mr. Dickens's known views and tastes would permit him to accept, and that after more than one title of honor had been declined, Her Majesty desired that he would, at least, accept a place in her Privy Council."

Three days before this he had attended the levée and been presented to her son H. R. H. the Prince of Wales, introduced by the Earl De Grey and Ripon.

His daughter, Miss Dickens, was presented at court to Her Majesty on the 10th of the following month, introduced by the Countess Russell.

As recently as the 17th of May last, among the names appearing in the "Court Circular"

as having attended the State Ball at Buckingham Palace on that day, were those of Mr. and Miss Dickens.

The fact of Mr. Dickens going more into society than usual during the past spring, and entertaining his friends—always with the utmost hospitality—rather more frequently than was his custom, had been observed by those who knew him. But he continued to complain that he was not well, and when he felt a little of his old robust health returning to him he seemed to desire the recreation of society, the company of friends. Literary composition was a task—not a pleasure, as formerly.

As showing his great fondness for the stage, it may be mentioned that almost the last—if not the very last—occasion on which he appeared in London society, was in connection with an exhibition of amateur theatricals given at the house of Mr. Freake, at South Kensington, only a very few days before his death.

"The Mystery of Edwin Drood," we are told, gave its author more trouble than any of his former works. He complained of this, perhaps with a sad presage of the truth. He had, he thought, told too much of the story in the early numbers, and his thoughts did not flow so freely as of yore.

The personal friend, who has before assisted us with his reminiscences, shall tell the rest :

"Unquestionably he had very much aged in appearance during the two previous years; the thought-graven lines in his face were deeper, the beard and hair were more grizzled, the complexion ruddier, but not so healthy in hue. He walked, too, less and less actively—latterly, indeed, dragging one leg rather wearily behind him. But he maintained the bluff, frank, hearty presence, and the deep cheery voice; his hand given to his friend had all its affectionate grip, and the splendid beauty of the dark eyes remained undimmed to the last.

"How that last came about is now well known. He returned home to Gad's Hill, where, during his absence, some ornamental alterations, which he had previously planned, had been carried out, on Tuesday, the 31st of May. He was not then in good health, and complained that his work fatigued and worried him. On Wednesday, while sitting at dinner with his sister-in-law, Miss Hogarth, a change came over the expression of his face, which alarmed his companion. She proposed to send for medical assistance, but he refused, putting his hand to his face, complaining of toothache, and desiring that the window might be shut. It was shut at once, and he rose to leave the room, but after taking a few steps, he fell heavily on his

---

* Immediately on his return from Balmoral, Mr. Helps wrote to Mr. Dickens, in pursuance of Her Majesty's desire; but the letter that contained so remarkable a tribute to the great novelist could only have reached Gad's Hill while he lay unconscious and dying.

left side, and remained unconscious until his death, which took place at ten minutes past six, on Thursday, June 9, 1870, just twenty-four hours after the attack. Medical assistance had been summoned; Mr. Frank Beard, Mr. Steele, of Strood, and Dr. Russell Reynolds all saw him, but he was beyond the reach of science.

"He died of apoplexy—an effusion of blood on the brain—and an attack of this kind must have been apprehended by Mr. Frank Beard, when he caused such prompt and decisive measures to be taken last year at Preston."

That he died from over-work is now too clear. The day preceding his death had been passed at the desk in literary composition and correspondence, and already three letters written by him on that day have been published.

Only a few weeks before he wrote to a friend: "I have 'placed' your touching poem, 'The God's Acre,' which will appear in the next number." The poem describes a very old man and a very young child in a church-yard on a sunny Sunday; the old man reflecting, the child gathering flowers; and predicts that, as the "old, old fruit has ripened, death will not tarry long." Contrary to probability, it is the little child that dies within a few days, and not the octogenarian. The verses conclude with a reflection that, in the after-light shed upon it by Mr. Dickens's early death, possesses a mournful interest:

"Whom the gods love die early:
Our Father knoweth best,
And it is wrong to murmur
At the high behest.
Sleep gently, blighted blossom;
Sleep, and take thy rest."

When Mr. Helps received the news of Dicken's death he immediately telegraphed the fact to her Majesty at Balmoral, and received the subjoined sympathetic response: "From Colonel Ponsonby to Mr. Helps, Council Office—The Queen commands me to express her deepest regret at the sad news of Charles Dickens's death."

He died on the anniversary of the dreadful Staplehurst railway accident, and the shock his nerves received on that occasion it is believed he never entirely got over.

"The friends in the habit of meeting Mr. Dickens privately recall now the energy with which he depicted that dreadful scene, and how, as the climax of his story came, and its dread interest grew, he would rise from the table and literally act the parts of the various sufferers to whom he lent a helping hand. One of the first surgeons of the day, who was present soon after the Staplehurst occurrence, remarked that 'the worst of these railway accidents was the difficulty of determining the period at which the system could be said to have survived the shock, and that instances were on record of two or three years having gone by before the sufferer knew that he was seriously hurt.'"

As if with a presentiment of what was coming, he completed his will just seven days before he was struck down. After his wishes had been put into legal form by his solicitors, he copied out the entire document in his own handwriting. By a codicil to this document he bequeathed the whole of his interest in "All the Year Round" to his acting editor and eldest son, coupling the bequest with such private instructions as would, he believed, insure the character and merit of the periodical remaining unchanged after he had gone. Mr. John Forster, who had been on intimate terms with Dickens for more than thirty years, and Miss Hogarth, his sister-in-law, "and the best friend I ever had," to use his own words, were his appointed executors.

His affairs had been left in perfect order—in that order which, to the great man throughout life, was law. Concerning the disposition of his remains clear instructions were also left behind. He desired no publicity about his funeral, none of the well-meant assembling of friends when his remains should be committed to the earth. It is understood that he had expressed a wish to lie in his own favorite Rochester, as near as possible to the ruins of the old castle there, and in a spot which he had already pointed out. The burial-ground referred to is adjacent to the walls of the castle, and belongs to the parish of St. Nicholas, Rochester. It has been closed for some time, and for it to be reopened permission of the Secretary of State would have to be obtained.

But immediately following the sad intelligence of his death came the universally expressed desire that his remains should rest in Westminster Abbey — in that Poet's Corner which has been consecrated to the greatest, the wisest, the best of our countrymen. Dean Stanley at once communicated with the family, and in an interview with Mr. Charles Dickens, Jun., begged that the national wish might be complied with. This was on Friday. From that time until Monday evening the matter was under earnest consideration. Mr. Dickens's family took counsel with their father's dearest and oldest friends, and after due deliberation and consultation on the terms of the written instructions they held, asked the Dean of Westminster whether it would be possible to have certain conditions complied with if they consented that the interment should be at Westminster?

The answer was satisfactory, and arrangements were at once made for the funeral to take place in the most private manner possible, on the following day, Tuesday, the 14th June, 1870. A special train, bearing his remains, left Rochester early in the morning. At the Charing Cross station a waiting-room had been set apart for the mourners, and on the arrival of the body, three plain mourning coaches, having none of the feathers or dismal frippery of the undertaker, drew up to receive those personal friends and relatives who were to witness the burial of the great man. In coming to the Abbey, in the first coach were the late Mr. Dickens's children—Mr. Charles Dickens, Jun.; Mr. Harry Dickens, Miss Dickens, Mrs. Charles Collins. In the second coach were Mrs. Austin, his sister; Mrs. Charles Dickens, Jun.; Miss Hogarth, his sister-in-law; Mr. John Forster. In the third coach, Mr. Frank Beard, his medical attendant; Mr. Charles Collins, his son-in-law; Mr. Ouvry, his solicitor; Mr. Wilkie Collins; Mr. Edmund Dickens, his nephew.

Upon reaching the Abbey, the doors were immediately closed and the coaches dismissed. The ceremony was at once proceeded with. The Dean read our solemn burial-service in a manner which showed how strong were his own emotions; and the great organ chimed subdued and low. The solemnity of the scene was indeed striking—the vast place empty, save for the little group of heart-stricken people by an open grave. A plain oak coffin, with a brass plate bearing the inscription :

CHARLES DICKENS,
BORN FEBRUARY 7TH, 1812;
DIED JUNE 9TH, 1870,

a coffin strewed with wreaths and flowers by the female mourners, and then—dust to dust, and ashes to ashes!—such was the funeral of the great man who has gone. There were no cloaks, no crapes, no bands or scarfs—none of that mocking paraphernalia of the professional undertaker which Dickens so strongly objected to. When the subject of his funeral was being discussed, Mr. Ollier told us how strongly the great man had objected to take part in the ceremony which was performed over the grave of Leigh Hunt, in Kensal Green, during the past summer.

"In August last," writes Mr. Ollier, one of the honorary secretaries of the Leigh Hunt Memorial Fund, "I requested Mr. Dickens to inaugurate the monument in Kensal Green Cemetery, and to deliver a short address on the spot—a task which was afterwards excellently performed by Lord Houghton." To this the great novelist replied:

"MY DEAR MR. OLLIER,—I am very sensible of the feeling of the committee towards me, and I receive their invitation (conveyed through you) as a most acceptable mark of their consideration. But I have a very strong objection to speech-making beside graves. I do not expect or wish my feeling in this wise to guide other men; still it is so serious with me, and the idea of ever being the subject of such a ceremony myself is so repugnant to my soul, that I must decline to officiate. Faithfully yours always,
"CHARLES DICKENS.
"EDMUND OLLIER, Esq."

But the most energetic protest against the hideous fineries of the undertaker is to be found in an article entitled "Trading in Death," which appeared in "Household Words" about November, 1852. It is not generally known that this article—which produced much comment at the time—came from his pen.

On Sunday, the 19th June, Dean Stanley preached the funeral sermon in Westminster Abbey. An announcement to this effect had been made in the daily journals, and long before the hour appointed for the service a vast body of people had assembled at the doors. Immediately these were opened every available seat was taken, and many thousands of persons remained in distant parts of the building until the conclusion of the sermon. Among the many distinguished individuals present, the two who attracted most notice were the Poet Laureate and Mr. Thomas Carlyle. Mr. Dickens ever respected the great genius of Tennyson, and the poet has always expressed the highest admiration for the writings of Charles Dickens. It was fitting, therefore, that the surviving author should be present at this last ceremony over the great novelist's remains. The poet was accommodated with a seat inside the sacrarium; Mr. Carlyle sat in the body of the building. The family and relations of Mr. Dickens were in the gallery to the north of Poet's Corner. Dean Stanley was not well; indeed, he had for some days been complaining of severe indisposition, but, in spite of physical weakness, he determined to carry out the duty of the day. He took as his text the verses in the 15th and 16th chapters of St. Luke, which embody the parable of the rich man and Lazarus: "He spoke this parable. There was a certain rich man, which was clothed in purple and fine linen, and fared sumptuously every day: and there was a certain beggar named Lazarus, which was laid at his gate, full of sores, and desiring to be fed with the crumbs which fell from the rich man's table: moreover the dogs came and licked his sores."

The eloquent and impressive sermon which followed was listened to with breathless attention, and many a cheek was moist with tears during its progress. There was in the whole scene something unusually impressive — the enormous congregation covering every inch of ground in choir, and sacrarium, and transepts; the unbroken silence, or broken only by sobs; the careworn, delicate face and attenuated form of the preacher, struggling against overwhelming bodily weakness to reach the congregation that hung on his lips.

After commenting at some length upon the parables of the New Testament, and especially upon the one selected for their consideration that morning, the preacher thus applied the text:

"It is said to have been the distinguishing glory of a famous Spanish saint that she was the advocate of the absent. That is precisely the advocacy of this divine parable, and of those modern parables which most represent its spirit —the advocacy, namely, of the poor, the absent, the neglected, of the weaker side, whom, not seeing, we are tempted to forget. It was the part of him whom we have lost to make the rich man, faring sumptuously every day, not fail to see the presence of the poor man at his gate. The suffering inmates of our work-houses—the neglected children in the dens and caves of this great city—the starved, ill-used boys in remote schools, far from the observation of men—these all felt a new ray of sunshine poured into their dark prisons, and a new interest awakened in their forlorn and desolate lot, because an unknown friend had pleaded their cause with a voice that rang through the palaces of the great as well as through the cottages of the poor. In his pages, with gaunt figures and hollow voices, they were made to stand and speak before those who had before hardly dreamed of their existence. But was it mere compassion which this created? The same master-hand which drew the sorrows of the English poor drew also the picture of the unselfishness, the kindness, the courageous patience, and the tender thoughtfulness that lie concealed under many a coarse exterior, and are to be found in many a degraded home. When the little work-house boy wins his way, pure and undefiled, through the mass of wickedness around him—when the little orphan girl, who brings thoughts of heaven into the hearts of all around her, is as the very gift of God to the old man who sheltered her life—these are scenes which no human being can read without being the better for it. He labored to teach us that there is even in the worst of mankind a soul of goodness—a soul worth revealing, worth reclaiming, worth regenerating. He labored to teach the rich and educated how this better side was to be found, even in the most neglected Lazarus, and to tell the poor no less to respect this better part of themselves—to remember that they also have a calling to be good and great, if they will but hear it.

*　　*　　*　　*　　*　　*

"There is one more thought that arises on this occasion. As, in the parable, we are forcibly impressed with the awful solemnity of the other world, so on this day a feeling rises in us before which the most brilliant powers of genius and the most lively sallies of wit wax faint. When, on Tuesday last, we stood beside that open grave, in the still deep silence of the summer morning, in the midst of this vast solitary space, broken only by that small band of fourteen mourners, it was impossible not to feel that there is something more sacred than any worldly glory, however bright—or than any mausoleum, however mighty—and that is the return of the human soul into the hands of its Maker. Many, many are the feet that have trodden, and will tread, the consecrated ground around his grave. Many, many are the hearts which, both in the old world and the new, are drawn towards it as towards the resting-place of a dear personal friend. Many are the flowers that have been strewn—many the tears that have been shed—by the grateful affection of the poor that have cried—of the fatherless—and of those that have none to help them. May I speak to them a few sacred words, that will come perhaps with a new meaning and a deeper force, because they come from the lips of their lost friend—because they are the most solemn utterances of lips now closed forever in the grave? They are extracted from the will of Charles Dickens, dated May 12, 1869, and will now be heard by many for the first time. After the most emphatic injunctions respecting the inexpensive, unostentatious, and strictly private manner of his funeral—injunctions which have been carried out to the very letter—he thus continues:

"'I direct that my name be inscribed in plain English letters on my tomb. I conjure my friends on no account to make me the subject of any monument, memorial, or testimonial whatever. I rest my claim to the remembrance of my country on my published works, and to the remembrance of my friends in their experience of me in addition* thereto. I commit my soul to the mercy of God, through our Lord and Saviour Jesus Christ; and I exhort my dear children humbly to try to guide themselves by the teaching of the New Testament, in its broad spirit, and to put no faith in any man's narrow construction of its letter here or there.'

"In that simple but sufficient faith he lived and died. In that simple and sufficient faith he bids you live and die. If any of you have learnt from his works the value—the eternal value—of generosity, of purity, of kindness, of unselfishness, and have learnt to show these in your own hearts and lives, then remember that these are the best monuments, memorials, and testimonials of the friend whom you have loved, and who loved with a marvellous and exceeding love his children, his country, and his fellowmen. These are monuments which he would not refuse, and which the humblest and poorest and youngest here have it in their power to raise to his memory."

The beautiful anthem, "When the ear heard him," was then sung, and the remainder of the service was gone through. The dispersion of the congregation was a work of time, for, although three doors were open, nearly every person present passed out by Poet's Corner, in order to take a last look at Charles Dickens's grave.

He lies, without one of his injunctions respecting his funeral having been violated, surrounded by poets and men of genius. Shakspeare's marble effigy looks upon his grave; at his feet are Dr. Johnson and David Garrick; his head is by Addison and Handel; while Oliver Goldsmith, Rowe, Southey, Campbell, Thomson, Sheridan, Macaulay, and Thackeray, or their memorials, encircle him. Thus "Poet's Corner," the most familiar spot in the whole Abbey, has received an illustrious addition to its peculiar glory. Separated from Dickens's grave, by the statues of Shakspeare, Southey, and Thomson, and close by the door to "Poet's Corner," are the memorials of Ben Jonson, Dr. Samuel Butler, Milton, Spenser, and Gray; while Chaucer, Dryden, Cowley, Mason, Shadwell, and Prior are hard by, and tell the by-stander, with their wealth of great names, how

"These poets near our princes sleep,
And in one grave their mansion keep."

APPENDIX.

UNDER this heading a few detached anecdotes, and some additional particulars, are given:

THE FIRST HINT OF "PICKWICK."—A great deal has been said as to the origin of "Pickwick," and in the chapter devoted to a consideration of this favorite work the present writer has stated from whence the name, at least, was taken. He did not, however, for the moment remember a conversation upon the subject which he had with a friend not long since, which conversation was shortly followed by a letter from him upon this same topic. The letter runs thus, and the compiler of this little book trusts he may be pardoned for quoting it:

"When I stated to you that Dickens took his ideal of novel-writing from the works of Mr. Pierce Egan, I had nothing but internal evidence to go upon. When he began to write, the most popular fictions were the descriptions of 'Life in London' connected with the names of 'Tom' and 'Jerry.' The grand object of Dickens, as a novelist, has been to depict not so much human life as human life in London, and this he has done after a fashion which he learned from the 'Life in London' of Mr. Pierce Egan. If you remember that once famous book, you will call to mind how he takes his heroes—the everlasting Tom and Jerry—now to a fencing-saloon, now to a dancing-house, now to a chop-house, now to a spunging-house. The object is not to evolve the characters of Tom and Jerry, but to introduce them in new scene after new scene. And so you will find with Dickens. He invents new characters, but he never invents them without, at the same time, inventing new situations and surroundings of London life. Other novelists would not object to invent new characters appearing in the same position of life as the characters in some preceding novel, and trusting for novelty to the newness of the surroundings and the situation. Dickens insists upon putting the new characters into a new and unexpected trade—doll-making perhaps, or news-vending—and he has always in view some new phase of London life which he is far more anxious to exhibit than the characters without which it is impossible to bring the phase into prominence. If you look to his writings, or if you talk to him, you will find that his first thought is to find out something new about London life—some new custom or trade or mode of living—and his second thought is to imagine the people engaged in that custom or trade or mode of living. Now this is Pierce Egan's style—and Dickens, with rare genius, and with large sympathies, has followed in grooves which the once celebrated Pierce laid down. Pierce Egan had no wit, and his conversations are not worth mentioning. Dickens riots in wit, and what Pierce would have shown in a description, Dickens makes out in a conversation. But the objects of the two men to magnify London life, and to show it in all its phases, were the same."

Upon examining Pierce Egan's "Finish"—a sequel to his "Life in London"—we certainly find the characters somewhat similar to those in "Pickwick." In other matters, too, a parallel may be drawn—thus, the Bench instead of the Fleet, and the archery match instead of the shooting party. But the most curious coincidence is that the "Fat Knight"—the counterpart of Mr. Pickwick—is first met by Corinthian Tom at the village of *Pickwick!**

DICKENS AND THE "MORNING CHRONICLE."—Various and conflicting accounts of Dickens's earliest "Sketches" have been given, and of the circumstances under which he first contributed to the evening edition of the "Morning Chronicle;" but the following extract, which we have been permitted to make from a long unpublished letter, will set the question at rest. The letter was addressed to the late Mr. George Hogarth, then connected with the "Morning Chronicle," and was the beginning of a friendship between the two which ended in Mr. Dickens marrying Mr. Hogarth's daughter:

"* * * As you begged me to write an original sketch for the first number of the new evening paper, and as I trust to your kindness to refer my application to the proper quarter, should I

---

* The writer thinks it scarcely necessary to say that these remarks upon the origin—the first hint—of "Pickwick" are not to be understood as intended in any way to detract from the great novelist's fair fame for originality. On the contrary, it is believed that the time has now come when it will be a delight with students to trace his reading, and, if possible, catch some glimpse of the origin of those inimitable characters which will live forever in English fiction.

be unreasonably or improperly trespassing upon you, I beg to ask whether it is probable that if I commenced a series of articles under some attractive title for the "Evening Chronicle," its conductors would think I had any claim to *some* additional remuneration—of course, of no great amount—for doing so.

"Let me beg you not to misunderstand my meaning. Whatever the reply may be, I promised you an article, and shall supply it with the utmost readiness, and with an anxious desire to do my best; which I honestly assure you would be the feeling with which I should always receive any request coming personally from yourself. * * * I merely wish to put it to the proprietors—first, whether a continuation of light papers, in the style of my 'Street Sketches,' would be considered of use to the new paper; and, secondly, if so, whether they do not think it fair and reasonable that—taking my share of the ordinary reporting business of the 'Chronicle' besides—I should receive something for the papers beyond my ordinary salary as a reporter?"*

The offer was accepted, the then sub-editor informs us, and Mr. Dickens received an increase in his salary of from five guineas per week to seven guineas.

PORTRAITS OF DICKENS.—Besides those enumerated in the body of this book, there are others which should be mentioned. A very re-

DANIEL MACLISE, R.A.

Taken in 1839, and given as a frontispiece to "Nicholas Nickleby."

COUNT D'ORSAY.

From a pencil sketch made in 1841.

CHARLES LESLIE, R.A.

From his painting of Dickens as "The Copper Captain" in "Every Man in his Own Humor." 1846.

PHOTOGRAPH.

From the portrait considered by Mr. Dickens as his best likeness. 1870.

---

* Dated "13 Furnival's Inn, Tuesday evening, January 20, [1835]."

markable one was etched about 1837, with the name "Phiz" at the foot. It represents Dickens seated on a chair, and holding a port-folio. In the background a Punch-and-Judy performance is going on. The face has none of that delicacy and softness about it which are observable in the Maclise portrait. It looks, however, more like the real young face of the older man, as revealed in the photograph now publishing. This portrait is very rare, and it is understood that it was withdrawn from publication soon after it appeared. Mr. Hablot K. Browne, the genuine "Phiz," denies all knowledge of it.

There exists a portrait by S. Lawrence, which was lithographed by W. Taylor.

In 1856, Ary Scheffer's portrait of the great novelist was exhibited in the Royal Academy. It was hard and cold, and gave general dissatisfaction.

Mr. Frith painted a portrait of his friend, representing him writing his celebrated compositions at his plain, but workman-like, desk. This portrait is now the property of the great novelist's friend and executor, Mr. John Forster, and in due time will be hung on the walls of the National Portrait Gallery. In the Exhibition of the Royal Academy for 1857, Mr. Frith exhibited a picture (No. 125), "Kate Nickleby at Madame Mantalini's." Kate is holding a mantle, while Miss Knagg (reflected in the cheval glass) is trying on another.

THE NAMES OF DICKENS'S CHARACTERS.—It is well known that the quaint surnames of his characters, concerning which essays have been written, were the result of much pains-taking. Dickens, with a genius which might have justified his trusting it implicitly and solely, placed his chief reliance on his own hard labor. It is said that when he saw a strange or odd name on a shop-board, or in walking through a village or country town, he entered it in his pocket-book, and added it to his reserve list. Then, runs the story, when he wanted a striking surname for a new character, he had but to take the first half of one real name, and to add it to the second half of another, to produce the exact effect upon the eye and ear of the reader he desired.*

* * * In "Notes and Queries" for August 28, 1858 (this periodical takes its motto from one of Mr. Dickens's characters), it was suggested that the name of "Carker" was framed from the Greek, as so much is said of Mr. Carker's teeth. Mr. Dickens, however, replied to this, that the coincidence was undesigned. It has been further suggested that the name was made up from "canker" and "carking" (as in "carking care"), which are very expressive of the blighting influence possessed by Carker.

It has been stated that the Pickwickian names of Wardle, Lowten, and Dowler occur in the "Annual Register's" account of the Duke of York's trial, 1809.

Some inquiry is made as to the names of

---

* "Daily News," June 11, 1870.

Mr. Dickens's characters in an article on the novelist, in "Blackwood's Magazine," April, 1855.

DESCRIPTION OF "BOZ" IN 1844.—Mr. R. H. Horne, in his "New Spirit of the Age," gives this graphic description of him as he appeared when a young man : "Mr. Dickens is, in private, very much what might be expected from his works—by no means an invariable coincidence. He talks much or little, according to his sympathies. His conversation is genial. He hates argument ; in fact, he is unable to argue—a common case with impulsive characters who see the whole, and feel it crowding and struggling at once for immediate utterance. He never talks for effect, but for the truth or for the fun of the thing. He tells a story admirably, and generally with humorous exaggerations. His sympathies are of the broadest, and his literary tastes appreciate all excellence. He is a great admirer of the poetry of Tennyson. Mr. Dickens has singular personal activity, and is fond of games of practical skill. He is also a great walker,* and very much given to dancing Sir Roger de Coverley. In private, the general impression of him is that of a first-rate practical intellect, with 'no nonsense' about him. Seldom, if ever, has any man been more beloved by contemporary authors, and by the public of his time."

DESCRIPTION OF DICKENS IN 1852.—Miss Clarke, an American lady, who visited England in 1852 with Miss Cushman and a friend, in her "Haps and Mishaps of a Tour in Europe" (written under the assumed name of Grace Greenwood), says :

"He is rather slight, with a symmetrical head, spiritedly borne, and eyes beaming alike with genius and humor. Yet, for all the power and beauty of these eyes, their changes seemed to me to be from light to light. I saw them in no profound, pathetic depths, and there was around them no tragic shadowing. But I was foolish to look for these on such an occasion, when they were very properly left in the author's study, with pens, ink, and blotting-paper, and the last written pages of 'Bleak House.'"

BOZ'S TABLE HABITS.—Some of the American newspaper paragraphs about his personal tastes gave him considerable amusement. Said a Temperance Journal :

"The prevailing idea that Mr. Dickens is accustomed to a very generous diet, which has mainly arisen from the jovial tone of his writings, is quite incorrect, for we are credibly in-

---

* "So much of my travelling is done on foot that, if I cherished betting propensities, I should probably be found registered in sporting newspapers under some such title as the Elastic Novice, challenging all elevenstone mankind to competition in walking. My last special feat was turning out of bed at two, after a hard day, pedestrian and otherwise, and walking thirty miles into the country to breakfast.—("Sly Neighborhoods," "Uncommercial Traveller.")

THE MS. OF "OLIVER TWIST."—A portion of the MS. of "Oliver Twist," which originally appeared in "Bentley's Miscellany," is still in Mr. Bentley's possession. It has been suggested that it might fittingly be placed in the British Museum by the side of the MS. of Sterne's "Sentimental Journey."

DICKENS'S BENEVOLENCE.—The late Sheridan Knowles, in a letter to a friend, gave an instance of his generosity: "Poor Haydn, the author of the 'Dictionary of Dates' and the 'Book of Dignities' (I believe I am right in the titles), was working, to my knowledge, under the pressure of extreme destitution, aggravated by wretchedly bad health, and a heart slowly breaking through efforts indefatigable, but vain, to support in comfort a wife and a young family. I could not afford him at the moment any material relief, and I wrote to Charles Dickens, stating his miserable case. My letter was no sooner received than it was answered—and how? By a visit to his suffering brother, and not of condolence only, but of assistance—rescue! Charles Dickens offered his purse to poor Haydn, and subsequently brought the case before the Literary Society, and so appealingly as to produce an immediate supply of £60. I need not say another word. I need not remark that such benevolence is not likely to occur solitarily. The fact I communicate I learned from poor Haydn himself. Dickens never breathed a word to me about it."

HOOK AND DICKENS.—"A comparison seems almost to force itself upon our notice between the writings of Hook and those of a still more popular author, Mr. Charles Dickens. We shall not be tempted to pursue it farther that to remark that, their subject-matter being in some measure the same, the former seems to survey society from a level more elevated and more distant than his competitor; his delineations are in consequence genial and sketchy, those of the latter more technical and minute. Hook gives you a landscape, while 'Boz' is tracing every leaf of a particular tree. The same analogy holds good as regards their moral teaching. Hook is pithy, pointed, and offhand; the reflections of Mr. Dickens are elaborated with a care that occasionally, perhaps, detracts from their effect. Hook has undoubtedly the advantage of more experience of the world, but the palm of originality must, we should think, be awarded to his rival."—BARHAM's *Life of Theodore Hook.*

METHODICAL HABITS AND PERSEVERANCE.—One who knew him well says: "He did not work by fits and starts, but had regular hours for labor, commencing about ten and ending about two. It is an old saying that easy writing is very difficult reading; Mr. Dickens's works, so easily read, were by no means easily written. He labored at them prodigiously, both in their conception and execution. During the whole time that he had a book in hand, he was much more thoughtful and preoccupied than in his leisure moments."

⁎ Another friend has written: "His hours and days were spent by rule. He rose at a certain time, he retired at another, and though no precisian, it was not often that his arrangements varied. His hours for writing were between breakfast and luncheon, and when there was any work to be done no temptation was sufficiently strong to cause it to be neglected. This order and regularity followed him through the day. His mind was essentially methodical; and in his long walks, in his recreations, in his labor, he was governed by rules laid down for himself by himself, rules well studied beforehand, and rarely departed from. The so-called men of business, the people whose own exclusive devotion to the science of profit and loss makes them regard doubtfully all to whom that same science is not the main object in life, would have been delighted and amazed at this side of Dickens's character."

⁎ "No writer set before himself more laboriously the task of giving the public the very best. A great artist, who once painted his portrait while he was in the act of writing one of the most popular of his stories, relates that he was astonished at the trouble Dickens seemed to take over his work, at the number of forms in which he would write down a thought before he hit out the one which seemed to his fastidious fancy the best, and at the comparative smallness of manuscript each day's sitting seemed to have produced. Those, too, who have seen the original MSS. of his works, many of which he had bound and kept at his residence at Gad's Hill, describe them as full of interlineations and alterations."

MANNER OF LITERARY COMPOSITION.—A writer in a weekly journal says: "I remember well one evening, spent with him by appointment, not wasted by intrusion, when I found him, according to his own phrase, 'picking up' the threads' of 'Martin Chuzzlewit' from the printed sheets of the half volume that lay before him. This accounts for the seeming incompleteness of some of his plots; in others, the design was too strong and sure to be influenced by any outer consideration. He was only confirmed and invigorated by the growing applause, and marched on, like a successful general, with each victory made easier by the preceding one. It seemed hardly to come within his nature to compose in solitary fashion, and wait the event of a whole work. No doubt this resulted in part from his character as a journalist; and so did his utter disdain of the shams which it is the express province of journalism to detect and expose.

"His composition, easy as it seems in the reading—indeed, so natural that it would be difficult to substitute any truer word in any place—was, we are told, elaborate and slow. But in his happier days the process was by no means wearisome. It was the love of the idea, that could not let it go till he had nursed it to its utmost growth. In this he resembled many of the greatest humorists, whose enjoyment of their own fancies is evidenced by the impossibility of passing them into print while a single mirth-stirring thought or word could be added to make the picture perfect. The result was invaluable. With the exception only of Shakspeare, among English writers of drama and fiction, no other author than Dickens yields so many sentences on each page of sterling value in themselves; no other author can be read and re-read with such certainty of finding fresh pleasure on every perusal. Nowhere, with the one exception, does so much thought go to finish the production. It is jeweller's work, inlaying and enriching every part."*

"THE CHIEF."—In his own immediate literary circle, and among those who were on the most familiar terms with him, the name "Mr. Dickens," or "Mr. Charles Dickens," or even "Charles," with his most intimate friends, was never heard. The respect felt for his genius—his superiority—took a more striking, although more familiar form. He was invariably spoken of as "the Chief!" At "All the Year Round" office, the question was never, "Is Mr. Dickens in?" but "Has the 'Chief' arrived?" "Is the 'Chief' in?"

BLUE INK.—The present habit among literary men—especially among those formerly connected with "Household Words," and more recently with "All the Year Round"—of using *blue* in preference to black ink, arose with Mr. Dickens. "The Chief" disliked the necessity of blotting his MS. in the progress of composition, and on finding that a certain make of blue ink dried almost immediately it left the pen, he invariably used that kind ever after; and thus began the fashion for blue ink among London journalists.

DICKENS IN PRIVATE LIFE.—One who was intimately acquainted with him says: "To those who never saw Dickens, and who ask whether he was like his works, we answer emphatically, Yes. When in congenial society, his humor was so abundant and overflowing, that the impression it gave the listener was that it would have been painful to check it; while in nobility and tenderness, in generous sympathy for all that is elevating and pure, in lofty scorn of the base, in hatred of the wrong, Dickens the author and Dickens the man was one. The stories of his goodness and generosity are endless. His was the common fate of having to bear the burdens of others as well as his own, and those who knew him under circumstances of trial unite in testifying to the open-handed justice of the man."

* * * * *

"Never was human being more 'thorough.' His friendship was a fervent reality, and he spared no pains and withheld no exertion to serve those whom he thought worthy, and to whom his countenance was valuable. The whole energy of his nature—and the passage in 'David Copperfield,' in which the hero attributes whatever success he has acquired in this life to his faculty of devoting his whole strength and thoughts to the subject in hand, whatever it might be, precisely describes Charles Dickens himself—was given to the friend as readily and fully as to the day's work; and it would be impossible to say more. Again, this kindly helpfulness was more valuable in Dickens than in most men, from his shrewd common sense, his worldly wisdom, his business habits, his intense regard for accuracy in detail. Whatever he said should be done, those who knew him regarded as accomplished. There was no forgetfulness, no procrastination, no excuse, when the time for granting a promised favor came."*

SYMPATHY WITH WORKING-MEN.—A friend, writing in the "Observer," says: "He took a certain honest pride in receiving and returning the salutations of working-people personally unknown to him as he walked along the city's streets or the country roads, and he was greatly pleased by the reception at Christmas-time of numberless small presents, generally of provisions, sent to him, 'in honor of the season,' by humble and anonymous admirers."

A BEGGAR'S ESTIMATE OF HIS GENEROSITY.—Dickens has, like others in this world, been made to suffer every now and then for his good nature. High up on a list, taken from the pocket of a begging-letter writer, of persons easily induced to give money to those who pleaded distress, was found the name of "Charles Dickens," in company with that of an equally kindly, but more wealthy, charitable person, Miss Burdett Coutts. His own account of how he has been victimized by the clever tales of systematic impostors has been told in his own inimitable way in "Household Words."

PARAGRAPH DISEASE.—Writing to a friend in Boston, Dickens said: "I notice that about once in every seven years I become the victim of a paragraph disease. It breaks out in England, travels to India by the overland route, gets to America per Cunard line, strikes the base of the Rocky Mountains, and, rebounding back to Europe, mostly perishes on the steppes of Russia from inanition and extreme cold."

DICKENS AND THACKERAY.— Mr. Hodder tells us that "Thackeray did not keep copies of his own books. I was at his house when he

---

* "Weekly Dispatch," June 18, 1870.

* "Daily News," June 11, 1870.

had completed the 'Newcomes,' and, on looking at the book-shelves in his studio, I saw a newly-bound copy of that work, but neither 'Vanity Fair,' 'Pendennis,' nor 'Esmond.' I spoke of this strange want in his library; 'for (said I) Charles Dickens has all his own works neatly bound in the order of publication.' 'Yes,' answered Thackeray, 'I know he has, and so ought I; but fellows borrow them or steal them, and I try to keep them, and can't.'"

₊ "In the mere matter of literary style there is a very obvious difference. Mr. Thackeray, according to the general opinion, is the more terse and idiomatic, and Mr. Dickens the more diffuse and luxuriant writer.. There is an Horatian strictness and strength in Thackeray which satisfies the more cultivated taste, and wins the respect of the severest critic; but Dickens, if he is the more rapid and careless, on the whole, seems more susceptible to passion, and rises to a keener and wilder song. Referring the difference of style to its origin in difference of intellectual constitution, critics are accustomed to say that Thackeray's is the mind of closer and harder, and Dickens's the mind of looser and richer, texture—that the intellect of the one is the more penetrating and reflective, and that of the other the more excursive and intuitive."—Masson's "British Novelists and their Styles."

₊ An anonymous writer says: "The first time I heard Mr. Thackeray read in public, he paid a tribute to 'Boz.' It was the night after the Oxford election, in which Mr. Thackeray was an unsuccessful candidate, and the kindhearted author hastened up to town to fulfill a promise to give some readings on behalf of Mr. Angus Reach.* I well remember the burst of laughter and applause which greeted the opening words of his reading. 'Walking yesterday down the streets of an ancient and well-known city, I—' but here the allusion to Oxford was recognized, and he had to wait until the merriment it created had ceased. In alluding to Charles Dickens, Mr. Thackeray, after speaking with abhorrence of the impurity of the writings of Sterne, went on to say: 'The foul satyr's eyes leer out of the leaves constantly; the last words the famous author wrote were bad and wicked—the last lines the poor stricken wretch penned were for pity and pardon. I think of these past writers, and of one who lives amongst us now, and am grateful for the innocent laughter, and the sweet and unsullied pages, which the author of "David Copperfield" gives to my children.' The author of 'David Copperfield' was taken by surprise, and looked immensely hard at the ceiling, as if trying to persuade himself that he was unknown to the audience. On the same night I heard Thackeray read Hood's celebrated lines, 'One more unfortunate,' etc."

* The writer is here in error. The lecture was not delivered on behalf of Mr. Reach, but for the fund then being raised to the memory of the late Douglas Jerrold.

Anecdote of Abraham Lincoln.—Mr. Arthur Locker says that the following sad story was related to Mr. Dickens by the late Mr. Edwin Stanton, the famous Secretary of War in the United States Cabinet. On Good-Friday, 1865, there was a Cabinet meeting at Washington, and Mr. Stanton chanced to enter the council chamber some time after the other members had assembled. As he entered he heard the President say, "Well, gentlemen, this is only amusement. I think we had better now turn to business." During the meeting he noticed that Mr. Lincoln was remarkably grave and sedate; and that, instead of strolling about the room, as was his usual wont, dealing out droll remarks, he sat bolt upright in his chair. On leaving the Cabinet, Mr. Stanton asked one of the other Members why the President's manner was so peculiar, and received the following explanation: "When we assembled to-day, Mr. Lincoln said, 'Gentlemen, I dreamt a strange dream last night for the third time, and on each occasion something remarkable has followed upon it. After the first dream came the battle of Bull Run [Mr. Dickens could not remember the second event], and now the dream has come again. I dreamt that I was in a boat on a lake, drifting along without either oars or sails, when—' At this moment you," said the Member, addressing Mr. Stanton, "opened the door, whereupon the President checked himself, and said, 'I think we had better turn to business.' So we have lost the conclusion of the dream."

And it was lost forever. The council met at half-past two, and on the same evening President Lincoln lay dead, slain by the pistol-shot of Wilkes Booth.

The Contributors to "Household Words."—The earliest contributor to "Household Words" may be said to have been Mrs. Gaskell, for, after the beautiful little introductory address by Charles Dickens, the new periodical opened with a fine story from her pen. Many of the small band of writers who had rallied round Mr. Dickens, and who formed what may be called the staff of the journal, were comparatively unknown; some were altogether novices, whom Mr. Dickens's quick discernment of talent had marked out as useful *collaborateurs*. More than one young writer, whose name has since become familiar to the public, made his *début* here. One of the first contributors was Mr. W. H. Wills, who had been editor of "Chambers's Journal," and who for years acted as Mr. Dickens's working editor and confidential secretary. Besides the contributors enumerated on p. 60, there were Mr. R. H. Horne, the author of "Orion," Douglas Jerrold, and Mr. James Hannay, who wrote most of the sea-sketches. Mr. Sala's "Key of the Street," published here, was, we believe, his first appearance as a magazine writer. Among other regular contributors may be mentioned Percy Fitzgerald, Wilkie and Charles Collins, Sidney Blanchard, Mrs. Gaskell, Walter Thornbury, Mrs. Linton, Robert Brough, Miss Amelia Edwards, Mr. J. C. Parkinson, Blanchard Jerrold, W. Allingham. The names of all the contributors to the journal, however, would occupy more space than we have at command.

"THE MYSTERY OF EDWIN DROOD."—Concerning the completion of this, Messrs. Chapman & Hall, the publishers, have addressed the following letter to the "Times:"

"SIR,—We find that erroneous reports are in circulation respecting 'The Mystery of Edwin Drood,' the novel on which Mr. Dickens was at work when he died. It has been suggested that the tale is to be finished by other hands. We hope you will allow us to state in your columns that Mr. Dickens has left three numbers complete, in addition to those already published, this being one-half of the story as it was intended to be written. These numbers will be published, and the fragment will so remain. No other writer could be permitted by us to complete the work which Mr. Dickens has left."

** A letter had been sent to Mr. Dickens relative to a figure of speech in Chapter X. of "Edwin Drood," which figure of speech, the writer stated, had been taken from the description of the sufferings of our Saviour, as given in the New Testament, and applied in a way to wound the feelings of Christian readers. The author of "Edwin Drood" wrote the following reply the day preceding his death. It has already been published as "his last words."

"DEAR SIR,—It would be quite inconceivable to me, but for your letter, that any reasonable reader could possibly attach a scriptural reference to a passage in a book of mine, reproducing a much-abused social figure of speech, impressed into all sorts of service, on all sorts of inappropriate occasions, without the faintest connection of it with its original source. I am truly shocked to find that any reader can make the mistake. I have always striven in my writings to express veneration for the life and lessons of our Saviour; because I feel it, and because I re-wrote that history for my children—every one of whom knew it from having it repeated to them, long before they could read, and almost as soon as they could speak. But I have never made proclamation of this from the housetops. Faithfully yours,
"CHARLES DICKENS."

** It has been remarked that the concluding words of the last number of "Edwin Drood,"*

" *Comes to an end—for the time,*"

have a mournful significance, when read in the light of after events.

But it may be mentioned that "Edwin Drood" is also having an independent issue* in America; and it is somewhat remarkable that the last words in the part issued there should likewise have an almost prophetic meaning:

"There, there! there! Get to bed, poor man, and cease to jabber! With that he extinguished his light, pulled up the bed-clothes around him, *and with another sigh shut out the world.*"

** Relative to the sketch of opium-smoking which occurs in "Edwin Drood," Sir John Bowring has written to the "Daily News:" "Connected with the name and history of Charles Dickens, and illustrative of his habits of observation, it may not be amiss to record that on the publication of 'Edwin Drood's Mystery' I wrote to him explaining what appeared to me an inaccuracy in his description and picture of opium-smoking, and sent to him an original Chinese sketch of the form of the pipe and the manner of its employment in China. Expressing much gratification with my communication, he informed me that before he wrote the chapter he had personally visited the eastern districts of London, in the neighborhood of the docks, and had only recorded what he had himself seen in that locality. No doubt that the Chinaman whom he described had accommodated himself to English usage, and that our great and faithful dramatist here as elsewhere most correctly portrayed a piece of actual life."

GAD'S HILL HOUSE.—It has been suggested

GAD'S HILL PLACE, NEAR ROCHESTER (1860-'70).

[Mr. Dickens's last residence. Here "Great Expectations," "Our Mutual Friend," "The Uncommercial Traveller," and portions of "Edwin Drood," were written. As is well known, he died here, 9th June, 1870.]

---

* June 1, 1870.   * "Every Saturday," June 9, 1870.

APPENDIX.

THE SWISS CHALET.

[Presented to Mr. Dickens by his English friends in Switzerland. It forms a summer-house in the grounds at Gad's Hill.]

that Charles Dickens's favorite abiding-place should be purchased by a general subscription, and kept as a national memento of the author. It is further suggested that the house should be retained by Mr. Dickens's family for a term, to be named by themselves, at the expiration of which, with their consent, the place should merge in trustees. Dickens passed the morning and afternoon of his last day on earth in the châlet presented to him by a few Swiss admirers two years since, which is erected in the shrubbery opposite his residence, and approached by a tunnel underneath the turnpike road. This châlet, embosomed in the foliage of some very fine trees, stands upon an eminence commanding a magnificent view of the mouth of the Thames and the opposite coast of Essex. It was a favorite retreat of Dickens.

THE END.

FRANKLIN SQUARE, NEW YORK, September, 1870.

HARPER & BROTHERS'
LIST OF NEW BOOKS.

☞ HARPER & BROTHERS *will send any of the following books by mail, postage prepaid, to any part of the United States, on receipt of the price.*

HARPER'S CATALOGUE, *with* CLASSIFIED INDEX OF CONTENTS, *sent by mail on receipt of Six Cents in postage stamps, or it may be obtained gratuitously on application to the Publishers personally.*

HARPER'S COMPLETE EDITION OF THE LIFE AND WORKS OF THE REV. F. W. ROBERTSON. In Two Volumes. $1 50 each.

    LIFE, LETTERS, LECTURES ON CORINTHIANS, AND ADDRESSES OF THE LATE FREDERICK W. ROBERTSON, M.A., Incumbent of Trinity Chapel, Brighton, 1847–1853. With Portrait on Steel. Large 12mo, 840 pages, Cloth, $1 50.

    SERMONS PREACHED AT BRIGHTON BY THE LATE REV. FREDERICK W. ROBERTSON, the Incumbent of Trinity Chapel. With Portrait on Steel. Large 12mo, 838 pages, Cloth, $1 50.

The publishers take pleasure in commending to public favor their complete and uniform Edition of the Life and Works of this gifted preacher, as more compact and neat than any other in the market, while its extraordinary cheapness puts it within the reach of many who have been heretofore prevented by their high price from possessing this author's life and writings.

* * * A more thoughtful, suggestive, and beautiful preacher never entered a pulpit; a simpler and braver man never lived; a truer Christian never adorned any religious community. His life and death were *vicarious*, as he himself might have put it. He lived and died for others, for us all. The sorrows and agonies of his heart pressed rare music out of it, and the experience of a terribly bitter life leaves a wealth of thought and reflection never more than equaled in the history of men.—*Morning Star* (London).

Here is a book which has gone through as great a number of editions as the most popular novel. It has all those marks of arduous service which are only to be seen in books which belong to great public libraries. It is thumbed, dog-eared, pencil-marked, worn by much perusal. Is it then a novel? On the contrary, it is a volume of sermons. A fine, tender, and lofty mind, full of thoughtfulness, full of devotion, has herein left his legacy to his country. It is not rhetoric or any vulgar excitement of eloquence that charms so many readers to the book, so many hearers to this preacher's feet. It is not with the action of a Demosthenes, with outstretched arms and countenance of flame, that he presses his Gospel upon his audience. On the contrary, when we read those calm and lofty utterances, this preacher seems seated, like his Master, with the multitude palpitating round, but no agitation or passion in his own thoughtful, contemplative breast. The Sermons of Robertson have few of the exciting qualities of oratory. Save for the charm of a singularly pure and lucid style, their almost sole attraction consists in their power of instruction, in their faculty of opening up the mysteries of life and truth. It is pure teaching, so far as that ever can be administered to a popular audience, which is offered to us in these volumes.—*Blackwood's Magazine.*

CHARLES DICKENS: THE STORY OF HIS LIFE. By the Author of "The Life of Thackeray." Portraits taken at various times, and Views of his Residences. 8vo, Paper, 50 cents.

A record of the incidents in a career full of labors, full of triumphs, and almost exceptionally full of friendships. * * * The volume, in truth, is a faithful account of every event in the life of Dickens, social, domestic, or literary, which can interest the reader.—*London Daily Telegraph.*

A great deal of information and entertainment may be derived from this volume.—*London Daily News.*

SPEECHES, LETTERS, AND SAYINGS of CHARLES DICKENS. To which is added a Sketch of his Life by George Augustus Sala, and Dean Stanley's Sermon. With Portrait on Wood. 8vo, Paper, 50 cents.

As a deliverer of what the French would call "a speech of occasion," no one is more happy.—*Percy Fitzgerald.*

His capital speeches. Every one of them reads like a page of "Pickwick."—*Critic.*

THE GENIAL SHOWMAN. Being Reminiscences of the Life of Artemus Ward and Pictures of a Showman's Career in the Western World. By EDWARD P. HINGSTON. Two Illustrations. 8vo, Paper, 75 cents.

THE UNITED STATES INTERNAL REVENUE AND TARIFF LAW (passed July 13, 1870), together with the Act imposing Taxes on Distilled Spirits and Tobacco, and for other purposes (approved July 20, 1868), and such other Acts or Parts of Acts relating to Internal Revenue as are now in effect; with Tables of Taxes, a copious Analytical Index, and full Sectional Notes. Compiled by HORACE E. DRESSER. 8vo, Paper, 50 cents.

HARPER'S HAND-BOOK FOR TRAVELERS IN EUROPE AND THE EAST. Being a Guide through France, Belgium, Holland, Germany, Austria, Italy, Egypt, Syria, Turkey, Greece, Switzerland, Tyrol, Russia, Denmark, Sweden, Spain, and Great Britain and Ireland. With a Railroad Map and 44 other Maps and Plans of Cities. By W. PEMBROKE FETRIDGE. New Edition: Ninth Year. Large 12mo, Leather, Pocket-Book Form, $7 50.

COCKER'S CHRISTIANITY AND GREEK PHILOSOPHY. Christianity and Greek Philosophy; or, the Relation between Spontaneous and Reflective Thought in Greece and the Positive Teaching of Christ and his Apostles. By B. F. COCKER, D.D., Professor of Moral and Mental Philosophy in Michigan University. Crown 8vo, Cloth, $2 75.

A work of learning and ability, and of wide research; dealing with its problems and difficulties according to modern philosophic methods, and pervaded throughout with a devout Christian spirit.—*Lutheran Observer*.

The problems proposed for discussion in this volume are some of the most profound and most important which can engage the attention of the human mind. Dr. Cocker is disposed to see, both in the heathen religions and the teachings of the philosophers, a much clearer apprehension of the Deity as one and supreme than is commonly admitted, and to recognize this as the result of that apprehension of himself which God has given to all his intelligent creatures. His book is written vigorously, and adapted to the comprehension of intelligent readers, and the notes have been prepared with reference to the wants of those who do not read Latin and Greek.—*Standard* (Chicago).

MEMOIR OF DR. JOHN SCUDDER. Memoir of the Rev. John Scudder, M.D., Thirty-six Years Missionary in India. By the Rev. J. B. WATERBURY, D.D. Portrait. 12mo, Cloth, $1 75.

The letters and journals give the reader an insight into Dr. Scudder's interior life and experience. The extent of his bishopric, the itinerant character of his labors ("like the Apostle Paul, he was ever in motion, penetrating the interior of heathendom and preaching the Gospel to princes and to the people"), and his medical skill, his genuinely apostolical combination of healing of the body and healing of the soul, give to the story of his life's labors a peculiar interest.—*Independent*.

ORTON'S ANDES AND THE AMAZON. The Andes and the Amazon; or, Across the Continent of South America. By JAMES ORTON, M.A., Professor of Natural History in Vassar College, Poughkeepsie, N. Y., and Corresponding Member of the Academy of Natural Sciences, Philadelphia. With a New Map of Equatorial America and numerous Illustrations. Crown 8vo, Cloth, $2 00.

A more charming book of travel than that of Professor Orton on the Equatorial regions of South America has not appeared for years, in England or America. A man of thorough scientific attainments, he is yet not so wholly absorbed in his observations of natural phenomena as to lose sight of those phases of social life under an effete civilization which the reader most desires to have presented to him; nor does any aspect of beauty in the passing cloud or the glittering mountain peak escape him.—*N. Y. Evening Post*.

ABBOTT'S QUEEN HORTENSE. The History of Hortense, Daughter of Josephine, Queen of Holland, Mother of Napoleon III. By JOHN S. C. ABBOTT, Author of "The French Revolution," "History of Napoleon Bonaparte," &c. With Engravings. 16mo, Cloth, $1 20. (*Uniform with Abbotts' Illustrated Histories*.)

BAKER'S NEW TIMOTHY. The New Timothy. By WM. M. BAKER, Author of "Inside," "Oak Mot," "The Virginians in Texas," "Life and Labors of Daniel Baker," &c. 12mo, Cloth, $1 50.

DIXON'S FREE RUSSIA. Free Russia. By W. HEPWORTH DIXON, Author of "Her Majesty's Tower," &c. With Two Illustrations. Crown 8vo, Cloth, $2 00.

This is a more important and remarkable work upon the great Muscovite Empire than any foreign traveler has ever even attempted, much less accomplished. Thanks to the writer of this splendid volume, "Free Russia" is brought clearly, boldly, vividly, comprehensively, and yet minutely, within the ken of every intelligent reading Englishman. The book is in many parts as enthralling as a romance, besides being full of life and character.—*Sun* (London).

We claim for Mr. Dixon the merit of having treated his subject in a fresh and original manner. He has done his best to see with his own eyes the vast country which he describes, and he has visited some parts of the land with which few even among its natives are familiar, and he has had the advantage of being brought into personal contact with a number of those Russians whose opinions are of most weight. The consequence is that he has been able to lay before general readers such a picture of Russia and the Russian people as can not fail to interest them.—*Athenæum* (London).

WINCHELL'S SKETCHES OF CREATION. Sketches of Creation: a Popular View of some of the Grand Conclusions of the Sciences in reference to the History of Matter and of Life. Together with a Statement of the Intimations of Science respecting the Primordial Condition and the Ultimate Destiny of the Earth and the Solar System. By ALEXANDER WINCHELL, LL.D., Professor of Geology, Zoology, and Botany in the University of Michigan, and Director of the State Geological Survey. With Illustrations. 12mo, Cloth, $2 00. (*New Edition now ready*.)

Professor Winchell presents a popular view of some of the important discoveries and conclusions of modern science, and has succeeded in making a book of much interest. There are very many persons who desire some knowledge of the origin, construction, and development of the earth and of its relations to the other bodies in the solar system, yet have neither the time nor the patience to master the details of the subject. Those details so burden ordinary geological treatises that this class of inquirers is repelled from their study. They will find this summary of the matter better adapted to their purpose than almost any thing else that has appeared.—*Brooklyn Eagle*.

THE BAZAR BOOK OF DECORUM. The Care of the Person, Manners, Etiquette, and Ceremonials. 16mo, Toned Paper, Cloth, Beveled Edges, $1 00. (*New Edition now ready*.)

A series of sensible, well-written, and pleasant essays on the care of the person, manners, etiquette, and ceremonials. The title *Bazar Book* is taken from the fact that some of the essays which make up this volume appeared originally in the columns of *Harper's Bazar*. This in itself is a sufficient recommendation—*Harper's Bazar* being probably the only journal of fashion in the world which has good sense and enlightened reason for its guides. The "Bazar Book of Decorum" deserves every commendation.—*Independent*.

MARCH'S ANGLO-SAXON GRAMMAR. A Comparative Grammar of the Anglo-Saxon Language; in which its Forms are Illustrated by those of the Sanskrit, Greek, Latin, Gothic, Old Saxon, Old Friesic, Old Norse, and Old High-German. By FRANCIS A. MARCH, Professor of the English Language and Comparative Philology in Lafayette College; Author of "Method of Philological Study of the English Language," "A Parser and Analyzer for Beginners," &c. 8vo, Cloth, $2 50.

THE NEW NOVELS

PUBLISHED BY

HARPER & BROTHERS, New York.

Man and Wife. By Wilkie Collins,
Author of "Armadale," "Moonstone," "The Woman in White," &c. With Illustrations. 8vo, Paper, $1 00; Cloth, $1 50.

True to Herself. By F. W. Robinson,
Author of "Stern Necessity," "For Her Sake," &c. 8vo, Paper, 50 cents.

Recollections of Eton. By an Etonian.
With Illustrations. 8vo, Paper, 50 cents.

A Dangerous Guest.
By the Author of "Gilbert Rugge," &c. 8vo, Paper, 50 cents.

Estelle Russell.
By the Author of "The Life of Galileo." 8vo, Paper, 75 cents.

Put Yourself in His Place. By Charles Reade,
Author of "Hard Cash," "Griffith Gaunt," "Never Too Late to Mend," White Lies," &c., &c. *From the Author's early sheets.*

HARPER'S OCTAVO EDITION. With all the Illustrations, including the characteristic Vignettes. Paper, 75 cents; Cloth, $1 25.

HARPER'S DUODECIMO EDITION. Uniform with the Household Edition of Charles Reade's Novels, and bound in Green Morocco Cloth. Illustrated. $1 00.

Kilmeny. By William Black,
Author of "In Silk Attire," "Love or Marriage?" &c. 8vo, Paper, 50 cents.

John: a Love Story. By Mrs. Oliphant,
Author of "Agnes," "Brownlows," "Chronicles of Carlingford," "Miss Marjoribanks," "Laird of Norlaw," &c., &c. 8vo, Paper, 50 cents.

The Vicar of Bullhampton. By Anthony Trollope,
Author of "Doctor Thorne." Illustrated. 8vo, Paper, $1 25; Cloth, $1 75.

Stern Necessity. By F. W. Robinson,
Author of "For Her Sake," "Carry's Confession," &c. 8vo, Paper, 50 cents.

A Brave Lady.
By the Author of "John Halifax, Gentleman," "A Noble Life," "Woman's Kingdom," &c. With Illustrations. 8vo, Paper, $1 00; Cloth, $1 50.

Miss Thackeray's Writings, Complete.
The Writings of Anne Isabella Thackeray. Illustrated. 8vo, Paper, $1 25; Cloth, $1 75.

Gwendoline's Harvest.
By the Author of "Carlyon's Year," &c. 8vo, Paper, 25 cents.

Miss Van Kortland.
By the Author of "My Daughter Elinor." 8vo, Paper, $1 00; Cloth, $1 50.

☞ HARPER & BROTHERS *will send any of the above works by mail, postage prepaid, to any part of the United States, on receipt of the price.*

VOLUME 41.
NUMBER 244. } HARPER'S MAGAZINE. { NEW YORK
SEPT., 1870.

WITH the June Number HARPER'S MAGAZINE entered upon its *Forty-first Volume*. The old-established features that have made the Magazine so popular hitherto are retained, while new attractions are continually being added. Regarding the popular character and variety of its contents, the attractiveness of its illustrated articles, the timeliness of its occasional articles upon current topics, the instructiveness and importance of its Historical and Scientific papers, and the conduct of its special Editorial Departments, the Publishers of HARPER'S MAGAZINE may confidently challenge comparison of its present with its previous record, and claim that they are generously fulfilling the promises which they have given in the past. In the July Number was commenced a serial story, "*The Old Love Again*," by ANNIE THOMAS, printed from the author's manuscript and beautifully illustrated. "*Anteros*," by the Author of "Guy Livingstone," will still be continued. In the present Number is commenced a serial story, "*Anne Furness*," by the Author of "Mabel's Progress," "Aunt Margaret's Trouble," etc.

Published Monthly, with profuse Illustrations.

VOLUME
XIV. } HARPER'S WEEKLY. { For
1870.

HARPER'S WEEKLY is an illustrated record of, and commentary upon the events of the times. It will treat of every topic, Political, Historical, Literary, and Scientific, which is of current interest, and will give the finest illustrations that can be obtained from every available source, original or foreign.

Published Weekly, with profuse Illustrations.

VOLUME
III. } HARPER'S BAZAR. { For
1870.

HARPER'S BAZAR is a Journal for the Home. It is especially devoted to all subjects pertaining to Domestic and Social Life. It furnishes the latest Fashions in Dress and Ornament; describes in-door and out-door Amusements; contains Stories, Essays, and Poems—every thing, in brief, calculated to make an American Home attractive. "*The Cryptogram*," by Prof. DE MILLE, now being published in the BAZAR, is after "Man and Wife," the most interesting story of the season.

Published Weekly, with profuse Illustrations.

HARPER'S MAGAZINE, WEEKLY, and BAZAR,
One Copy of either for One Year, $4 00.

The three publications, the MAGAZINE, WEEKLY, and BAZAR, will be sent to any address, for One Year, for $10 00; any two of them for $7 00.
An Extra Copy of either the MAGAZINE, the WEEKLY, or the BAZAR will be supplied gratis to every Club of Five Subscribers who send $4 00 each in one remittance; or Six Copies, without extra copy, of either publication, for $20 00.
The Volumes of the WEEKLY and BAZAR commence with the year. When no time is specified, it will be understood that the subscriber wishes to commence with the Number next after the receipt of his order.
The Volumes of the MAGAZINE commence with the Numbers for June and December of each year. Subscriptions may commence with any Number. When no time is specified, it will be understood that the subscriber wishes to begin with the first Number of the current Volume, and back Numbers will be sent accordingly.
Bound Volumes of the MAGAZINE, each Volume containing the Numbers for Six Months, will be furnished for $3 00 per Volume, sent by mail, postage paid. Bound Volumes of the WEEKLY or BAZAR, each containing the Numbers for a Year, will be furnished for $7 00, freight paid by the Publishers.
The Postage within the United States is for the MAGAZINE 24 cents a year, for the WEEKLY or BAZAR 20 cents a year, payable yearly, semi-yearly, or quarterly, at the office where received. Subscriptions from Canada must be accompanied with 24 cents additional for the MAGAZINE, or 20 cents for the WEEKLY or BAZAR, to pre-pay the United States postage.
Subscribers to the Magazine, Weekly, or Bazar will find on each wrapper a Number following their name which denotes the time their subscription expires. Each periodical is stopped when the term of subscription closes. It is not necessary to give notice of discontinuance.
In ordering the Magazine, the Weekly, or the Bazar, the name and address should be clearly written. When the direction is to be changed, both the old and the new one must be given.
In *remitting by mail*, a **Post-Office Order** or **Draft** payable to the order of HARPER & BROTHERS is preferable to Bank Notes, since, should the Order or Draft be lost or stolen, it can be renewed without loss to the sender. The Post-Office Department recommends that, when neither of these can be procured, the money be sent in a **Registered Letter**. The registration-fee has been reduced to fifteen cents, and the present registration system, the postal authorities claim, is virtually an absolute protection against losses by mail. *All Postmasters are obliged to register letters when requested.*
The extent and character of the circulation of HARPER'S MAGAZINE, WEEKLY, and BAZAR render them advantageous vehicles for advertising. A limited number of suitable advertisements will be inserted at the following rates: In the *Magazine*, Full Page, $250; Half Page, $125; Quarter Page, $70; for lesser spaces, $1 50 per line. In the *Weekly*, Outside Page, $2 00 a line; Inside Pages, $1 50 a line. In the *Bazar*, $1 00 a line; Cuts and Display, $1 25 a line.

Printed in Poland
by Amazon Fulfillment
Poland Sp. z o.o., Wrocław